WITHDRAWN

Madness and Leadership

NEW HORIZONS IN LEADERSHIP STUDIES

Series Editor: Joanne B. Ciulla, *Professor and Coston Family Chair in Leadership and Ethics, Jepson School of Leadership Studies, University of Richmond, USA*

This important series is designed to make a significant contribution to the development of leadership studies. This field has expanded dramatically in recent years and the series provides an invaluable forum for the publication of high quality works of scholarship and shows the diversity of leadership issues and practices around the world.

The main emphasis of the series is on the development and application of new and original ideas in leadership studies. It pays particular attention to leadership in business, economics and public policy and incorporates the wide range of disciplines which are now part of the field. Global in its approach, it includes some of the best theoretical and empirical work with contributions to fundamental principles, rigorous evaluations of existing concepts and competing theories, historical surveys and future visions.

Titles in the series include:

Madness and Leadership

From Antiquity to the New Common Era

Savvas Papacostas

The Cyprus Institute of Neurology and Genetics, Cyprus

NEW HORIZONS IN LEADERSHIP STUDIES

 Edward Elgar
PUBLISHING

Cheltenham, UK • Northampton, MA, USA

Published by
Edward Elgar Publishing Limited
The Lypiatts
15 Lansdown Road
Cheltenham
Glos GL50 2JA
UK

Edward Elgar Publishing, Inc.
William Pratt House
9 Dewey Court
Northampton
Massachusetts 01060
USA

A catalogue record for this book
is available from the British Library

Library of Congress Control Number: 2015935903

This book is available electronically in the Elgaronline
Business subject collection
DOI 10.4337/9781784719586

ISBN 978 1 78471 957 9 (cased)
ISBN 978 1 78471 958 6 (eBook)

Typeset by Columns Design XML Ltd, Reading
Printed and bound in Great Britain by T.J. International Ltd, Padstow

To the memory of my parents,

Symeon and Loulla,

and of my brother,

Costas

Contents

Acknowledgements

Many people have contributed to the writing of this book with encouragement and useful suggestions. Of these, I should mention my colleagues as well as my students at the School of Molecular Medicine and the University of Cyprus whose constructive criticism and ideas helped shape the arguments of the book. I would like especially to thank my friends and collaborators, Vassos Neocleous, Fofi Constantinidou and Evridiki Papastavrou who agreed to review selected portions of the manuscript, while still in preparation, and make useful and well taken comments through which the final product became comprehensive and readable. I would also like to thank my colleague Yiannis Laouris for his encouragement and guidance through the process of finishing a book, selecting a publisher, and overcoming the hurdles and particulars of such an endeavour. My scientific secretarial assistants Elena Polycarpou and Christina Hadjiyianni were invaluable in helping me put the manuscript together and structure it according to the publisher's instructions. My commissioning editor, Benedict Hill was helpful along the way with useful information, answers, and help regarding the final version of the book. In fact, I was impressed with the professionalism, patience and the impeccable approach of the staff at Edward Elgar Publishing who were involved in the production of this book. I would especially like to mention Harry Fabian, editorial assistant; Damian Penfold, copy editor; and Robert Pickens, desk editor. Their help and support are much appreciated.

Last but not least, I must acknowledge my immediate family, my wife Maria, son Symeon, and daughter Andriana for their support, patience, and willingness to forgo valued family time with me in order to allow me the pursuit of this project.

1. Introductory remarks about leaders and leadership

> Leadership is one of the most observed and least understood
> phenomena on earth.
>
> James McGregor Burns

I.

Our world is in crisis. In this era of restructuring and reshuffling the world order, when values and priorities are reconsidered, and the globe is becoming truly 'global', there is a desperate need, and demand, for leaders and managers with a perspective that goes beyond parochial, national and even regional boundaries to encompass emerging international urgencies. I call our times The New Common Era because, I feel, it resembles the original one, that of the early Christian world, which encompassed the diverse geographical areas of the Mediterranean basin, Asia Minor and Roman Europe. As in those days, ours are rapidly becoming truly interdependent and interconnected.

The original Common Era related to a time and place that redefined the basis of our civilization and gave it its characteristic Western feel, borrowing and merging the values from Judaeo-Christianity and the Graeco-Roman world. The outcome was the replacement of old Rome by its politico-religious successor, the Catholic Church, that eventually split into the Western (Roman-dominated) lands of Europe and the Eastern theocratic Byzantine Empire. Those initial divisions continued to split and subdivide geographically, ideologically, politically and culturally over the ensuing centuries down to the present day, which is characterized, again, by pluralism and multiculturalism. Subsequently we are reaching a state of new unification as a result of technological advances, economic interdependence and the necessity to share resources. Thus a New Common Era is again upon us promising, as well as threatening, to consume national and regional identities into a world 'melting pot' resulting in a new world order with new political and economic realities.

1

The way forward, and our success or failure, will depend on the role that our emergent leaders will be called upon to fulfil. The importance therefore of the choices we make in appointing and following our leaders becomes paramount. A leader in this new Common Era, as in the original one, will have to be able to balance the needs of his specific constituents to those of the world at large and to walk the fine line between regionalism (nationalism if you will) and internationalism since our interdependence gets progressively deeper. Consider the example of the recent European financial crisis. As the Northern economies are striving to remain stable, they need to fork out part of their wealth towards their needy Southern partners in order to maintain their (pseudo) political and financial union. A similar situation arose a couple of centuries ago between the northern and the southern United States when the visionary leadership of the American founding fathers and subsequent presidents helped glue that union together.[1] The role of leaders, then and now, remains central in determining the outcomes that follow.

Nowadays the world is morphing into regional spheres of political and economic interests. The Americas, the European Union, the Organization of the Petroleum Exporting Countries (OPEC) countries, and the former Soviet Republics are but a few examples. Even between such regions, however, there is an increasing tendency for collaboration and co-existence, due partly to an appreciation of the world's limited natural resources and the imperative for developing sustainable ones. Such tendencies are contrasted with the feeling, and evidence, that different world ideologies and regions are on an inevitable course of collision and that disaster lurks maliciously in our future.

Whether we co-exist or co-destruct, our future hangs on threads and strings tangled by people we appoint to be in charge of our affairs. Can we collectively take charge and guide our leaders to take wise decisions or are we desperately dependent on their own initiatives and understanding of what course of action must be taken? We can begin to answer this question with an attempt to understand the phenomenon of leadership, the characteristics of successful leaders, and their relationship to followers.

---

[1]   Following the end of American Civil War the North, under the guidance of Republicans, set up reconstruction governments in many Southern states in order to help them rejoin the Union and advance politically, economically and socially (Foner 1990).

II.

It was said that history is written by the masses and individuals merely succumb to the will of the multitude. Such an idea may be psychologically appealing to most of us because it provides support to our egocentric predispositions, as well as meaning, in what sometimes appears to be a purposeless state of being. It constitutes a cosy and comfortable feeling of worthiness and importance, not to mention collective participation in progress. The alternative view of course is that history is driven by a few individuals, or gifted leaders who, by the mere radiance of their character, their personality, and the timing of their appearance, determine the choices and fates of their societies. The former paradigm was the essential factor considered by the Marxist ideology in prophesizing the ultimate victory of the proletariat against another, albeit smaller multitude, that of the bourgeoisie. The latter paradigm, which holds that individuals, and not the masses, make the difference, provides an explanation for different groups of people reaching greatness at certain historical times. Such an example would be the well-known golden age of Athens ushered in after the defeat of the Persians; Pericles is thought to have skilfully led the ancient Athenians into an era of unparalleled creativity, political progress, and artistic output, that has continuously influenced western civilization, and beyond, ever since (Kagan 1998). He swayed his co-citizens into accepting pre-conceived notions that had already fermented in his mind, with such skill in rhetoric, that they were proudly adopted as their own democratically formed decisions.

Such skill in leadership, according to Stephen Denning (2007), requires, first and foremost, the ability to communicate the type of language that 'feels fresh and inviting, energizing and invigorating, challenging and yet enjoyable, lively, spirited, and fun, as when equals are talking to equals'. A similar notion was put forth in antiquity by Aristotle in his *Politics* (2001) when he spoke about government, which he considered to be 'not like the rule of a shepherd over his sheep, but the rule of equals over equals'. Of course, equals are not talking to equals since in every relationship automatically there will be a leader and a follower or followers. In fact, 'leader-follower structure emerges spontaneously even when groups set out to be leaderless' (Bass 1954). The latter however may confer leadership qualities onto the former, and can withdraw it as they see fit; thus, Foucault's (1978) saying that 'in a certain way, one is always the ruler and the ruled', becomes instructive.

The skill of a leader should ensure that he appears, and persuades followers, that their association is a legitimate, if not an egalitarian one.

Leadership therefore can be seen as a 'process of influence', which nevertheless induces folk ideas that appear to emphasize persuasion rather than coercion as its main strategy (Hogan, Curphy, and Hogan 1994). Therefore the role of language in bringing about persuasion that enhances political action assumes clear significance. In that respect, language is a fundamental aspect of the leadership process, shaped by both leaders and followers as they interact (Bligh, Kohles, and Meindl 2004). According to Warren Bennis (2003), 'Leadership is quite simple. It is the way great leaders communicate that sets them apart'. The role language plays in the formation of leader–follower relationships will be central to this book.

The question about which factor is important in driving society forward, the crowd or the individual leader, is not new and has been the subject of hotly debated arguments throughout history. This basic but ever-present question will be the topic of this diatribe approached from a bio-psycho-social perspective. The bio- part will refer to genetics and evolutionary perspectives regarding the phenomenon of leadership; the psycho- part will refer to personality traits and putative character pathologies that leaders possess; and the social part will refer to the cultural context in which leaders emerge.

In other words, we will attempt to answer whether such phenomena as democracy and new religious movements came about as a collective culmination of social progress, or as the guided process of charismatic leaders. Were Christianity, Islam, or the Magna Carta, to use but a few examples, steps forward of a society at large, or brainchildren of prophets and able civil magistrates? And if we assume that history is written by few special individuals, what attributes should they have in order to carry out their leadership potential? Do they represent the average individual in their society, who just happened to be at the right place at the right time, or do they come with some unusual and exceptional qualifications? Obviously, their presence needs to be signalled out to the people who will become followers and the followers themselves must be attuned to their potential leader's presence; Halpern and Lubar (2003) discuss this presence, which they define as 'the ability to connect authentically with the thoughts and feelings of others'. In other words, to use such language and mannerisms that will signify to others that a leader is speaking. To reiterate, language, that unique human characteristic, will be central in the discussions that follow in this book as we explore the characteristics that leaders should have in order to lead effectively.

As we said, the above questions are hardly novel ones; many historians, social scientists, philosophers, and other students of humanity have pondered these very issues. And, as is usually the case, there are competing theories and explanations, opposing views, and middle of the road positions. Karl Marx, for example, as a result of his intense preoccupation with class struggles and economic forces in society, had a tendency to ignore the individual, in favour of the masses. As he put it (1978 [1857–58], p. 247), 'society does not consist of individuals, but expresses the sum of interrelations, the relations within which these individuals stand.' On a different occasion (1978 [1845], p. 145) he wrote that 'the human essence is no abstraction in each single individual. In its reality it is the ensemble of the social relations.' Economic forces, according to this paradigm, are driving society, as well as history at large, and they are embodied in the multitude leaving little room for individual action let alone choice. Marx is therefore a constructionist in his views; the constructionist paradigm holds that reality, and therefore the necessity of leadership, is the product of human constructs, which attain meaning through social, political, and other culturally-defined interactions (Hickman and Couto 2006). In contrast, essentialists hold that the world, and reality, exist in their own right, and individuals perceive them through their senses (Rosenblum and Travis 2008). According to the constructionist paradigm, the notion of the so-called 'great men of history' is nothing but a misconception, an illusion of nineteenth-century romantic thinkers. Engels proceeds even further in stating, 'that such and such a man and precisely that man arises at a particular time in a particular country is, of course, pure chance. But cut him out and there will be a demand for a substitute, and this substitute will be found ... If a Napoleon had been lacking, another would have filled the place' (Engels 1978 [1894], p. 767-8).

Contrast these views with those opposing ones of Thomas Carlyle (1972 [1840], p. 101) who wrote that:

> Universal history, the history of what man has accomplished in this world, is at the bottom the history of the Great Men who have worked here. They were the leaders of men ... the modelers, patterns, and in wide sense creators, of whatever the general mass of men contrived to do or to attain; all things that we see standing accomplished in the world are properly the outer material results, the practical realization and embodiment of Thoughts that dwelt in the Great Men sent into the world: the soul of the whole world's history, it may justly be considered, were the history of these.

Unmistakable nineteenth-century prose, that nonetheless makes the point quite clear; the history of the world is the history of great individuals. Great events occurred because, and precisely because, these men willed them.

Similarly, Sidney Hook (1943) considers an individual leader's style and personality as important factors that are causal on the development of historical events. Certainly, and he makes the argument, the course of the Bolshevik revolution was influenced by Lenin's leadership and would have turned out differently if another man had taken his place; we can make the same claim for Alexander the Great and Macedonia, Napoleon and France, or Hitler and Germany. These personalities emerged within certain 'situations and conditions' and brought about remarkable results. Therefore, and as Chiari (1975) argues about social phenomena 'there is always a residuum of uniqueness which does not fit the abstractions and generalizations in which the scientist would like to enclose it'.

Similar to Great Man theory, trait theory proposed that leadership depended on the personal qualities of the leader, but unlike the Great Man theory, it did not necessarily assume that leadership resided solely within the grasp of a few heroic men (Terman 1904). On the other hand, and following attempts to portray a notable leader's 'typical' profile, House and Aditya (1997) concluded, that 'there were few, if any, universal traits associated with effective leadership … [and] that the search for universal traits was futile'. We will argue in the rest of this book that there are, indeed, social and biological traits (such as certain psychopathologic traits including paranoia), that fit the bill of the personality of leadership. Genetic studies have begun to tilt the pendulum towards the direction of biological determinism with, perhaps, the identification of putative leadership genes (De Neve *et al.* 2013).

Tucker (1981) reminds us that the argument is as old as civilization. He contrasts Socrates, the mentor, who focused on the power of the city, the collective citizens of Athens, the *Demos*, and therefore de-emphasized the individual, with his pupil Plato, whose notion of the *philosopher king* proposes that man is in charge of his destiny and determines his political development. Therefore, even close associates, teachers and pupils, have taken differing approaches to the issue.

Conciliatory views have also been proposed. William McKinley Runyan (1988a) is critical of both extremes and tries to reconcile them in a middle-of-the-road, reciprocal approach:

> It is, unquestionably, simplistic to claim that 'History=Biography' or that history can be reduced to nothing more than the aggregation of individual biographies, since this leaves out the impact of ecological and demographic factors, ignores the evolution of economic, political, religious, educational, and other institutions, and neglects the complex interactions between institutions and social groups. It is, however, equally reductionistic to claim that an understanding of individual persons and their psychological processes has

nothing to contribute to an analysis of the history of groups, social movements, institutions and nations. Only a dogmatic reductionism would maintain that the personality and life of Hitler had nothing to do with the course of World War II; of Lenin, with the Russian revolution; of Gandhi, with India's struggle with the British; or of Martin Luther King, Jr., with the civil rights movement.

Obviously history is neither biology nor pure economics, and world events need to be understood within their temporal, socio-political, cultural, and biological contexts in order to make sense out of them, as well as interpret them through a meaningful exegesis. Our concern here is with the overall 'tendencies' within these contexts and the source of influence that governs them; society at large, the individual leader, or a balanced dyadic relationship? Post (2004) states precisely this point, and expresses current thinking which sees the leader in context, not in isolation from his group, neither as an undifferentiated member. Contingency theorists (Fiedler 1972), also focus on the context of leader emergence as well as the leader's personal characteristics. Contemporary thinking considers leadership a process that can be learned and coached, borrowing from behavioural and cognitive psychology; leadership style and such distinctions as *task-oriented* (Stogdill 1957) versus *people-oriented* (Bales and Slater 1945) leaders emerge as important factors. In addition, internal processes of both leaders and followers, as affected by cultural, historical, but also individual psychological factors, need to be taken into account (Ayman and Chemers 1983). Even more recently, moral theories of leadership, and leader–follower relationships, proposed a common cause, and a contract between equal parties, to attain it (Burns 1978). The concepts of *servant, citizen,* and *transformational* leadership, grew out of these moral theories (Greenleaf 1977, Burns 1978, Couto 1992). We will discuss these issues further on in subsequent parts of this book.

III.

Leadership–followership patterns, according to some scientists, may have emerged in social species, including humans, in order to solve coordination problems and they represent social strategies that have been selected for by virtue of their success in fostering collective action (Van Vugt 2006). They therefore contribute to the success of groups in addition to that of individuals; at the group level, followers might fare better than individuals in groups without leaders or poorly functioning leaders (Van Vugt 2006). Leadership, then, has emerged in human evolutionary history, because between-group selection pressures were stronger than within-group selection pressures (Sober and Wilson 1998).[2]

All in all, however, it is the appearance of the phenomenon of leadership that is the driving force behind change, accomplishment, and fulfilment. Whether it is the product of a 'lone ranger' type of leader or the result of a social consensus, it is manifested as 'a function of the group', beyond which it is only '[a] realm of the potential' (Green 2006). Michael Harvey (2006) also reminds us of the ancient Greeks (Aristotle) who knew that 'we are really social animals who make sense of the world together. No man is an island of thought.' Similarly, Giddens (1976) argues that 'the production and reproduction of society ... has to be treated as a skilled performance of its members'.

We will argue subsequently that culture moulds the individual's personality, which, in turn, moulds culture. By the same token, it can be said that groups mould (and choose) their leaders who, in turn, mould the very groups that select them in a reciprocal and mutually dependent, symbiotic way. This is analogous, as we will see later on, to the notion of evolutionary brain development that produced that unique organ and set humanity apart from the rest of the animal kingdom; tools enhanced the progressive sophistication of the human brain, which, in turn, produced more complex tools; these in turn produced more sophisticated brains; and on, and on ...

The leader in context, as stated above, is the current way to view leadership in general, borrowing notions from cultural anthropology but taking into account its biological aspects as well. What's important to understand, however, is that within the right context, it is the individual leader who shapes his group's actions. As Bennis (2003) states, 'just as no great painting has ever been created by a committee, no great vision has ever emerged from the herd'. Stephen Denning (2007) speaks of transformational leaders who:

> Change the world by generating enduring enthusiasm for a common cause. They present innovative solutions to solve significant problems. They catalyse shifts in people's values and ideologies. They demonstrate willingness to sacrifice personal interests when necessary. They help others get through critical moments of crisis. They inspire people to want to change, so that positive energy sustains the change over time.

---

[2] This argument resembles the group selection logic for the evolution of altruism (Sober and Wilson 1998).

Personality or trait models assume the presence of distinct personality traits reliably distinguishing leaders from non-leaders, whereas situational or state theories of leadership emphasize the importance of the decision situation in determining who emerges as a leader (Van Vugt 2006).

Whichever model one adheres to, the unavoidably obvious question that follows is how they bring about this transformation. Communication skills constitute the critical tool to get the message across. Language, then, becomes the sole significant means by which a leader can attract his followers. Such communication may be oral, written, or electronically conveyed, as President Barack Obama and his team have recently showed by the flood of electronic mailings that have been sent to rally support for health care reform and other issues.

In order to delve further into the above questions we need to briefly digress into the history of man and his cultures, which, for our purposes, may be understood as the by-product of a genetic endowment that determines behaviour in ways more subtle than obvious. In other words, we will consider human behaviour, and human achievement, as a biologically determined phenomenon that obeys all the laws and rules by which living organisms exist. In the case of humans, biology produced two characteristics that have changed our terms of existence in remarkable ways; these two characteristics, of course, are language and culture. Both, we will argue, are biologically determined and are associated with other qualities when they create an environment suitable for leaders to ascend. After all, recent evidence has tilted the scale in favour of nature *via* nurture as far as human behaviour is concerned (Ridley 2003). But to make our argument convincing, we must consider social and behavioural phenomena that have remained constant (universal) across cultures and through time, thus lending credence to putative genetic causations. My own biological biases will become rather obvious on many occasions throughout this book. I hope to convince my readers as well.

Among the few cultural universals that one can find in the study of human behaviour is what philosopher Adam Smith (1776) called our strife to continually improve the means of our subsistence. Be it the primitive man's attempt to sharpen his arrows (thus procuring a better yield of game), or modern times' ever increasing efforts to produce sustainable energy resources, the ultimate goal is to improve our conditions of living. This phenomenon has been going on since the dawn of history and, assuming that we somehow manage to avoid annihilating ourselves in the process, will most likely go on forever. The consequence of this fact is a constantly changing social, technological and political milieu, which itself issues from the constant struggle to improve our lives. In other words, a cultural constant induces a continuous process that is none other than change. No society has remained immutable for ever so that 'change and continuity is an endless cycle' (Harvey 2006). Even among the most traditional cultures, change is ever-present, albeit very slow. The ubiquitous nature of this phenomenon supports the idea that, at its basic level, it is biologically determined. 'Nothing endures but change' was written by Heraclitus (Barnes 1982).

What, then, drives this inescapably constant change in our historical existence, appears to be hard-wired into our genetic programming, resulting in an almost deterministic (and futile) nature that was shaped millennia ago to ensure our survival as a species. Our beliefs and behaviour (that constellation of our attitudes about ourselves and our environs and the way we act upon them), may leave fewer personal liberties of choice than our anthropocentric views of reality are comfortable with. Recently conducted research (Custers and Aarts 2010) suggests that our choices and actions are controlled by our brain on a subconscious level long before they manifest behaviourally; this is the end result of brain evolution and sheds doubts on the existence of free will. Consequently, our choices and actions may owe more to our primordial milieu than our current (but ever-changing) concepts of social norms. Darwinian evolution and its underlying mechanism of natural selection have long ago cemented the explanations of these actions and reactions to the various vicissitudes of our daily lives. They have also set the limits into which the ranges of observable human behaviours are to be found given the finishing touches of nurture. Mat Ridley (2003) says that 'culture will often reflect human nature rather than affect it'.

A basic function of culture is to set limits on behaviour by establishing norms. Normal and abnormal behaviour may be seen as the ends of a continuum that are statistically clustered around a mean, with standard deviations setting the limits of tolerance outside of which our actions are deemed unacceptable or, at the very least, strange. Behaviours closely approaching this mean are considered 'normal' whereas the farther away they get from it, the more intolerantly the social group reacts towards them. Each group of people establishes its own set of values that determine which type of behaviours are acceptable; thus they reinforce a clustering of normal behaviours around their statistical average and increase their probability of occurrence. Throughout history one can find numerous examples of such intolerance and the attempts of society at large to contain that which was thought of as deviant. Medieval society, to use but one well-known example, dramatically witnessed such intolerance in the infamous institution of the Inquisition, which ran for the better part of 600 years, and sought to protect Christian orthodoxy from all false dogmas by such means as persuasion, torture, and the burning stake! Moreover, when different cultural groups meet, the more diverse is their behaviour, the more likely their instinctual clash will be. The point was poignantly illustrated by Samuel Huntington (2002) in his much acclaimed and highly controversial book *The Clash of Civilizations*, in which he argues that different world ideologies are on an inevitable collision course, with destructive consequences. Is the world currently becoming polarized along religious lines? Only time will tell. However, there is undeniable evidence that such a development is currently taking shape and peoples are siding with one or the other camp, not only figuratively but literally as well. Recent world events, realignment of alliances and toppling of old-world establishments, are all in the making and necessitate a deeper understanding of human leadership and its relationships with followers, since this is the level at which such change occurs.

Culture, the most immutable universal phenomenon of human behaviour, provides the vehicle through which those characteristics that set us apart from other mammals are formulated and developed. Humans, write Leakey and Lewin (1992), 'become human through intense learning – not just of survival in the practical worlds, but of customs and social mores, kinship and social laws. In other words: culture. Culture can be said to be *the* human adaptation'. Social organization is not of course only privy to humans; birds and bees, ants and fish, amphibians and primates, all form and exhibit complex systems of behaviour, pecking orders, and survival strategies. They do not, however, record their history, agonize about their future, or undergo existential crises. Moreover, their amazing and remarkable patterns of behaviour are immutable from one generation to the next, because they are hardwired into their DNA. Human-like attributes in their behaviour are just the result of evolution. For example they 'have genes for altruism, and those genes have been selected in the evolution of many creatures because of the advantage they confer for the continuing survival of the species' (Lewis 1984). Birds that fly south for the winter ensure their survival but this process is accomplished instinctively and automatically through the actions of their genes at critical climactic moments year after year; these birds could not decide one winter to devise the means by which to produce enough heat up north and stay put. It takes the long and slow process of natural selection to favour certain mutations and bring about change.[3] But by then we are

---

[3]   This change may be phenotypic and/or behavioural.

dealing with an altogether new and different species which many times bears little phenomenological resemblance to its progenitor.

Homo sapiens (our scientific name which means, perhaps euphemistically, wise man) on the other hand, appears to have diversified his behaviour, adapted to widely varied environments, developed a plethora of tongues and ideologies, and modified his social behaviour with each successive generation; all of this was accomplished in the short time span of his existence that amounts roughly to 50 millennia. Perhaps it is our genomic makeup that programmed us for such unprecedented behavioural diversity, and it would not be unreasonable to assume that this genetic background has evolved precisely to allow behavioural diversification as an ultimate aid to survival. Let me quote Leakey and Lewin again:

> *Homo sapiens* is a cultural creature, to an extent and in a manner unmatched by any other species. This extra dimension of behaviour essentially creates another world, one that may be constantly reshaped. The generation-to-generation transmission of ideas and knowledge means that we all take part in a cumulative expression of our species. Our view of the world, and the material trappings we enjoy in it, depend in a very direct way on what was done one generation back, a hundred generations back. Today, we are the beneficiaries of our distant ancestors in a way not experienced by any other species.

That, in turn, may be the necessary precondition to keep us on this planet. And yet, even though we have been subdivided into different races in response to the environments that nurtured us, we remain a single species. This fact supports the idea that our behavioural diversity is actually a derivative of genetic programming and natural selection. Examples of cultural universals, such as language and culture, must have entered our genes prior to, or just simultaneously, to our division and break off from our hominid (human-like) relatives. Writing about Man and his culture, de Duve (2010) states that 'Unlike other living species, [men] have not achieved their successes by developing appropriate physical adaptations; they have done it with their intelligence.' Moreover, he also asserts that 'we are indeed, of all living beings on Earth, the only ones that are not slavishly subject to natural selection. Thanks to our superior brains, we have the ability to look into the future and to reason, decide, and act in the light of our predictions and expectations, even against our immediate interest, if need be, and for the benefit of a later good'. The value of delayed gratification is hammered into the brains of schoolchildren and students in order to induce them to forgo many options for immediately available types of fun, so that they can reap greater satisfaction later on. Most religions promise greater goods in the afterlife as a counterbalance to suffering in this life.

Culture, therefore, may be thought of as that adaptive dimension that has allowed man to become the dominant species on earth. Culture also gave us our identity, language, and those social characteristics that define who we are and where we belong. Culture, in this sense, can be thought of as the ultimate product of human evolution that defines not only who we are, but what we may one day become. It was written that 'in the process of natural selection, then, any device that can insert a higher proportion of certain genes into subsequent generations will come to characterize the species' (Wilson 1975). Humans are characterized by the genetic capacity to produce culture. It is the ultimate tool we have in our constant struggle against the ever-present destructive force of nature, a force physicists call *entropy*. The ubiquitous process of entropy threatens to consume us if left unchecked. Let's examine it closer.

When the universe was formed about 10 billion years ago, it consisted of a primordial mass that contained all of the elements that make it up today. A terrific explosion took place that is now known as the Big Bang and initiated a continuing expansion that is occurring to this very day.[4] Throughout the millennia, the heavenly bodies appeared; the stars, planets, and galaxies as we know them today. As a consequence of this continuing expansion, the galaxies and other heavenly bodies keep moving away from each other resulting in a condition of ever-increasing disorder. This universal disorder is called entropy and, as far as scientists can discern, it is constantly increasing and applies to everything in the universe. Culture is man's attempt to counteract it. Culture, in this respect, may be considered the end result of a long evolutionary process that began millennia ago, and is the ultimate tool to aid in our survival. According to Andrew McClary (1975):

> Entropy, the obstinate tendency for matter and energy to spread out into even distribution in the environment, seems a characteristic of both the living and nonliving. Is there no way to avoid entropy? If there is, it will probably be found in that product of human evolution we call culture. For it is basic to the character of life, and man in particular, to wage an endless war on entropy.

---

[4] Physicist Stephen Hawking (1988) has called this explosion a singularity because, in the life of this universe, it occurred only once. The study of what happened from that point in time onward, some people consider to fall into the realm of science; whereas what 'happened' before, that of theology.

An example that is closer to home, and illustrates entropy clearer, is the situation in a 'normal' adolescent's bedroom. No matter how orderly it may get after a visit by the housekeeper, in a matter of days (if not hours), it becomes a place of disorder. Entropy, then, is universal change on a grand scale. Societal change can be thought of as entropy on a smaller, more restricted scale, and leaders, according to Bennis (2003), thrive on it since it lets their true colours come through; in other words, they manage it masterfully well since it provides them with a chance to deal with it head on and, through it, channel their energies into forming new realities for their societies. They break away from what Alexis de Tocqueville described when he wrote about democracy in America: 'I am tempted to believe that what we call necessary institutions are no more than institutions to which we have become accustomed. In matters of social constitution, the field of possibilities is much more extensive than men living in their various societies are ready to imagine'. Leaders become leaders precisely because they have the capacity to imagine those other possibilities and guide their people there. Michael Harvey (2006) writes that 'Leadership draws on who we are, but it also shapes what we might be – a kind of alchemy of souls that can produce both Lincoln's "better angels of our nature" and Hitler's willing executioners'. To attain such imagined worlds, however, a leader must understand what Kurt Lewin (1951) calls, 'the totality of coexisting facts which are conceived as mutually interdependent', weigh all the possibilities, and chart a due course of action. The outcome will determine the greatness, or not, of the leader.

IV.

It is not the purpose of this book to discuss the theory of evolution in great detail, but a basic understanding of its premises is needed in order to follow the rationale of the arguments that will be presented later on. This is important because, as William McKinley Runyan (1988b) wrote, 'An evolutionary perspective directs attention to the interaction among biological evolution, the development of psychological structures and processes, and growth and change in sociocultural systems.' This triad of perspectives is my approach to the phenomenon of leadership.

Evolution is probably the most misunderstood theory that was ever put forward. It does not, as popular belief holds, propose that we evolved from the apes. It does suggest that we and the apes have a remote common ancestor, which is quite a different concept. But let's take things from the beginning. Given the presence of oxygen, nitrogen, hydrogen, carbon, water, sunlight and time, life evolved in the primordial seas in simple forms that gradually became more complex. The change occurred secondary to the everlasting need of living organisms to adapt to an ever-changing physical environment. One necessary ingredient was the spontaneous occurrence of mutations, small genetic alterations that brought about structural and behavioural changes in an organism. Most of these accidental changes were actually deleterious and incompatible with survival or resulted in disease. Every so often, however, these changes conferred such characteristics to an organism that actually helped it survive better in the world. Having a better chance to survive meant that this organism had also a better chance to produce offspring that would also bear those changes and reproduce more adapted individuals. Given enough time, the animals with the new characteristics might become the majority whereas the rest became extinct. Thus, a new life form evolved. Recently, a gene known as FOXP2 was identified that is present in many animal species; a mutant form of this gene is somehow associated with the development of language in humans (Enard *et al.* 2002).[5] It was so successful in conferring survival capabilities on humans, that it has replaced all previous forms of it, which might have been previously considered to be the normal state. This 'aberration' then gave rise to a new successful species by allowing a more efficient type of communication. Environmental pressures 'select' different mutations that enhance survivability and reproduction. A fine gradation is often observed in the characteristics of a species as it adapts to gradually differing surroundings. As Darwin (1859) himself observes:

> I have stated, that in the thirteen species of ground-finches [in the Galapagos Islands], a nearly perfect gradation may be traced, from a beak extraordinarily thick, to one so fine, that it may be compared to that of a warbler. I very much suspect that certain members of the series are confined to different islands; therefore, if the collection had been made on any one island, it would not have presented so perfect a gradation. It is clear, that if several islands have each their peculiar species of the same genera, when these are placed together, they will have a wide range of character.

An evolutionary analysis asserts that there should be benefits associated with a particular trait or behaviour to evolve through natural selection (Betzig 1986, Schmitt and Pilcher 2004). In summary, then, two basic factors are necessary for evolution to occur; spontaneous mutations

---

[5] The same author has recently reported (Enard *et al.* 2009) that the humanized form of this gene, transjected into mice, alters the type of squeaks that mice produce.

(producing inter-species variations), and environmental pressures that select them out of other alternatives.[6] This process is known as natural selection. It works as the environment changes so that the organisms that evolve are well suited and adapted to these changes. Climactic changes are usually what we mean as we talk about environmental pressures. As Leakey and Lewin (1992) write:

> Such climactic changes break up habitats, and may drive pulses of extinction throughout the plant and animal worlds. But they may also cause speciation, the development of new species from isolated populations, adapting to new conditions.

One may not help wonder what will result from the recent environmental (climactic) changes that the Earth is going through, as far as humans and other organisms are concerned. De Duve (2010), in discussing our options to save our habitats, hopes that 'with increasing awareness of the disaster we are facing if we do not change course, future initiatives could meet with greater success'. Such initiatives of course will have to come about by the leaders we will choose and their personality traits will be of paramount importance in order to allow them, and us, to make the necessary and imperative decisions, even against our immediate interests, for the benefit of all humanity, the planet, and the rest of living organisms. The main thesis of this book is that to be successful, a leader must have a degree of paranoia in his personality. If a healthy dose of paranoia or other psychological trait is needed in order to accomplish this, then so be it. Subsequent chapters hopefully will help to alert readers in the choices we all make for our leaders and our future. US Republican resistance in bringing about the necessary changes in order to ensure our future in a clean environment, may be seen as an example of paranoia against too much and too fast a change brought about by what they consider to be leftist liberals.

One should not erroneously think that mutations are determined *a priori* or that they occur in a teleological (that is, towards a specific goal) fashion. They just occur by chance and occasionally they happen to be advantageous to an organism.[7] A rough sequence of organismal appearance on Earth is as follows; from single-celled (that is, amoebae) to

---

[6]   As biologists like to refer to them, Darwinian Theory comprises of two basic premises; that of continuing change and that of natural selection.

[7]   Alternatively, a religiously inclined person might see 'the hand of God' in this occurrence and many theologians have argued that, if evolution is true, then it must be guided by divine intervention. Even the Scriptures however, hint at

multiple-celled organisms; from the water to marshes to land; from fish to amphibians to reptiles; the latter gave rise to both birds and mammals.[8] All evidence suggests that life initially developed in the sea. Even today, animals, including man, are made up mostly of water, and in fact, of saltwater, reflecting the primordial environment that surrounded our ancestral life forms.[9]

An interplay between the human brain, culture, tools, and language appears to have set the stage for the evolution of large convoluted brains, especially on the surface (what we colloquially call the grey matter), and even more so its frontal part known as the forebrain[10] that sub-serves such things as language, personality, and social skills. Those characteristics, in other words, that set us apart from other animals and made us human. Of these, language appears to have had the lion's share in importance. As Leakey and Lewin (1993) put it:

> When we contemplate our origins, we quickly come to focus on language. Objective standards for our uniqueness as a species, such as our bipedality and our relatively enormous brain, are easy to measure. But in *many ways it is language that makes us feel human. Ours is a world of* words. Our thoughts, our world of imagination, our communication, our richly fashioned culture – all are woven on the loom of language. Language can conjure up images in our minds. Language can stir our emotions – sadness, happiness, love, hatred. Through language we can express individuality or demand collective loyalty. Quite simply, language is our medium.

---

evolution in the famous story of Noah who, having exhibited the 'right' characteristics, was able, following divine providence, to survive the cataclysmic environmental change of the flood, and inaugurate a new generation of a different – dare I say evolved? – human race. Matt Ridley (2003) on the other hand uses the term Gene Organizing Device – GOD – to describe the process.

[8] Interestingly, a similar sequence is presented in the Bible and has been taught by theologians and Sunday school teachers for centuries. Therefore, the recently observed animosity between the so-called creationists and the evolutionists may, ironically, be more the result of misunderstanding than an actual conceptual difference.

[9] In the popular TV science fiction series *Star Trek: The Next Generation*, Captain Picard and his crew encounter a crystalline – thus perfectly symmetrical – life form on a distant planet, which, after they managed to communicate with each other, described humans as 'ugly bags of mostly water!'

[10] Telencephalon, meaning end-brain, is the scientific term used to describe this part of the anatomy of the nervous system to emphasize its relatively recent development in evolution and the – almost teleological – fact that it is found only in humans.

Chomsky (1965) proposed in the 1960s that the brain possesses a *language acquisition device* that is uniquely human and operates through similar mechanisms in people of all languages, and sub-serves the rules of grammar and syntax. This device, if it exists, would constitute the evolutionary development that set us apart from the apes.[11]

It may be interesting to note here how these functions were discovered. Sometimes we appreciate the function and usefulness of a structure by its absence; that is, after it is somehow damaged. This is actually how the function of the various parts of the brain, including the frontal lobes, was initially delineated; by experimentally ablating each part (in animals, of course), and reassessing the resulting loss of function. In humans, early neurologists would similarly study the effects of strokes, accidents, destructive tumours, and other processes that caused an ablation of a part of the brain. As Gazzaniga (2008) states, 'focal brain lesions produced discrete and specific deficits in patients. If a specific part of the brain is damaged, there are specific disorders of language, thought, [perception, attention, and so on]. And nowhere were such phenomena more dramatic than in split-brain patients, proving that the left side of the brain is specialized for one set of capacities and the other side for another kind.' We will return to the notion of brain (hemispheric) specialization again later on. An industrial accident, which occurred in the nineteenth century, gave us the first clues about the function of the frontal lobes. The case is briefly described below.

Phineas Gage was an energetic, responsible young American man with initiative at his work that commanded the respect of his superiors. He was the foreman of a railway construction crew. Unfortunately he was involved in a freak work-related accident when he was using a steel rod to ram a charge of blasting powder into a hole that was carved into a rocky surface. The charge exploded unexpectedly and sent the rod into his cheek, through his frontal lobe, and out of the top of his skull. The accident had destroyed a good part of his frontal lobes and he came close to dying. He did survive however and appeared to have sustained no long term consequences initially. But with time it became obvious that he was not the same person as before the accident. He began acting irresponsibly, erratically, with disrespect for others, and, at times, recklessly. His personality had made a complete turnaround as a result of the damage he had suffered in his frontal lobes (Damasio 1994). In fact, there is

---

[11] This 'device' would not be an anatomic location in the brain but a functional network of neurons organized accordingly, following the activation and inactivation of genes, in order to bring about the acquisition of speech and language.

evidence that lesions anywhere in the frontal lobes of the brain will cause behavioural symptoms as well as personality changes, especially executive dysfunction, meaning affectation of the ability to make decisions, reason, and plan appropriate actions (Tullberg *et al.* 2004). The importance of the frontal lobes for our humanness is thus obvious. Suffice it to mention that the speech centre is also located in the frontal lobes; this is an important component of language, perhaps the single most important characteristic that made us human and enabled the development of culture.

V.

Pre-humans (including primates) used tools in their everyday activities. As we saw above, evolution selected out those brains that used tools more efficiently according to the mechanisms described earlier. Gradually, larger brains appeared that manufactured more complex tools. They also, through mutations, produced language and abstract ideas that were advantageous for survival; and, subsequently, culture.[12] The English anthropologist Edward Burnett Tylor (1889) wrote that 'culture is that complex whole which includes knowledge, belief, art, morals, law, custom, and any other capabilities and habits acquired by man as a member of a society', whereas, more recently, Ashley Montague (1968) defined culture as follows; 'With the creation and usage of organized systems of symbols man created a new dimension of experience ... we call culture. Culture is man-made. It is the environment which man creates in order the better to control as much of the environment as he desires.' Domestication of animals and plants through culture, helped develop a surplus, a sedentary life, and the rise of specialists (McClary 1975). Through culture came the development of such things as social stratification, roles and division of labour, and expectations about appropriate behaviour (social norms and codes). In addition, the limits of normal and abnormal behaviour as they related to and enhanced the survival chances of the group at large in specific environments were set. These could be diametrically opposite in different environments but perfectly appropriate for their own needs and circumstances; to abandon ailing grandma in a hospital or nursing home in Western cultures is an example of deplorable and despicable behaviour; to abandon ailing grandma in an Eskimo igloo is an example of expected, accepted, and

---

[12] Culture in this context is thought of as one of the most, if not the key, genetic determinants of what constitutes humanness.

appropriate behaviour when her small kinship group will need to get on in search of food in harsh environmental conditions, and this is typically the behaviour that is traditionally seen.

An evolutionary legacy we have retained from our biological ancestors is the need to form social hierarchies and orders. To have them functioning in an orderly way, a leader or group of leaders (elders, senators, parliamentarians, and what have you) are found on top. Such a development became necessary in order to manage the increasingly more complex cultural systems that arose around the globe. Evolution would not have left the selection of leaders to chance, but it would have developed such social behaviours, so that the most appropriate member of any given group would rise to the top. That leader would consequently enhance the group's survival.

We now return to our initial question; has evolution produced a species that is genetically programmed to take on its destiny on an individual basis, or as a multitude that is pre-destined to follow leaders? And if the latter is true, which characteristics in a leader are those that the crowd has been genetically programmed to be attracted to? An individual alone cannot of course make significant strides in progress. He must clearly act within a social group in order to have an impact with his contributions.[13] Aristotle wrote that man is a social animal. As the first biologist, he was echoing future concepts about genetic determinants of behaviour including the formation of social groups. Any innovation must be adopted and accepted by, as well as get incorporated into a social context, in order to affect behaviour in some way. Ridley (2003) wrote that 'A solitary human mind cannot secrete culture'. Therefore, interplay takes place between the group and the individual. The question to answer is which of the two in this relationship assumes the leading role and which follows. As Samuel Johnson (Bloom 1986) observed in the eighteenth century, 'No two people can be half an hour together, but one shall acquire an evident superiority over the other'. Moreover, another issue to tackle would be whether the same process holds for all group-to-individual relationships or whether different circumstances create variable arrangements.

In every historically important moment of human affairs, there appear to have appeared great individuals that led the way. As the old English expression goes, 'Cometh the hour, cometh the man' the implication is

---

[13] Cultural traits can also diffuse across cultures and effect changes in the receiving group. Again, this is accomplished between social contexts and has the same effects as those new traits that are introduced into a group by an individual within.

that each circumstance requires its particular leader. From Abraham to Caesar, from Christ to Muhammad, from Constantine to Washington, from Stalin to Hitler, all these individuals have led their 'people' into destinies that they had not foreseen. The list is endless. Could there be a common underlying factor that determines the process of their advance, and if there is, could it be biologically explained? Birds for example that submit to a pecking order are so programmed biologically; and so are the ones doing the pecking (the leaders). Some trait puts both the pecker and the ones being pecked on notice about their respective place in the system. Wild herds are also known to form hierarchies that, once they get established, are adhered to until another animal in the herd (which itself usually rates high on the hierarchy), challenges the order. Primates are no exception to this phenomenon. The trait, I will argue subsequently, is a form of mental state (illness if you will), known as paranoia; it characterizes many psychiatric and psychological conditions, yet it confers leadership qualities on its bearers by producing a certain kind of personality that has a natural propensity to lead. Mental illness, like many other kinds of illnesses, has its biological substrate and as such, is subject to the laws of genetics and inheritance. In that respect I will attempt to convince my readers that, as William H. Hampton and Virginia Schroeder Burnham (1990) claimed, 'Paranoia has promoted and yet restricted our evolution in the development of the family, communities, and nations. It was part of the process by which human beings progressed from a primitive to a cultured civilized state. Paranoia is also responsible for the evolution of politics, religions, war, peace, science and tech-nology.'

Paranoia was once considered to be a characteristic of only mental illness; however, recently conducted studies have been revealing that paranoia may be much more common than previously thought; it may affect up to one in three people in the general public and may also be on the rise (most likely as an evolutionary triggered adaptive mechanism), in recent times, given the rise of world terrorism, the fall of communism, the fall of capitalism, and the global disintegration of values. Daniel Freeman *et al.* (2008) conducted an experiment in which he simulated the situation that exists in the London Underground and discovered that up to 40 per cent of his volunteer study group harboured at least one unfounded paranoid thought towards neutral others. As he puts it, 'Paranoid thoughts are often triggered by ambiguous events such as people looking in one's direction or hearing laughter in a room.' As an explanation he states that 'at the heart of all social interactions is a vital judgement whether to trust or mistrust, but it is a judgment that is error-prone. We are more likely to make paranoid errors if we are anxious, ruminate, and have had bad experiences from others'. Our time, the New Common Era, is rife with anxiety and misgivings. Such a condition likely triggers an evolutionary-determined gene-activating process that puts individuals into hyper-alert states, in order to maximize their defences and chances for survival. This would explain the unfortunate event of the shooting by police of an innocent man in the London Underground shortly after the 7 July 2005 bombings that shocked the British nation. I will not deal further with the mechanistic process of human evolution or its differentiation from other primates, except when such a discussion would be illustrative of my primary thesis regarding the relationship of language, mental illness and leadership. Recently published extensive treatises have adequately expounded on the topic (Leakey and Lewin 1992, Ridley 2003, Gazzaniga 2008).

Moreover, I will take it for granted that most political leaders have been on the odd end of the personality spectrum, as this fact is well accepted by most people without question. This also applies to leaders in general. Recently, I was following a conversation regarding the late Prime Minister of Greece, Andreas Papandreou, and his late-life escapades.[14] What an eye-opener it was for me to find out that he was chronically on treatment with lithium, a drug used to curtail the exacerbations of manic depressive (bipolar) illness.[15] This individual was holding his country's fate in his hands for decades. Post (2003) uses the term 'terminal machismo' in discussing Papandreou's personality – a term that could be applied to the rest of the bunch. Alexander, Ceasar, the Roman Emperor Constantine, Pope Clement VII, Napoleon Bonaparte, Vladimir Lenin, Adolf Hitler, Winston Churchill, Josef Stalin, Saddam Hussein and Osama bin Laden, to name but a few leaders readily recognized by everyone, need no introduction when their personality peculiarities are under discussion. I will not devote much space to character or biographical descriptions of individual leaders, political or otherwise, except briefly to illustrate my claims. Many books have been written on illustrious historical as well as current leaders. The interested reader may find a plethora of them through a brief perusal of any bookstore or the internet. I will mention names as the need arises to make my points clear.

The basic tenet of the book is that leaders are qualitatively different from followers; that these differences are biologically (genetically)

---

[14] In his 70s, he divorced his wife of many years and married an airline stewardess.
[15] Bipolar illness is discussed fully in Chapter 8.

determined; that an important difference lies in their use of language; that language itself is a uniquely developed human characteristic which is evolutionarily associated with the appearance of psychiatric disorders; and that we probably possess the capacity to activate certain genes at times of crisis which 'allow' us to appoint paranoid leaders in charge, because they appear to possess the 'right stuff' to see us through our troubles. It is reasonable to assume, then, that some biologically determined traits that have survived across species that live in teams, including man, enhance their structuring and stratification in an orderly and systematic way. Humans appear to have retained these traits as well, and Aristotle is proved correct in his ancient pronouncement (see above).

We may now bring biology and sociology together to help explain this phenomenon. What makes some humans leaders, others followers, and why our leaders' personalities fall outside the average of observable behaviours, will be discussed in the rest of this book.

2. Genes, behaviour, and the human speciation event

> It is in our genes to understand the universe if we can, to keep trying even if we cannot, and to be enchanted by the act of learning all the way.
>
> Lewis Thomas

I.

The question whether human behaviour is genetic (instinctual) having been determined by the principles of evolution through the millennia, or the result of cultural learning, can be approached from two somewhat opposing points of view, even though there are as many shades of answers as people who pondered the subject. Historically, there were those scientists who viewed behaviour as mostly genetically determined and hard-wired into our biological substance; and there were those who upheld the view that it is the product of an active learning process dependent upon upbringing, learning and social practices. The former are known as *ethologists* whereas the latter as *social scientists*. Ridley (2003), in a somewhat conciliatory approach, claimed that 'genes are designed to take their cues from nurture'; he advocated experience (nurture) as the trigger of gene expression (nature) and called the former by such names as nativists, geneticists, hereditarians, or naturians, and the latter as empiricists, environmentalists, or nurturists. He claimed that 'the more we lift the lid on the genome, the more vulnerable to experience genes appear to be'. As he puts it elsewhere in the same book, 'nature and nurture are not opposed to each other but work together'. Such a fact has become increasingly more obvious as the field of epigenetics has shed light onto the biological processes by which experience affects the structure and function of genes on the DNA level.[1]

---

[1] A simple and understandable definition of epigenetics is the following: epigenetics in biology is the study of heritable changes in gene expression or cellular phenotype caused by mechanisms other than changes in the underlying DNA sequence (Bird 2007); it refers to functionally relevant modifications to the

Epigenetic regulation is therefore critical in the interplay between nature and nurture by bringing about alterations in the DNA by methylation as well as histones modifications and microRNA expression (Ventura-Junca and Herrera 2012). Such patterns could explain the emergence of personality types but, also, abnormal behaviours secondary to early stressful events.

Ethology grew out of the study of animal behaviour in their natural habitats and has, subsequently, spilled over to the study of man. The first ethologists were zoologists (animal biologists) who observed that much of animal behaviour was, in fact, instinctual and not learned. This proved to be true particularly in such behaviours as courting, mating, and aggression to establish dominance. Even complex patterns of behaviour appeared to be genetic. Soon this type of approach was applied to humans as well and convincing evidence was gathered that, to a great extent, their behaviour was mostly instinctive rather than learned. Andrew McClary (1975) writes that ethologists 'contend that such diverse behaviour patterns as grooming, flirting, being submissive to superiors, pair bonding, and aggression all have an instinctive base'. If such behaviours, they reason, were naturally selected in animals in response to environmental pressures, and to ensure survival and reproduction, then why not in humans as well? Bouchard *et al.* (1990) report the illustrative case of identical twins separated at birth, who were adopted and raised apart by families that differed in their socio-economic status. They were reunited years later as adults; both had become firemen, married similar-looking women, and enjoyed the same hobbies. Coincidence? Perhaps. Then again, who's to say that both men, with their identical genetic makeup, had not developed tastes that were pre-ordained unbeknownst to them and that, in fact, their adoptive families had little influence on the moulding of their personalities? If indeed this case illustrates the extent of the control that is exerted on behaviour by genes, we can then begin to appreciate the magnitude of the role that genetics played, through natural selection and evolution, in shaping our personalities. The flip side of the argument is that we are just the vehicles by which genes survive; they are the ultimate masters of our existence and, as such, they produce the types of phenotypes, including leaders and followers that maximize their immortality. Haruki Murakami (2013) has put it eloquently:

---

genome that do not involve a change in the nucleotide sequence. Examples of such changes are DNA methylation and histone modification, both of which serve to regulate gene expression without altering the underlying DNA sequence (Spector 2012).

> Human beings are ultimately nothing but carriers – passageways – for genes. They ride us into the ground like racehorses from generation to generation. Genes don't think about what constitutes good or evil. They don't care whether we are happy or unhappy. We're just means to an end for them. The only thing they think about is what is most efficient for them.

The evidence is actually compelling and more than anecdotal as one might construe regarding the firemen case above. Well-designed studies have time and again provided similar conclusions; comparing the rates of schizophrenia in people who were adopted away during childhood, and whose parents were either normal or contained at least one schizophrenic parent, we find that the former exhibited little psychiatric disability, as well as lack of any significant talents or achievements; the latter, however, and in contrast to children of 'normals', contained significantly more psychiatrically impaired individuals, as well as creative achievements, leadership abilities, musical skills and an interest in religion (Heston 1970, Kety *et al.* 1994). Frequently we hear psychiatrically impaired people being described as talented and intelligent pre-morbidly. We will argue later on that relatives of schizophrenics and those with milder forms of mental illness may possess characteristics and abilities that express our human nature, and that, in fact, the presence of schizophrenia in the general population confers evolutionary advantages, including the phenomenon of leadership and the advent of language.

More evidence comes from the small and isolated population of Iceland where, due to a legacy of accurate record keeping and family-tree reconstruction, mental illness could be traced for generations. What stands out in Icelandic studies is the fact that families of schizophrenic individuals also contained people with other major psychiatric illnesses such as manic depression, alcoholism, psychopathy, and personality disorders. Moreover, the same families produced high achievers, talented and creative individuals, as well as leaders (Karlsson 1966, 1974, 2001). As Horrobin (1998) says, 'madness, badness, creativity and leadership all seemed to go together in the same family trees'.

Let's now turn to leaders and followers. Patterns of submissiveness and recognizing leaders may also be considered to be a genetically pro-grammed behavioural pattern, just as the tendency to assume leadership can. In other words, leaders and followers behave as leaders and as followers because their genetic endowment makes them do so. We have all come across people we felt were in the wrong position or role at work, precisely because their position did not match their character. This mismatch results when a genetically 'programmed' follower is given, for one reason or another, the role of a leader or, *vice versa*, a leader is put in a subordinate relationship. An aggressive person will not do well as a follower, the same way that a follower will make an ineffective leader. The paranoid or otherwise personality disordered individual (in the schizotypal/psychotic spectrum of pathology that will be discussed later on in Chapter 8), will be more likely to exhibit aggression in order to assume leadership and force his ideas on others who are more readily willing to follow without much aggression. In the animal kingdom these relationships and hierarchies are genetically controlled, and include aggression, the means by which pecking orders are established. Even though it may not be obvious at first, humans, who also belong to the animal kingdom, must also exhibit biologically determined patterns of behaviour that are character-specific and include the assumption of their 'proper' roles in society. M. Harvey (2006) reminds us that 'we find pronounced hierarchies in every human community anthropologists have ever observed'. Such a pattern would be the result of natural selection as an adaptive mechanism to enhance survival and reproduction, the two vital goals of all living organisms. Without hierarchy we might have withered away millennia ago.

Aggression, whether real or symbolic (linguistic for our purposes), may be one such characteristic that is seen as desirable by groups of people just as it is among animals. Aggression is tightly linked to reproductive prowess, symbolically as well as physiologically; the same brain structures are activated during both an aggressive act as well as copulation.[2] There appears to be '[a] continuous entanglement of sexuality and aggression, those two fundamental drives that make history' (Gay 1988). An aggressive person may be unconsciously seen by others as a better candidate to ensure survival and reproduction, not only for him, but also for the whole group. Hence his chances to become a leader are enhanced, since he is seen as the right individual to see the group (the followers) through the vicissitudes and demands of a given situation or a changing world. As Robert Ardrey (1971) put it, 'Aggressiveness is the principal guarantor of survival ... It is the innateness of the aggressive potential which guarantees that obstacles will be attacked, the young defended, new feeding grounds found when old lie waste, that orthodoxies give way to innovation when environment so demands'. The environmental demands may consist of a drought in sub-Saharan Africa, an

---

[2]   These structures are known as the amygdala and are found in the temporal lobes of the brain, where they also are closely linked to the so-called limbic system that sub-serves our emotional reactions.

invading army in another country, resurgence of terrorism, or the need for a strike in a production plant in Akron, Ohio.

Emergent leaders must provide enough aggressive dispositions to have their followers put their trust in them and thus establish their own symbolic pecking order. A successful outcome for their cause will ensure survival, and survival ensures success in reproduction. For primitive societies such outcomes were concrete and critically understood as their ultimate goal. Research in traditional societies shows a direct link between (male) leadership and reproductive success (Chagnon 1997) and perhaps, indirectly, that spills over onto followers as well. Men in leadership positions have, on average, more children and more wives than their subordinates (Chagnon 1997). Even though such issues may not appear as urgent or immediate for more advanced societies, and aggression may be expressed in more symbolic than actual forms, its effects on the collective consciousness of these societies is as real as in their primitive counterparts. When urgencies subside, aggressiveness may be sublimated into more creative activities. What better example would one need than the most obvious sublimation for aggression, sports, to understand this phenomenon? Christian de Duve (2010) reminds us that:

> Even in peace, competition has remained, directly or by proxy, the most widely, passionately, and, sometimes, violently practiced form of entertainment, with arenas, stadiums, and sports fields replacing bloody battlefields as outlets for our thirst for competition ... All these manifestations, whether bellicose or peaceful, are rooted in the depths of our being. The warring instinct is embedded in human nature.

Unfortunately, sublimation alone does little to avert actual aggressive skirmishes that often enough develop into major wars. Maybe the world could use more symbolism and sublimation to vent its aggressive tendencies. Aggression and its athletic substitutes also carry over into sexual attraction for the reasons analysed above. Heroes and champions have always prided themselves in their sexual escapades. Again, the attraction may lie in our ultimate biologically programmed wish to propagate our genes. If not actually, then symbolically, athletes and heroes are leaders in people's minds and as such are consciously or unconsciously given attributes of sexual prowess, admixed with their putative leadership qualities. Winning begets status and status begets power. Harvey (2006) reminds us that when it comes to males, power and sexual aggression are linked and, ultimately, both enhance survival. Like Harvey, I would also like to quote Machiavelli's famous passage from *The Prince* (2001b [1532]):

It is better to be impetuous than cautious, because fortune is a woman; and it is necessary, if one wants to hold her down, to beat her and strike her down. And one sees that she lets herself be won more by the impetuous than by those who proceed coldly. And so always, like a woman, she is the friend of the young, because they are less cautious, more ferocious, and command her with more audacity.

We will return to Machiavelli's ideas and political thinking in later chapters. Aggression is in fact one of the best studied phenomena both in animals as well as in man. Whereas in the wild aggression does not usually result in death (as in animals establishing a pecking order), in humans this process has gone off-track to the point of creating violent interpersonal conflicts and international wars that have cost millions of lives and destruction on an unprecedented scale. This is abnormal behaviour that, according to Desmond Morris (1969), has resulted from maladjustment of our instinctual predispositions, and which are adaptive up to a point, to a rapidly changing technological world. To illustrate, in his own words:

Under normal conditions, in their natural habitats, wild animals do not mutilate themselves, masturbate, attack their offspring, develop stomach ulcers, become fetishists, suffer from obesity, form homosexual pair-bonds, or commit murder. Among human city-dwellers, needless to say, all of these things occur. Does this, then, reveal a basic difference between the human species and other animals? At first glance it seems to do so. But this is deceptive. Other animals do behave in these ways under certain circumstances, namely when they are confined in the unnatural conditions of captivity.

In other words, abnormal behaviour as exhibited by humans, is to be encountered in societies that have advanced technologically from more primitive ways of life that were simpler and more adjusted to nature. The concept of the 'Noble Savage' described by French philosopher and sociologist Jacques Rousseau (2001 [1755]) is driving home the exact same point.[3] He advocated a return to the nostalgic times of human

---

[3] Rousseau holds that 'uncorrupted morals' prevail in the 'state of nature' and he especially praised the admirable moderation of the Caribbeans in expressing the sexual urge despite the fact that they live in a hot climate, which 'always seems to inflame the passions'. This has led Anglophone critics to erroneously attribute to Rousseau the invention of idea of the noble savage, an oxymoronic expression that was never used in France and which grossly misrepresents Rousseau's thought. The expression, 'the noble savage' was first used in 1672 by British poet John Dryden in his play *The Conquest of*

naiveté and simplicity as a way to overcome the ills of the 'civilized' society of his times which he considered to be a fraud. For Rousseau, the noble savage 'satisfies his hunger under an oak tree, quenches his thirst at the first stream, finds his bed at the foot of the same tree that supplied his meal; and thus, all his needs are satisfied'. One can only guess what his reaction might have been had he had a glimpse of the twenty-first century. The issue, however, is not whether we should return to less technologically advanced times, an unrealistic if not chimerical proposition, but how to make our times tolerable and humane, thus creating a better place to live. To achieve this we need to choose leaders who are capable to see us through our problems and crises with wisdom and foresight. After all, Morris's and Rousseau's ideas have been challenged in recent years as more research in the wild has revealed 'unnatural' behaviours among non-human primates in addition to our own species. Let's consider Matt Ridley (2003) again:

> Saint Augustine said we were the only creature to have sex for pleasure rather than procreation. (A reformed libertine would know.) Chimpanzees begged to differ, and their southern relatives, bonobos, were soon to blow the definition to smithereens. Bonobos have sex to celebrate a good meal, to end an argument, or to cement a friendship. Since much of this sex is homosexual or with juveniles, procreation cannot even be an accidental side effect.

So much for sex as only an instinctual, reproductive process in the wild. Not only are older theories toppled by these recent findings, our own uniqueness, negative or positive, is challenged as well; the inescapable insinuation here is that some of our behavioural characteristics seem to have appeared in our primate ancestors prior to our definite emergence. Our speciation may have been a protracted, gradual process with characteristics acquired along the way. Sex for the sake of sex may also have appeared as an adaptive phenomenon, perhaps as a 'rehearsal' for actual reproduction.

At the other end of the spectrum are those social scientists in whose view the mind is considered to be a *tabula rasa*, a blank sheet upon which experiences shape personality. In their views genetics plays but a minuscule part in human behaviour by setting the limits into which our potential manifests. It basically determines our biological characteristics whereas society shapes our behavioural ones. This has been a more

---

Granada. The French word 'sauvage' means 'wild', as in 'a wild flower', and does not have the connotations of fierceness or brutality that the word 'savage' does in English, though in the eighteenth century the English word was closer in connotation to the French one (Wikipedia accessed 2013).

appealing (and hopeful) theory since it gives people more control as well as responsibility about their behaviour. The role of society, education and politics, then, becomes paramount and behavioural deviants can be held responsible for their actions. Education is considered imperative, as an extension to families, in order to shape 'proper' personalities in children and future adults so that they exhibit appropriate and constructive behaviour. When these techniques fail, correctional facilities become a main instrument of social control and applied punishments hold the individual ultimately responsible for the aberrant behaviour. At the same time, they attempt to deter others from committing similar crimes. Capital punishment is often encountered in those societies that consider behaviour to be the ultimate responsibility of the individual and not the result of genetics or heritable traits; these societies, therefore, tend to resist the abolition of such extreme punishments.

Social scientists, including sociologists, anthropologists, and comparative psychologists, give such emphasis to upbringing, rearing techniques and the environment (including the social milieu), that the ideas of an instinctual basis to behaviour is often offensive to them. They particularly resist the idea that aggression is biologically determined. The famous American anthropologist Ashley Montague (1968) voiced this opposition quite explicitly:

> The myth of early man's aggressiveness belongs in the same class as the myth of 'the beast', that is, the belief that most if not all 'wild' animals are ferocious killers. In the same class belongs the myth of the 'jungle', 'the wild', 'the warfare of Nature', and, of course, the myth of 'innate depravity' or 'original sin'. These myths represent the projection of our acquired deplorabilities upon the screen of 'Nature'. What we were unwilling to acknowledge as essentially our own making, the consequence of our own disordering in the man-made environment, we saddle upon 'Nature', upon 'phylogenetically programmed' or 'innate' factors ... What, in fact, these writers do, in addition to perpetrating their wholly erroneous interpretation of human nature, is to divert attention from the real sources of man's aggression and destructiveness, namely, the many false and contradictory values by which, in an overcrowded, highly competitive, threatening world, he so disoperatively attempts to live. It is not man's nature, but his nurture, in such a world, that requires our attention.

And so it is not only the nature versus nurture argument that surfaces here, but also, the idea of the noble savage. Andrew McClary (1975) states that 'some primitive cultures are very warlike and aggressive; others are not'. Thus, according to social scientists, there is anthropological evidence that aggression is not a cultural (and therefore instinctual) universal. Turnbull (1972) studied a peculiar primitive people on the mountains of northeastern Uganda, the Ik, which, as a contrast to the 'noble savage' concept, were characterized by sadism towards their fellow tribesmen. The suffering of others was the greatest and perhaps only source of fun for them, leading Turnbull, unbefitting an anthropologist, to abhor the people he was studying. Be that as it may, we should keep in mind that anthropologists study primitive societies at a particular point in their social evolution and, from that point on, all bets are off since the contact with technologically more sophisticated cultures changes them forever.

Moreover, the work of Steven Pinker (2002), *The Blank Slate*, goes a long way in discrediting the notion of the noble savage as well as the view of the mind as a *tabula rasa*. Pinker also argues that modern science has challenged, in addition to the above, the notion of 'the ghost in the machine', which holds that each of us has a soul that makes choices free from biology. He explains such 'false' beliefs on unfounded fears of inequality, imperfectability, determinism and nihilism but considers them to be non-sequiturs and argues that equality does not require sameness, but the acceptance of different people as individuals with rights; that moral progress does not require the human mind to be void of selfish motives, but to have other motives by which to counteract them; that responsibility should not consider behaviour to be undetermined but that it would have the capacity to respond to social criticism or praise; and that a satisfying and meaningful life should not result from a teleological development of the brain, but only that it, the brain, must have goals. He also predicts that if we ground our moral values on claims of a blank slate that would open up the future possibility of having it overturned by empirical and scientific discoveries.

In order to establish whether early man was naturally aggressive or not, we need to turn, again, to our closest relatives, the primates, and their social interactions that may shed some light on the issue. Leakey and Lewin (1992) describe the story of two chimpanzees in a zoo in Arnhem, the Netherlands, and the way they formed an alliance, plotted against, and killed the alpha male chimp of their camp; the murdered chimp had previously used cunning and wit in order to win over an older male, one of the two murderers. Therefore, not only aggression, but murder as well appears to form part of the great apes' *modus operandi*. Both Morris (1969) and Ashley Montague quoted above would readily argue that this abnormal behaviour was exhibited in captivity and not in the animals' natural habitat and could not, therefore, be indicative of their true biology. However, there exist now many reports about violence among apes in their natural niches, not only between competing males but also between older chimps and the newborn offspring of other males

(Williams *et al.* 2008). Violence has also been described between females competing for foraging fruit in overlapping niches (Leakey and Lewin 1992). Recent research has revealed that, indeed, animal violence is exhibited in instances that are independent from purely defensive contexts and adaptive forms of aggression, indicating perhaps an evolutionary significance (Natarajan and Caramaschi 2010). As a biological marker of this behaviour, low levels of pre-frontal serotonin levels have been reported (Takahashi *et al.* 2012).[4]

Another major factor that has recently emerged in determining the expression of violence is the need for territorial expansion to gain access to more resources (food and females) in order to survive and reproduce (Mitani *et al.* 2010). Unfortunately, even in our modern-day 'civilized' world, such actions can galvanize people on opposite sides. Modern-day Turkey has recently been threatening the tiny island of Cyprus, itself a European Union member state, to curtail drillings in its exclusive economic zone in search of natural gas and oil, claiming that such an act is illegal (Arsu 2011); and this, in spite of an international cry against Turkey and a call to respect international law and order. What ultimate motive other that expanding its territory and resources could be operating? Such violence-for-expansion findings have been reported among chimpanzees in the wild, but can easily be extrapolated to humans as well, given our close genetic make-up, and can be seen as having survived in both populations to enhance survival. The history of the world is largely the history of one group of people usurping another group's resources. There is genetic evidence that such behaviour may be influenced by the kinds of genes one carries. For example, Beaver *et al.* (2010) reports that boys carrying a particular variant of the MAOA gene that codes for the monoamine oxidase A (MAOA) enzyme, are unusually prone to joining gangs. The variant results in low levels of the neurotransmitter MAOA in the brain. Low activity MAOA variants have been linked to various types of sociopathic behaviour and the gene has been called the 'warrior gene' by some scientists. When such tendencies enter world politics, however, the stakes get high enough to threaten peace and established order. At times of tension a paranoid leader could influence followers and turn them into a mob searching for real or imagined enemies. Recent insurgences by Muslim militants against Christians in the Middle East attest to this fact. It remains to be seen whether Pinker's

---

[4] Serotonin is a neurotransmitter believed to be involved in such functions as mood regulation, appetite, sleep, and cognition among others. Low brain levels of serotonin have been correlated with depression, aggression, pain, and learning.

assertion (2011) that violence has been declining significantly in the world, is a historical fact or just wishful thinking.

What these examples clearly demonstrate is not only the violent predispositions of non-human primates in their natural environments, but, in addition, the beginnings of political thinking, action and process, and the struggle to be on top of the social hierarchy with all the benefits and prestige it encompasses. And, to reiterate, these behaviours evolved in order to help these animals survive and reproduce. Some scholars even go so far as to suggest that such behaviour is hard-wired into human males in order to help them assert power by committing acts of violence and sexual aggression (Harvey 2006). Sublimating such violence with sports may have been a strategically targeted survival policy of early human behaviour, in order to avert greater acts of aggression. The war-like behaviour and physiological arousal that one observes during football matches, as well as the unfortunate violence that occasionally accompanies them, attests to this fact. Worldwide events such as the Olympic Games thus assume a significance of national urgency and pride. Fukuyama (1998) notes that both humans as well as pre-human primates live in male dominated, patrilineal – father (male)-dominated – societies in which males routinely engage in acts of violence and aggression, another fact supporting our biological/evolutionary legacy. Such behaviour would eventually prove conducive to the emergence of violence-prone leaders. To use a term coined by Wrangham and Peterson (1996), the most 'demonic' of these humans will rise to the top. There is evidence that even among women leaders, those who exhibit male-like behaviour have more chances to succeed in their roles (Eagly and Karau 2002).

We humans have retained this legacy and our leaders embody it in their social as well as their biological lives. Leaky and Lewin (1992), however, also point out that unquestionable evidence of human warfare is not present before about 10,000 years ago, when agriculture developed and sedentary lifestyles became necessary in order to produce farming goods and surpluses. Of course, that is not to say that the biological trait had not been bequeathed to the species. As we argue elsewhere, genes are turned on or off by the environmental conditions that nurture them (Ridley 2003) and the gene for aggression may have remained latent until the time when competition was necessary in order to defend the territory where food was produced, and so may have our genetic tendency to form hierarchies. Some of us naturally (biologically driven) lead, whereas others follow.

Our leaders carry biological characteristics that may appear to have been socially determined but, nonetheless, alert us about their leadership potential and abilities; followers, on the other hand, fall in place as their own social biology determines, an arrangement cemented by evolution to aid survival. Power, in this respect, becomes the social force through which our leaders accomplish their leadership demands. We will discuss this issue subsequently in Chapter 7. For now we should remember that what might appear on the surface to be a socially driven and determined behaviour on the part of our leaders, is actually a 'socialization' of hard-wired biological traits, manifesting as behavioural patterns of this very socialization process. This is a way for leaders to attain, maintain, and use power, in different forms, so that their goals (and ours) are accomplished. Again, the ultimate goal is that of survival, and its attainment by means of social organization was programmed into our genome millennia ago.

Power as used by leaders may take several forms and its underlying aggressive underpinnings may not be readily apparent. Thus, leader personality and style enter into the equation of the relationship with their followers, and this is also biologically driven. Psychologists French and Raven (1959) define power as 'the ability of an "agent" [leader] to alter the beliefs, attitudes, or behaviours of one or more "targets" [followers]', and in their influential writings categorized it in six possible manifestations, which may be used by leaders in order to rally or induce the support of their people; these categories are rewards, coercion, legitimacy, expertise, reference, and information (Raven 1965). Using these kinds of power, leaders turn or camouflage their aggression into more legitimate, thus more acceptable, forms of power, which, at the end, enhance the achievement of their goals.

More and more however, evidence is mounting that our behaviour, as well as the way we turn out to be, is the result of interplay between biology and the environment. Genetics sets the limits and the environment determines where actually within those limits a particular behaviour manifests. According to British zoologist Richard Dawkins in his book *The Selfish Gene* (1976), 'We are survival machines ... robot vehicles blindly programmed to preserve the selfish molecules known as genes'. Dawkins believes that genes, not individuals or populations or species, are the driving force of evolution. Let's turn to Ridley (2003) again to recapitulate current thinking:

> It is genes that allow the human mind to learn, to remember, to initiate, to imprint, to absorb culture and to express instincts. Genes are not puppet masters or blueprints. Nor are they just the carriers of heredity. They are active during life; they switch each other on and off; they respond to the environment. They may direct the construction of the body and brain in the

womb, but then they set about dismantling and rebuilding what they have made almost at once – in response to experience. They are both cause and consequence of our actions.

A timely example is that of autism, which is a serious neurodevelopmental disorder characterized by severe deficits in social communication, language development, as well as repetitive, stereotypic behaviours (Strathearn 2009). It is estimated that as many as one in 150 children in the United States are currently affected, which is a dramatic increase in prevalence than previously estimated (Centers for Disease Control and Prevention 2007, Blaxill 2004). When it was first described in the 1940s by Kanner, it was attributed to faulty rearing and defective bonding techniques on the part of the mother. Actually, in his initial paper (1943), he echoed more current notions about the disorder, stating that it resulted from an 'innate inability to form the usual, biologically provided affective contact with people', upon which parenting styles acted to bring about the condition in children. It was in a later work (1949) that he attributed the condition exclusively to environmental influences. Treatment, therefore, was subsequently directed not towards the affected child, but towards the mother and attempted to 'correct' her rearing inadequacies. One can imagine the guilt this approach must have created in a mother who, having borne a disabled child, had to assume the responsibility for that unfortunate happening as well. Science has subsequently identified genetic and biological causes for this syndrome. The ultimate responsibility may still lie with one of the parents, but as part of his/her genetic legacy, and not through faulty behaviour.

This idea was initially challenged by psychologist Bernard Rimland (1964) who swung to the other extreme and attempted to explain autism by pure biological processes.[5] His theories were supported by epidemiologic studies that pointed towards genetic causes in a high percentage of cases (Bailey *et al.* 1995), even though it was also observed that fraternal twins did not exhibit autistic characteristics to a significantly greater extend that identical ones did (Le Couteur *et al.* 1996): This observation implied that epigenetic (that is, environmental and nurturing) factors also played a role. Currently, following whole genome analysis, we have found evidence that indeed multiple factors, genetic, environmental, experiential, and epigenetic play a role in the pathogenesis of autism (Rutter *et al.* 2007, Geschwind 2008). Through special educational programmes, and other types of interventions and medications, these

---

[5] Rimbland was the father of an autistic child himself and invested part of his career to absolve parents of these children from blame.

children can reach their full potential whereas, if left unattended, they usually end up in an institution. The effect of current treatments is not very impressive (Ospina *et al.* 2008), however further discoveries regarding the interplay between social and biological factors are expected to bring about improvements and increased effectiveness of therapy. To reiterate, nature sets the limits, and nurture sets the actual end-point. Genes are actually, as Ridley says, on our side, they just need the environmental cue to turn on certain functions, synthesize certain proteins, and shape the end result in a more favourable way than would otherwise occur. We will return to these concepts again towards the end of this book when we discuss what shapes the leaders of society.

Another example is that of schizophrenia. Whereas science has found numerous biological explanations for its symptoms, and it is now considered to be a brain disease, not long ago these patients were treated on a psychoanalyst's couch.[6] As we will see in detail in subsequent sections of this book, psychotic behaviour, as well as some related personality disorders, are most likely genetic having been selected by evolutionary pressures to provide traits necessary to assume leadership roles for such areas of human activitiy as religion, politics, the arts, and the military. In short, they were selected to provide us with better chances of survival. I will shortly argue that characteristics such as straight talk, inflexibility, and lacking humour (thus being always serious) are traits of rigid personalities that, under certain circumstances, attract others (followers) because they (the followers) perceive them as being capable leaders. It appears that biology predetermines these conditions, but whether they actually develop, and to what severity, is determined by nurture. This is true of many biologically inherited conditions. Ridley's argument (2003) on nature via nurture becomes a case in point.

Not to belabour the point, IQ scores are another example that reflects this interplay between biology (genetic endowment) and environment (nurture). Even though evidence is in favour of genetics, the role of experience cannot be overlooked. According to Ridley, who cites several twin studies, 'IQ is approximately 50 percent "additively genetic"; 25 percent is influenced by the shared environment; and 25 percent influenced by environmental factors unique to the individual'.

Humans alone, among all other species, are characterized by the fact that they constantly strive to overcome and control the forces of nature.

---

[6] A detailed review of either the biological or the psychological theories about autism and schizophrenia is beyond the scope of this book. The interested reader is referred to the bibliography for further reading.

No other species has ever attempted to do so. Even primitive man developed simple ways to subdue his environment. Other animals adjust or perish. We manipulate and alter nature, including our own. Genetic engineering, prenatal diagnostic testing, cloning and transplantations, all indicate our attempts to control our own nature. Greenhouses, reclaimed land, dams, fertilizers, stem cell research, and genetically modified crops are but a few examples of our attempts to alter Mother Nature. This characteristic probably rates quite high among those that set us apart as humans. Tools, increasing brain size, culture, technology, and language are all intertwined into what makes us human. The transition from an environmentally adapted and respecting species to an environment-controlling and arrogant one probably occurred sometime between our descent from our arboreal homes and adaptation as land-dwellers. The new environment selected those traits and attributes that would enhance our survival in our new homes. The first bands of people must have formed at that time, which subsequently increased in number and became better organized, and were able to conquer the Earth by spreading in all directions out of Africa, the continent that Charles Darwin called 'the cradle of mankind' (1859). In doing so, new kinds of environments were encountered that selected those individuals fittest to survive and repro-duce. Thus the different races evolved out of their primordial ancestor, the African *Homo sapiens* (Jones and Rouhani 1986, Wainscoat *et al.* 1986, Cann *et al.* 1987).[7] We remain, however, one species that has developed in a reciprocal relationship with its identity-defining culture. In other words, we create and develop our culture, but our culture also defines and determines how we develop and what our behaviour will be like. A person of Chinese descent, for example, may grow up in China and behave like most of his compatriots. He may also, for whatever reason, grow up in the United States and behave like most Americans, even though he looks Chinese. He will carry, in addition, some of his Chinese characteristics if his parents raise him in America. If non-Chinese Americans adopt him, he mostly resembles typical Americans (no offence intended). This is the great dilemma that many immigrant parents face when their children exhibit characteristics of their adoptive culture rather than that of the mother country. Don Ray in his book *The Reassuring Universe* (2011) uses graphic language to illustrate this point

---

[7] There is recent evidence that all humans living today actually descended from a small band of people who came out of Africa about 50,000 years ago. Moreover, some researchers believe that they have managed to reconstruct through genetic analysis our primordial ancestor, an African woman – Eve? – who lived 200,000 years ago! (Rohde *et al.* 2004, Oppenheimer 2004).

as well as the multitude of shades and possible combinations of individuals in producing a social-cultural group:

> Combining beyond family, with other families, into alliances and bonds and treaties and tribes, cultures, societies, traditions – but not merely combinations of individuals as done by other species to produce herds and flocks and pods, which are after all merely more of the same – but these humans now self-initiate new combinations resulting in yet more new forms of being.

Among the many legacies we all carry from our ancestors is the way we organize our societies in hierarchies with our leaders sitting at the top. This appears to be a cultural universal. On the other hand, however, there must be some biological universals that point to the commonality of our descent as well as our unity as a species. Population genetics and specific gene characteristics aid our understanding of both similarities as well as diversity among different groups of people. Physical anthropologists, for example, are able to trace ethnic relationships, patterns of descent, and even migrational routes of populations through the ages, based on specific genetic mutations pertaining to certain diseases that characterize them. In other words, by tracing the distribution of a specific mutation in a gene that is associated with a specific disorder in a geographical area (or throughout the planet for that matter) they can map out its past migrational trends, and distribution among different ethnic groups. These population differences occurred after the various human groups separated into distinct races. What we are interested in, however, are bio-cultural characteristics that all ethnic groups have in common and which were preserved since before such separation and splitting. One such purely human trait is the incidence of schizophrenia, a disease that appears to be related closely to our distinction as a species, as well as our capacity to be creative, assertive and communicative. We will turn to it next.

II.

It turns out that schizophrenia consistently affects approximately one per cent of the world's population across all cultures, races, and ethnic groups. What this fact tells us, then, is that on the one hand it likely represents a genetic trait that is common to all humans, and has therefore appeared in our primordial ancestors' genes before they branched off to the various subgroups; and on the other hand, that it was preserved by evolution because it likely sub-served an important factor both for our survival as well as our 'humanness'. As such, it may represent one of the few truly universal biological traits that affect us. We know of no other animal, primate or otherwise, that displays symptoms that may even remotely resemble psychosis or the clinical condition we call schizophrenia.[8] It deserves closer examination because it bears so much relevance to our discussion, both for what it is, as well as for its relationship to the odd and eccentric personality disorders which are of great interest in our theory of leadership. At this point we will consider schizophrenia from an evolutionary, ethological perspective, while in a subsequent chapter give a description of its characteristics as well as those characteristics of other milder but related conditions that, I am arguing, help produce many of our leaders.

As we have just argued, the biological determinants of schizophrenia must have evolved before humans divided into the different races, since it occurs at a relatively constant frequency throughout the world. In fact, there are scientists who believe that it is related to the very evolutionary event that made us human. This event is estimated to have occurred between 100,000 and 200,000 years ago. As Timothy Crow (1997a), an Oxford psychiatrist wrote, 'if schizophrenia [[9]] is independent of the environment (that is, the different races) ... it seems, [it] is a characteristic of human populations. It is a disease (perhaps the disease) of humanity.' Remember, we lack convincing evidence that other species are ever afflicted with it. Crow also goes a step further and associates this illness with another speciation event (that is, an occurrence in our evolution that helped delineate the separation of the human species from our human-like ape, or hominid, ancestors); that event is none other than the development of language. In other words, he proposes that language and schizophrenia (psychotic disorders in broader terms) have a common evolutionary origin and, moreover, that the price humanity has paid to develop language is in fact the immutable incidence of schizophrenia around the world. If this supposition could be corroborated by the scientific evidence, it would lend support to the hypothesis that effective leadership (which itself depends on communicative skills that are expressed through language), is also associated with the various psychotic disorders.

I would like to briefly review Crow's paper because it raises many of the arguments that have been made in this book, and which I consider pivotal to my thesis that madness and leadership are somehow connected through

---

[8]   Hence, the lack of consistent animal models of this disease that could be used by scientists to study it further, understand it better, and devise more effective treatments and a possible cure.

[9]   And consequently its related conditions such as the personality and bipolar affective disorders.

our biology as well as our culture.[10] He begins by arguing that all of the psychotic illnesses, as they will be described subsequently in this book, fall on a continuum. In this regard, schizophrenia, manic depressive illness and schizo-affective psychosis may be at times difficult to distinguish from one another because they share common features and they appear to blend in to one another. This observation is hardly new; as early as 1920 Emil Kraepelin, one of the most influential fathers of modern psychiatry, raised this issue that has plagued scientists ever since. As every rookie psychiatrist is taught, an acute episode of mania (one extreme of the manic-depressive or bipolar illness), may be indistinguishable from a psychotic one as it would occur in schizophrenia (Hayman and Tesar 1993). Crow goes on to say that the existence of this continuum implies a disorder intrinsic to the patient, which in itself represents an extreme of variation in the normal population. This represents the statistical method of defining abnormal behaviour that was alluded to earlier in the book and will be discussed fully in subsequent chapters. This argument, therefore, humanizes psychiatric illness because it places it at one end of observable behaviours on a continuum with normal or acceptable ones. In other words, it is considered abnormal because, statistically, it is less likely to be observed by the majority of humans; it falls outside two standard deviations from the mean of observed behaviours. Its difference with normal behaviour, then, is quantitative and not qualitative.

We saw that genetic and anthropological studies place the origin of humans somewhere in East Africa about 100,000–200,000 years ago (Stoneking *et al.* 1992). This origin (the so-called speciation event) produced a species so separate and distinct from its primate predecessors that it has enabled it to spread out in a diaspora that has engulfed the whole planet. *Homo sapiens* therefore, possessed some unique characteristics that helped him dominate his environment and most other living species. The all-encompassing vehicle for such achievements, of course, is culture. Its basic, and probably defining, attribute is language, something no other primate species has developed to any significant extent, but which is part of every human group and race. Again, this is a characteristic that is related, along with psychosis, to our speciation event. Human races have been separated for, at least, 50,000 years (Mowry *et al.* 1994). Yet, the disease continues to remain constant in all populations, despite the fact that it afflicts primarily young, otherwise healthy individuals who, as a consequence, are unable to contribute in

---

[10]   Readers with a background in the physical and biological sciences are strongly encouraged to seek the original article and read it.

any meaningful way to their society. From an evolutionary perspective this may appear on the surface to be somewhat of a paradox, especially if one considers the fact that afflicted individuals also exhibit reduced fecundity (a measure of birth rates). Clearly, one might think that this is not at all an advantageous situation for the survival of the species. There is evidence, according to Crow, that language and psychosis share common evolutionary origins and functions; otherwise, the genetic mutation responsible for schizophrenia should have been selected out of some, if not all, populations after they diverged. The fact that it remains constantly present suggests that it confers an evolutionary – Darwinian as was discussed in the introduction – advantage for our survival, and not a disadvantage as might appear at first glance. This advantage could be none other than language and its by-product, culture. But what is the evidence for this? Let us carry on with Crow's arguments. He states that:

> If the predisposition to schizophrenia is a part of variation that crosses the population as a whole, and it can be traced back to the origin of modern *Homo sapiens*, the conclusion is difficult to resist that this genetic variation is directly associated with the function that characterizes the species, that is, language.

In other words, he considers two immutable human constructs, language and schizophrenia, and joins them together in a commonly expressed and transmitted genetic substrate that must be inherited together if human nature is to be maintained. It turns out, then, that these individuals do contribute to humanity in a quite meaningful manner; they contribute language and other attributes such as the ability to lead through a partial bequeathing of their genome to relatives who may emerge as leaders possessing the personality type (paranoia) and the language necessary to be recognized as such. Furthermore, Crow asserts:

> Like the complexity of language itself, the capacity to represent appears to be intrinsic to *Homo sapiens*, and relatively constant across populations. The two abilities may reflect different aspects of a single genetic change that underlies the communicative potential of the human brain. Language has its origin in the change that gave rise to modern *Homo sapiens*, an event that introduced an innovation in the functional organization of the brain.

In other words, the two characteristics of the human species are thought of as two consequences of a single genetic mutation.[11] One characteristic,

---

[11]   By the term *single genetic mutation* we do not necessarily imply a single locus on a single gene but, rather, genetic characteristics which are co-expressed and are likely in some proximity on a gene.

language, was of such paramount importance in our speciation process, that its evolutionary advantages far outweighed the disadvantages conferred by the second (and genetically linked) characteristic of schizophrenia. One such positive characteristic, among many others, is the fact that human language is lateralized; in other words, it is preferentially localized in one of the two brain hemispheres, usually, in the majority of people, the left one. A peculiar fact about the organization of the nervous system is that one side of the brain controls the opposite side of the body. The left hemisphere, then, controls the right side of the body *and vice versa.* The fact that language is usually localized in the left hemisphere, explains why most people are right handed as far as writing and other motor skills (dexterities) are concerned. Writing, like reading, speaking, and comprehending, are all language functions. We refer to the left hemisphere as the *dominant* one since, in addition to language functions, it also controls fine motor skills. Population studies have shown that about 10 per cent of people have right hemisphere dominance and hence, are left handed. A small portion of individuals who are ambidextrous (possessing equal skills in both hands), are really at a disadvantage as far as language and other cognitive skills are concerned (Annett 1985), and they also appear to lack the well-known asymmetry that characterizes non-ambidextrous people (Witelson and Kigar 1988), whose brain width is greater on the right in the front, and on the left in the back (Foundas *et al.* 1995). Such asymmetry, Crow speculates, is determined by genetic factors.

The asymmetry of the two cerebral hemispheres is not something we find in other mammals or even hominids. It appears to have been a late evolutionary development, but one that has had great implications for the human species. One such implication is the so-called generativity of language. By this term we mean to express the capacity of a given language to generate an infinite number of word combinations and, hence, sentences, so that any person that possesses that language may understand them perfectly, so long as its rules are obeyed (Chomsky 1965). This generativity appears to derive from the 'allocation of function to one or other of the two hemispheres' (Crow 1997b), and it is precisely this hemispheric specialization that has resulted in the development of language, the faculty by which *Homo sapiens* has speciated. However, a complete split, or functional independence of the two hemispheres cannot be the case if one considers the presence of the *corpus calosum*, a large anatomic structure that is found between the two hemispheres; this consists of an abundant number of nerve fibres that run across it and connect the two sides of the brain in such a way that what happens in one affects the other. This is true for language as well. One side takes dominance, as we discussed above, with some components of language localized in each. To quote again from Crow, 'The increased inter-connectivity of diverse cortical areas relates to this core function; specific components of language must be located in each hemisphere. Language, therefore, is a whole brain function; it is bi-hemispheric. The key to the interaction between the hemispheres rests in the mysterious process of the establishment of "dominance."' The argument put forth here is that there are different aspects of language that are sub-served by the two hemispheres. They do work in unison but in ways that we are not readily aware of; thus, there are brain functions that occur, which determine the way we comprehend language but remain largely hidden from conscious awareness. These functions deal with language components that are not immediately obvious as are, for example, phonological and acoustic ones. There are other components such as visual and motor modalities, which also convey meanings and are independent from the putative primary areas of the brain that deal with language comprehension (Armstrong *et al.* 1995). The example of sign language illustrates this point well, since it consists of a system of visual and motor cues that convey language without the use of sound. These modalities are referred to as spatial ones, in contrast to the so-called temporal ones that depend on the (time-linked) transmission of sound to convey meaning. Crow (1997a), based on these notions, asserts:

> there are both temporal and spatial aspects to language … the two are segregated (in the two hemispheres), and … the interaction between them is central to the mode of operation of the human brain.

There is a time delay of approximately 25 milliseconds for transmission of messages through the *corpus calosum*, and this delay prevents the two sides from 'jamming' the signals, which are differentiated in the two sides. This mechanism 'precludes multiple inter-hemispheric passes in the course of single actions' (Crow 1997a). According to Ringo *et al.* (1994):

> these temporal limits will be avoided if the neural apparatus necessary to perform each high-resolution, time critical task is gathered in one hemisphere. If the, presumably overlapping, neural assemblies needed to handle overlapping tasks are clustered together, this would lead to hemispheric specialization.

Crow, then, postulates that:

the determining focus (a temporally organized sequence) is localized in one, presumably the dominant, hemisphere (and acts as a frame) but that this sequence also has access through commissural fibres to neural traces (contents), perhaps at multiple sites, in the other hemisphere. Such access would provide the basis for the recombinational generativity of the process.

This, one may argue, is a leap of faith. However, if it can be shown unequivocally that both hemispheres participate in the generation and comprehension of language, the hypothesis would become plausible. Such evidence has been made available through recent scientific developments that clearly show that such is, indeed, the case. Positron Emission Tomography (PET) scans depict the areas of the brain that get activated during a cerebral process by imaging their underlying metabolic activity. During language functions, parts of both hemispheres become active (Brown *et al.* 2006).

Language, then, depends not only on the collaboration of the two sides of the brain, but also on a selective inhibition of simultaneous access of one into the workings of the others. Strokes, which selectively destroy part of a hemisphere, give us clues about the function of each hemisphere. Whereas lesions in the dominant hemisphere produce more dramatic deficits, the non-dominant side also results in 'dysphasic' (abnormal language functions), symptoms indicating the distribution of functions in both sides (Ropper and Brown 2005).

The concept of hemispheric specialization and differentiation is hardly new. In 1844, A. L. Wigan wrote that 'a separate and distinct process of thinking ... may be carried out in each cerebrum simultaneously ... [and] each cerebrum is capable of a distinct and separate volition ... and these are very often opposing volitions'. The function of the non-dominant hemisphere is thus suppressed by the dominant one, at least at the level of conscious awareness, since both are needed to work in unison, albeit with certain time delays, in order to have normal function and language. That this may be true is also evidenced by victims of stroke who, at times, exhibit the so-called disconnection syndromes in which the two sides of the brain work independently. There are case reports of patients with disconnection syndromes who attempt to harm their wife with one hand while trying to protect her with the other (Carlson 2001); or, while trying to hold a book with the right hand to read, the left one is attempting to close it (Kandel *et al.* 2000). Psychodynamic explanations notwithstanding, the evidence is in dramatic favour of the concepts discussed above.

Readers may be wondering by now what all these notions have to do with the primary thesis of this book: that leadership and madness frequently go together. Well, this is precisely the point that I am making here; in attempting to support my thesis I have tried to digress into aspects of behaviour that may result from disordered types of cerebral function. I have used the illness of schizophrenia as the paradigm of psychotic or odd behaviour and attempted to correlate that with some of the characteristics of leaders. It will be stressed in subsequent chapters, when we study the spectrum of these disorders that schizophrenic patients themselves cannot rise up in social hierarchies due to the social marginalization they suffer as a consequence of their unfortunate illness. However, their close but unaffected relatives, who may possess milder forms of odd and eccentric behaviours, as well as personality disorders, may exhibit such behavioural patterns, so as to attract followers by consequence of their style. Such style will undeniably include their usage of a language, which will have its own characteristics and affectations as they result from their biological affinity to psychosis. That constitutes the evolutionary advantage of maintaining these people in human populations.

Schizophrenia, according to many scientists in the field, results when there is a failure to establish unequivocal dominance of one hemisphere of the brain over the other (Crow *et al.* 1996). Some authors support the view that schizophrenia is a regression to a more primitive time in our evolutionary development, before the establishment of hemispheric dominance, during which the functional roles of the two sides of the brain were largely undifferentiated, and the interaction between them was experienced as voices, something that today we would call auditory hallucinations (Jaynes 1990).[12] Nasrallah (1985) echoes much of the same when he claims that, in the normal state of brain functioning, there is an inhibition of any awareness by the dominant hemisphere, which is usually the left one, of any input and interaction from the non-dominant one. Crow (1997a) in paraphrasing Nasrallah states that:

> In schizophrenia, this function is disturbed with the result that the left hemispheric consciousness becomes aware of an influence from an 'external' force, which, in fact, is the right hemisphere ... delusions such as thought insertion and withdrawal, and delusions of control might arise in this way.

> From the fact that the flexibility (generativity) of language must be contributed from the other hemisphere, and that, in some sense, this contribution exists in a spacial or 'distributed' form, it follows that abnormalities of

---

[12] One might trace the origin of religion in primitive man to such a phenomenon.

inter-hemispheric connectivity will be associated with deviations in sentence production and the train of thought.

Such abnormalities may also be present, possibly in lesser degrees, in relatives with milder forms of psychosis and odd/eccentric personality disorders, who can be functional enough, nonetheless, to assume roles of leadership in their societies. Schizophrenia may be a by-product of our speciation event of inter-hemispheric asymmetry and functional differentiation; in other words, it is the price we pay to have language. A lesser price is the presence of milder forms of psychosis, such that they may be contributing to the making of our destiny precisely because of their psychopathology. In this case, that would be another advantage we gain by having schizophrenic people among us.

One may think of religious functionaries and religious adherents as belonging to such a rather 'primitive' group of people in that they may have retained some of the characteristics of early man, when inter-hemispheric dominance was not established. So they would have a different way of approaching the human condition in a more mystic or esoteric manner, a style that might influence others to follow in trust and hope. Recent studies suggest that religion may have evolved as a by-product of such pre-existing states (capacities), and has had such a strong hold on people because it inadvertently enhanced the stabilizing of cooperation between groups, as well as the codification of moral values to the point where the two became indistinguishable (Pyysiainen and Hauser 2010). It would eventually also become another means by which certain canny individuals could grab power.

Even in literary and non-scientific works, astute writers such as Sebastian Faulks propose a similar thesis. In his novel *Human Traces* (2006), which is set towards the end of the nineteenth century, he deals with the struggle of early psychiatrists to understand the workings of the mind and the cause of madness. Remember, Darwinian theories hadn't become widely accepted by the scientific community yet, and the understanding of the biological basis of most neuropsychiatric diseases was just beginning. I will quote the conversation between Dr Faverill, an older psychiatrist in a British asylum and Sonia, the sister of a young and ambitious doctor in training there:

[Sonia:] 'Do you no longer believe we will discover remedies [of madness]?'

[Dr Faverill:] 'Not until we understand what makes us who we are. My instinct, though I am pitifully far from being able to prove it true, is that what makes us mad is almost the same thing as that which makes us human.'

Sonia frowned. 'You mean that we are fallen? Imperfect? That God gave us the capacity to suffer more than other animals?'

'Yes', said Faverill. 'That is one way of explaining it. It is the price we pay for being favoured by the Almighty. Mr. Darwin might prefer to put it differently. If we were to borrow his language, we could say that when the brain one day developed the capacity that made the species *Homo sapiens*, it developed simultaneously a predisposition to kinds of insanity. Though since we are the only animals to have madness, you may regard what I have just said as no more than a simple tautology.'

'I see' said Sonia, not quite certainly.

'Whether you choose to explain it in the terms of the Bible or Mr. Darwin seems to me to make almost no difference,' said Faverill.

From *Human Traces* by Sebastian Faulks. Published by Vintage. Reprinted by permission of The Random House Group Limited

Sonia's brother, Thomas, years later lives in Germany and is a famous psychiatrist. He is piqued however by his dismal record in curing madness even though he runs a famous clinic along with his sister's French husband. He is reaching similar conclusions as those proposed several decades later by Nasrallah and quoted above. At the risk of writing a chapter by mostly using quotations and work by other authors, I still feel the need to reproduce here a couple of more pages from Sebastian Faulks' book to illustrate, in a literary manner, what scientists have been saying recently. So, we find Thomas in a church in Rothenberg, Germany, studying and pondering the altarpiece depicting the Last Supper:

[I]t seemed suddenly clear to Thomas what Christ's gift was. It was not that he was more developed or refined than the fishermen who were his Apostles; it was that he was less so. He alone possessed something their ancestors had lost: the power to hear voices and thus to commune with the unseen.

[T]he situation that confronted him at that instant ... was of a world in which millions of people worshipped something they could neither see nor hear. The explanation traditionally offered was that this not-being-there was central to the divine plan for human existence ... . But suppose, he thought, that there was a simpler and more credible explanation: that the absence was real ... . that something once present had genuinely disappeared.

Suppose that what had disappeared was the capacity to hear the voice or voices of the god. Once, all those fishermen would have heard a god: now only Christ could. For early humans separated from their group – the young man, for instance, dispatched to fish upstream – the ability to hear instructions, to produce under the influence of stress or fear the voice of the absent leader or god, had once been a necessary tool of survival; but as the capacity to remember and communicate through words had slowly developed, humans had lost the need for heard instructions and comment.

In this way the Bible all made sense, not as a ragbag of metaphor and myth, but as the literal story of a people crying in the wilderness for what had once been theirs. 'I will lift up mine eyes unto the hills, from whence cometh my help'. What was that if not the forlorn and agonized call of the solitary human whose once ever-present helping voice had left him?

Thomas felt quite calm as he gazed into the carving. At the beginning of the Bible, everyone – Noah, Abraham, Moses – seemed to hear God's voice externally; then it was heard only by a minority, who became priests; then the gift became rarer, so the infant Samuel could hear but the old priest Eli could not; and then by the time of the New Testament, Christ alone – and perhaps Paul – could hear voices.

From *Human Traces* by Sebastian Faulks. Published by Vintage. Reprinted by permission of The Random House Group Limited

Did Faulks read Nasrallah? If not this specific author, certainly others of the same school of thought. Faulks even claims later on that schizophrenia 'lies very close to the mental faculty that made us human'. The irresistible implication from the discussion above, then, is that if schizophrenia and other psychotic illnesses form part of the human experience as a genetic variation, they cannot be distinct pathological processes but, instead, an extreme variation that is part of the population as a whole; in other words, they are a shift from the mean behavioural patterns of the general population, a statistical deviation if you will (Crow 1997a). Recent biological studies (Crow 1997b) show in fact that, among other morphological changes, there is a loss of the hemispheric asymmetries that are characteristic of the average human brain! This also brings to mind the claim mentioned above that religion evolved from pre-existing mental capacities. Psychosis and language, then, appear to have developed through a common evolutionary mutation that continues to be selected into the gene pool precisely because of the survival advantages it confers on humans. It appears, therefore, that schizophrenia is a small price for humans to pay in order to have language, the characteristic that makes us who we are. As Faulks puts it through the words of his hero Thomas, 'It is almost as though they [schizophrenics] pay the price for the rest of us to be human.'

Horrobin (1998) carried the argument even further and has hypothesized that schizophrenia is not only the price humans pay for language, but, in addition, it *is* the illness that made us human! In his view, the process of developing the biochemical features of schizophrenia is what, ultimately, caused the appearance of our species. Quoting Horrobin, 'we are human ... because some members of the human race are schizophrenic'. As a true evolutionist, he asserts that several important biochemical steps took place, which, coupled with appropriate environmental factors, influenced the development of the human brain, which in turn, led to the appearance of culture as the ultimate aid for our survival. In doing so, he goes beyond such theories as anatomical and social explanations for the disease. For Horrobin, the basic events to account for the development of our brains are biochemical ones, concerning the very workings of this remarkable organ.

Unrelated specifically to brain size, since other hominid (that is, human-like), species are known to have existed that had larger brains than humans,[13] the development of culture must be the consequence of changes in function that began to occur around two-and-a-half million years ago. They culminated in the social and cultural achievements that have characterized us for the last 50,000 to 100,000 years and which were unaccompanied by significant increases in brain size. They were, however, accompanied by paramount functional-biochemical changes (Horrobin 1998), resulting in different levels of neural connectivity and organization. The time-sequence of events as described by Horrobin and corroborated by the archaeological record, shows enormously long periods of time without apparent behavioural change (for example, rudimentary tools remain the same throughout the world), followed by sudden surges in progress, and I quote:

> Technology developed quickly, as shown by the presence of more and more complex weapons constructed from varied structural elements ... Religion developed, as indicated by apparent ritual burials ... Art developed, as indicated by the extraordinary cave drawings and paintings and possibly by the finding of true musical instruments. Warfare perhaps developed, as indicated by tantalizing evidence of weapons and dismembered humans. Then around ten thousand to fifteen thousand years ago the pace of change increased again. Farming led to settlements which led to cities, states, the emergence of rulers governing large numbers, and to real war. Cultural, religious, linguistic and other diversity became exuberant.

All of the above developments were linked to important changes in the function of our brains. These changes were brought about by biochemical alterations that affected the connectivity of the various parts and cells (neurons) within the brain. If its size was not altered significantly in relation to body size, then its function must have become progressively

---

[13]   The Neanderthal brain, for example, was proportionally larger than ours.

more complex. For such a change to have occurred, Horrobin maintains, the connectivity between neurons increased tremendously, resulting in sophistication of thought, language, and action. At the cellular level of the brain, where these changes took place, an important role was played by the lipids (fat cells), which make up a large proportion of the brain. They provide structural and functional support in key areas of neurons. There are several types of these lipids, some of which are synthesized by the human organism and others that must be provided through the diet.[14] These lipids, when available, helped the brain keep its size up to that of our bodies but only up to a point. A more important function was to enhance the richness of connections between neurons and between different brain areas, thus contributing to increased levels of intelligence.[15] The rates of production and breakdown of these substances are, according to this theory, directly related to the orderly versus disorderly function of the brain and bear, ultimately, an association with dietary habits and the environment. Evidence exists that increased breakdown and reduced incorporation rates of these and other substances into the brain result in schizophrenia and, its putative relative, manic-depressive illness (Yao *et al.* 1996).

Since mammals, including humans, have a relatively limited capacity to manufacture these important substances on their own, their procurement through the food chain becomes of paramount importance. Their absence leads to brain growth retardation (Oloyede 1992). They are abundantly found in meat and animal as well as fish and sea products. They would therefore, dictate specific dietary habits those early ancestors of ours should have had in order to survive. Such dietary habits may have been possible in East Africa, where we presumably appeared, during hominid evolution (Horrobin 1996). Archaeological evidence suggests that most presumed human ancestor fossil sites were associated with water, where these types of foods would have been readily available (Morgan 1997). Thus, the primitive environment of our ancestors provided such nutritive substances that helped the growth and development of their brain to its human specifications.

Evolution operated through natural selection to favour those brains that could best utilize essential nutrients. The two surges in human brain size

---

[14] The latter are known as essential nutrients because they must absolutely be part of our diet, since we cannot manufacture them.

[15] The two lipids which Horrobin considers to be important in this respect, are arachidonic acid and docosahexaenoic acid; his discussion becomes rather involved at this point, but for the interested reader he provides a highly recommended and thought-provoking theory that is worth reviewing.

occurred around two million and half a million years ago respectively
and there is archaeological evidence that essential nutrients were in
abundance during these periods of time. These surges were the result of
natural selection assisting human brains to become more sophisticated.
One such way was the evolution that resulted from expanding the diet to
include animal meat, which as Bob Martin (1996) claims, is another
example of the interplay between tools, brain size, and better tools. By
improving on an important tool, thus creating a sharper stone flake, he
could hunt and kill animals larger than himself, opening up a new world
of nutrition. This nutrition provided high concentrations of calories, fats,
and proteins, which in turn resulted in facial structural changes that may
have enabled intonation and the production of various sounds, resulting
ultimately in the development of language (Martin 1996). Furthermore,
increases in brain size and reorganization, and the potential for language,
were enhanced. As Leakey (Leakey and Lewin 1993) puts it 'by taking a
crude hammer stone and striking it against a pebble to produce a small,
sharp flake, our earliest Homo ancestors began to control their world in a
way that no other creature had done before or has done since'. This is
another way to conceptualize Ridley's (2003) *nature via nurture* stance.
He brings in evidence from the human genome studies that organisms
evolve by adjusting what he calls thermostats, areas at the front of genes,
which then enable them to grow parts of their bodies in a differential way
(think brain hemispheric asymmetry). Thus, he delineates the mechanism
by which the same genes can act in different ways in response to nurture.
As he puts it:

> You can turn up the expression of one gene, the product of which turns up the
> expression of another, which suppresses the expression of a third, and so on.
> And right in the middle of this little network, you can throw in the effects of
> experience. Something external – education, food, a fight, or requited love,
> say – can influence one of the thermostats. Suddenly nurture can start to
> express itself through nature.

By now, however, the reader may by wondering again what, if anything,
these facts have to do with the subject of madness and leadership.
Horrobin contents that '[schizophrenia] is at the core of our humanity
and provides many of the characteristics which distinguish us from our
hominid ancestors'. And elsewhere, 'it frequently struck members of
families who are otherwise distinguished in many fields'. The biochemical basis of the illness, as exposed above, is also the same one that
is operative in the development of gifted individuals. I will, once more,
quote Horrobin extensively:

[L]ooking at the psychological and psychiatric characteristics of some non-psychotic family members where at least one individual is schizophrenic ... there are many individuals who are not formally mentally ill who have a spectrum of personality deviations which may be classed as schizotypal. These represent schizophrenia-like features but which are much milder than those in truly psychotic individuals. There may be an excess of suspicious-ness, a trace of paranoia, a difficulty in making easy social contact, the hearing of voices, great interest in religion and a good deal of eccentricity and magical thinking ... not only is there a continuum of illness between schizophrenia and manic-depression, there is also a continuum between schizophrenia, schizotypal personality and normality. If susceptibility to schizophrenia has a genetic basis, then many apparently near-normal people must be carrying the genes that convey that susceptibility.

Throughout this book I am calling the above near-normal individuals personality disordered. Also, as it was emphasized previously, with schizophrenia we also include manic-depressive illness, just as the authors quoted above do. The evolutionary legacy of major psychiatric illness, then, is the presence of mildly affected, but otherwise gifted, relatives who embody and reify many of our human characteristics. To reiterate, normality, mild mental illnesses, and severe mental illness, are positioned on a continuum; schizophrenia and other disorders are but extreme variations of the normal condition; to put it in statistical terms, they represent behaviours beyond two standard deviations from the average.

Horrobin provides evidence that the same kinds of biochemical altera-tions that operate in people with schizophrenia are also found, albeit in lesser forms, in their relatives with distinguished characteristics as described earlier. He also ties in such disordered individuals as dyslexics, manic-depressives, and schizotypal personalities all of which possess peculiar talents. The primary defect, as identified above, is decreased incorporation and increased breakdown of essential nutrients (lipids) that affects the structure and function of nerve cell (neuron) membranes, leading to schizophrenia and other related disorders. To use his own words:

three major events ... require explanation not just in social but in biochemical terms:

1. The increase in brain size: This alone could not have produced creativity but could have provided the background against which creativity might emerge.
2. The creativity which led to the hand axe cultures and the emergence of complex cooperative behaviour.
3. The creativity ... which emerged somewhere between fifty thousand and

two hundred thousand years ago and which was responsible for making us truly human.

My hypothesis is that each of these events was related to something new happening in lipid metabolism [16] ... associated with the introduction of increased activity of one or more phospholipases [17] ... [leading] to exuberant modeling, pruning, and remodeling of synapses. [18]

Attributes present in some members of such [schizophrenic] families are:

1. A tendency to hear voices and a tendency to be intensely interested in religion.
2. A tendency to have unusual spatial senses and visual art skills.
3. Extraordinary musical skills.
4. Paranoia may have been important in creating a sense of the value of kinship and the dangers of other social groups. Psychopathy and sociopathy, with their simultaneous understanding of, yet total lack of sympathy with, the needs of others, are features of ruthless *leadership*. [emphasis added]

Another long and tortuous quotation, which, however, has provided us with a synthesis of many important concepts and ideas put forth in this chapter: evolutionary changes that, in relation to the environment, have introduced such mutations in humans that enhanced the appearance of culture, sophistication, religion, art, music, and skills for leadership. In short, these are all the characteristics that distinguish us as human, and all are related to psychotic and paranoid traits. Thus, to be a human of consequence, as well as to possess leadership abilities, one needs to belong to a family that also includes psychiatrically impaired members.[19]

Language, another human characteristic, has its own qualities and attributes in such individuals in a way that it confers in them the ability to induce the formation of pecking orders or, more appropriately put, social hierarchies, often with themselves at the top. As Stephen Denning (2007) claims, 'The right words can have a galvanizing effect, generating enthusiasm, energy, momentum, and more, while the wrong words can undermine the best intentions and kill initiative on the spot, stone dead.' This is language in all its communicative manifestation functions; in addition, it connects us with people who lived in the past, and with those

---

[16]   Metabolism simply put refers to that process by which food is broken down in the body and reconstituted into useful substances.

[17]   Those compounds in our bodies which help break down and recycle phospholipids, which include lipids.

[18]   A synapse is one of multiple sites of communication between neurons.

[19]   The presence of an eccentric family background is further discussed in Chapter 9.

who will come. It sub-serves civilization and as Ray (2011) puts it, 'Language and writing. A growing massif of shared experience, observations, experiments, and edicts combined to result in ... structures, buildings, technologies, societies, civilizations.' The evolutionary process of language acquisition and its leadership-defining characteristics instil tremendous advantages to potential leaders; as Leakey and Lewin (1992) claim, 'an incremental and significant enhancement of spoken language may well have been part of the final evolution of modern humans'. I think the importance of language in the development of humans and culture cannot be overstated. Moreover, its relationship to both leader emergence and psychopathology is by now, I think, obvious.

3. Paranoia and historical interpretation

> And you know that a man who is deranged and not right in his mind will
> fancy that he is able to rule, not only over men, but also over the gods?
>
> Plato, *Republic*

I.

'Many are the wonders of this world but the most wonder-full of them is man'.[1] Thus spoke the Greeks in days of old but in ways that still ring true today. Of all the wonders of the cosmos – and as far as we know – man alone has such peculiar qualities as self-awareness, knowledge of his history, contemplation of his future and the quest for meaning. Only man has taken his destiny (or has he?) in his hands and has shaped his world according to his needs. And, as William Shakespeare (Craig 1914) wrote: 'What a piece of work is a man! How noble in reason! how infinite in faculty! in form, in moving, how express and admirable! in action how like an angel! in apprehension how like a god! the beauty of the world! the paragon of animals!'

As we have already argued, culture is a universal and ubiquitous phenomenon that results from and defines human behaviour. Whether primitive or modern, all cultures share certain characteristics such as a system of hierarchical arrangement that sets the rules of conduct of their members.[2] Even in purely egalitarian societies (if indeed there was ever such an unusual social arrangement), systems exist that rotate authority among the members of the group. Among the Amish societies of North America,[3] for example, the office of the Bishop is rotated among all males of the group and does not constitute a matriculated or permanent position (Kraybill *et al.* 2013). It is, however, a hierarchical, albeit

---

[1] Sophocles, *Antigone.*

[2] Even in purely egalitarian societies, systems exist that rotate authority among the members of the group.

[3] A Christian denomination that prefers to maintain and use the technology, behaviour and social organization of the seventeenth century, the time when they arrived in the New World.

transient, distinction that commands the respect of others and carries important administrative duties, such that ensure the smooth running of the group's day-to-day affairs. This type of arrangement probably fulfils some moral philosophers' radical approach to leadership, which they propose as a means to combat inequality between leaders and followers, or the extent to which they would tolerate it in order to achieve practical needs (Price and Hicks 2006).

All social groups, from the nuclear family, to social clubs, nations, and international organizations, create their own sets of rules, behaviour, and hierarchies. This pattern ensures both the survival of a group, but also, the safety of the leader; Hobbes (1991 [1651]) reminds us that even the strongest person, at least in nature, would be insecure without some measure of consent from his constituencies, which in turn, would delegate to their leader, the task of leading in order to attain their own safety. There is a double bind here; our need for autonomy on one hand, and our need for interdependence and sharing on the other (Harvey 2006). Both needs are biologically determined. The person who can balance these two needs – that is dominance and consent – has accomplished, according to Harvey, the 'highest achievement of leadership'. The person who can do it, is endowed to do so, by nature. As Price and Hicks (2006) state, 'leadership is so central a response to the human condition that it is difficult to imagine what we might do without it. Yet this relationship is distinctive in its tendencies towards hierarchy and inequality.' This situation conflicts with the views of moral philosophers, however, because, as already mentioned, it is biologically determined, and thus, inescapable. J. MacGregor Burns states that 'equality is the status quo in morality and deviations from the status quo require special justification'. The answer to this, again, rests in our biologically determined behaviour as a means for survival; and that constitutes its special justification! Harvey (2006) identifies three constituent parts of leadership, namely kinship, reciprocity, and command. To use his own words:

> From kinship it draws a sense of connection (if often exploited) between leaders and followers. From reciprocity it draws a sense of mutual exchange and belief (if often betrayed). But from command it takes its most visible aspect, for leadership is above all a social relation of dominance and consent (if often contradicted), yoked uneasily together.

In order to understand society and culture further, as well as the phenomena of leader ascent across various communities, we need to dwell briefly on representative examples of such leadership against the background of major social theories that have been proposed to explain human organization and its dependence on leaders. This historical survey will bring us up to date with current thinking and allow a further insight into the sociobiological determinants of behaviour including leadership. The obvious explanation is, of course, that a group can accomplish greater feats than an individual alone, in a safer and nurturing environment. Especially in traditional societies, it might benefit groups to have a leader in place to organize group defence and lead attacks against competing ones (Diamond 1998). Even in modern societies, urgencies need to be dealt with in an efficient and effective manner necessitating leader ascent and leadership permanence. This is evidenced in the wild, not only at the level of primates, but also in other animals, where inequality between the alpha male and female is rather pronounced and constantly attended to.

Our historical passage has not always been smooth and rosy; to the contrary, due to the leaders we have had the road was thorny, arbitrary, redundant and chaotic. Therefore, as Runyan (1988a) states, 'historical inquiry ... must attend not only to the ordered, structured, and lawlike [sic] aspects of human and social reality, but also to the disorderly, the particular, the idiosyncratic, the transient, and the random'. Let's briefly survey man's passage through the ages.

At the dawn of his history, man used to live in small bands of people engaging in hunting animals and gathering goods in order to survive. All members of the group were probably related and formed a kinship.[4] Even at this primitive level however, a hierarchy existed to oversee the distribution of labour and responsibility, as well as to settle disputes. Usually the elders assumed such roles, and being a senior commanded obedience and respect since, besides their leadership roles, they served as the repository of their group's wisdom, knowledge, and ethics. The kinship constituency described above by Harvey would be most recognizable here. It is unknown whether those leaders were set apart by madness even though the gene(s) coding for psychosis had already evolved and penetrated the human race. At that time the fringe people would more likely assume shamanistic and witchcraft roles, which, over the centuries, probably gave rise (evolved) to organized religion, medicine, politics, and law. In many instances they probably usurped the leadership of their societies, especially when the latter grew in size. Thus we have the appearance of the god-kings and the rise of empires such as that of Egypt. Thanks to Egyptian scribes we are in possession of

---

[4] A kinship is a group of people who share a bloodline and constitute a social unit.

detailed accounts for many pharaohs' lives to assess their personality type even though historical record-keeping and biographies were moulded in order to reinforce the god-like image of the kings and enhance national solidarity.

It is tempting to speculate about the actual personality of the founders of those dynasties but we must make do with what historical record there is and infer the rest. Sometimes reading between the lines can point towards traits and characteristics that make up a personality. In general we can assume that the pharaohs, like most other god-anointed kings, were aggressive and persuasive enough for others to submit to their will. Their god-like attributes (which themselves might have resulted from a psychotic predisposition), likely reinforced their image. In addition this perception on the part of the people 'acted as a strong unifying force, holding his country together as one nation, from Aswan to the Delta' (Payne 1992). Skill in battle, which in those days was an everyday affair, would have also consolidated their rule. After all, such skill would, ultimately, ensure their people's survival, and at the end of the day that mattered the most. Use of fear, which might have been directed both towards the leader but, also, by the leader towards an outsider group, would enhance the consolidation of his power, especially the command constituency. Hillman (1995) wrote that 'Of all the faces of power, fearsomeness seems to serve as a profound stabilizing principle … Shared fear unifies people.' The belief that pharaohs descended from half-mortal half-gods (the Hawk, the Scorpion, the Reed and the Bee demigods) only reinforced their fearsomeness (Payne 1992). When centuries later another pharaoh chose to alter this image he practically ruined the status of the kingdom, the kings, and the people's respect for the institution (see Amenhotep IV's story below).

What qualities, then, might an early leader possess to solidify his rule? Most probably, the same ones that every other despot had throughout history; that is, physical and verbal prowess coupled with an inflated self-image that came about as the result of a personality disorder trait.[5] Thus, we can explain the megalomania that characterized all those imperial leaders of antiquity. Whatever the circumstances in which a leader ascends, an important factor to consider is the issue of change; leaders might either initiate change (Burns 1978), direct it (Yarmolinski 2007), or modulate the levels of distress it causes in an otherwise stable

---

[5] We have argued in the previous chapter that there was a relationship between schizophrenia, a severe form of mental illness, and the development of language in humans.

system (Heifetz 1994). Perhaps change is either imminent or initiated. The skilful leader's personality attributes, including mannerisms and language use, must fit the needs of the specific circumstances and direct change to the advantage of all. Such must have been the lot of early despots.

The development of agriculture in Mesopotamia and the Mediterranean basin enabled people to form settled communities and allowed the accumulation of surpluses and wealth. This development, in turn, allowed the growth of populations to great numbers, something quite impractical in earlier times when small bands (kinships) of people wandered around in search of food. Thus we begin to observe the beginnings of cultural traditions and the solidification of practices that typically kept people from rapidly changing their social systems, especially if they had served a particular group's exigencies well in the past. This explains why societies resist dramatic changes in traditions; people through most of history have barely survived, with little or no surplus, giving them little or no margin for error if the new ideas and changes do not work (paraphrased from Butler 2007). The management of large settled populations, as well as the distribution of resources, land and wealth, necessitated the appearance of capable leaders, hierarchies, and political organization. Dynastical monarchies such as the Egyptian pharaohs and other Near-Eastern kings are the first examples of such stratification. Multiple socio-political systems subsequently developed. Their description is beyond the scope of this book, even though it is worth perusing over some of them in a cursory way in order to appreciate the role played by leaders in driving history forward. We will focus on Western culture.

Agriculture was the critical development that moved history forward and led to the creation of settled populations, villages, cities, and, inadvertently, civilization with both positive as well as undesirable consequences. According to Butler (2007):

> Settled agricultural life had dramatic effects on human society and the environment. First of all, farming required less cooperation and sharing than hunting and gathering did. Before, all members of a tribe had to hunt together and share the results. Since there was no private property or anything to fight over, hunting and gathering societies were (and still are) relatively peaceful and harmonious. In contrast, agriculture allowed individual families to farm their own lands. As a result, private property evolved which led to social classes and more conflict in society between rich and poor.

So we see the need for leadership arising, to arbitrate conflicts, as well as to organize and guide groups of people through their historical predicaments. Surpluses allowed large groups of people to settle and form the first cities that now became possible since agriculture could sustain them. Increasing numbers of city dwellers lessened the appreciation of kinship and blurred blood lines, resulting in a situation with strangers living among strangers. This also brought about divisions of labour, specialization and sub-specialization as a means for survival, a development that in turn diluted even further the sense of kinship. Thus, the possibility of conflict also increased along with the need for capable mediating leadership. Agriculture obviated the egalitarian need to engage solely in hunting and gathering by allowing farming occupations as well. It subsequently helped create a diversification of professions needed to sub-serve the growing numbers of groups (settlements) and their needs. The appearance of writing – another form of communication – and record-keeping, occurred in this setting. The rise of powerful priests and organized religion was the other development of this historical period.

> Civilization brought problems as well as blessings. For one thing, the continued expansion of population and farmland to feed it eventually led to cities clashing over new lands. With civilization came the first wars. Since priests were ill suited for fighting, they would choose a lugal, ('great man') to lead them in the fight. After the war, the lugal would be expected to resign his office. However, either because of ambition or the fact that another war was always around the corner, the lugal would keep his office. In time, he became a permanent official, the king, who led the city-state in war and administered justice in peacetime. (Butler 2007)

Certainly the above is not the only plausible explanation on how leaders appeared; they may have singled themselves out or allowed the priests to single them out. Once the office of the leader/monarch/governor appeared, it became part and parcel of organized society, characterized by all the attributes that are described in this book. Recent neuroimaging research lends support to such social ranking hierarchies as a brain-based system for recognizing and interpreting social status and rank-related information in interpersonal encounters (Beasley *et al.* 2012); it thus explains neurobiologically the leader–follower phenomenon.

The Babylonian king Hammurabi is one of the best-known personalities of early Mesopotamian history who, owing to his shrewd and austere character, led his city to excel among several other competitors. His paranoid predisposition was critical in defining his own goals, but also in identifying who his enemies were and his limits of tolerance towards them. He was, after all, surrounded by tough, ambitious, and violent enemies, vying to increase their groups' presence and influence in the same areas. Hammurabi rose to the Babylonian throne around 1750 BCE at the time when a leader was desperately needed to mobilize the crowds and see the city through its vicissitudes and threats from aggressive neighbours. Anybody else would have probably withered away along with his followers, just as his surrounding enemies did. As Butler (2007) puts it:

> Over the next twenty-five years, this Babylonian king masterfully maneuvered his city-state among all its hostile neighbors. At one point, he would ally with one state to eliminate another. Later on, he would make a new ally to help him destroy the first. In such a way, he steadily expanded Babylon's borders and swelled its army's ranks with troops supplied by subject cities. One final showdown with the city-state, Larsa, left him master of Mesopotamia and 'King of the Four Quarters.'

The title 'King of the Four Quarters' was most likely an attribute he bestowed on himself as a result of his successful campaigns on one hand, and his psychopathology on the other. He was, after all, seriously paranoid that his subjects were plotting against him (English 2011) and this was likely one of the reasons he issued his code of laws that spelled what was expected of his subjects and the punishments that trans-gressions would incur. The first ever systematic organization of a legal system arose out of one leader's paranoia towards his people. Of course, he also attempted to compensate for his despotic rule by providing prosperity to them, but only as a strategy to ensure their loyalty and obedience. More evidence regarding his psychopathology comes from his belief that he was chosen by the gods who often, he felt, addressed him by name and responded to his supplications; 'I have complained to Šamaš and Marduk,[6] and they have responded with a "yes". I did not attack without the approval of the god' (van de Meiroop 2005). Or, consider his captivating language: 'In order that the mighty not wrong the weak, to provide just ways for the waif and the widow, I have inscribed my precious pronouncements upon my stela' (Roth 2000). Any aspiring modern politician might use similar words in order to captivate his audience.

Most empires throughout history are dependent on the personality and leadership of their founders and fall apart soon after their deaths (Butler 2007). The stronger the personality of the leader, the harder it gets to maintain his empire afterwards. Examples such as that of Alexander the Great (see below) and Napoleon are convincing enough. On the other hand, the endowment of critical political thinking in a leader, which in

---

⁶ Šamaš was the Mesopotamian Sun-god, whereas Marduk was the national god of Babylon.

itself might be a by-product of paranoia, may help start a dynasty that outlasts its founder by several generations. Such were the kingdoms of ancient Egypt. Let us briefly turn to them next and consider representative leaders.

Thutmosis III (1479–1425 BCE) is one such example of a great leader, an able warrior, and a skilled administrator. Orphaned as an infant he inherited a throne that was controlled by Hatshepsut, his step-mother; she had led a peaceful reign withdrawn from the world outside Egypt in contrast to previous rulers, likely due to mistrust (paranoia perhaps) regarding foreigners (Payne 1992). She kept her stepson virtually without any power until his late teens when, following her death, he assumed his rightful place as a king. Because of his accomplishments he has been called the Napoleon of ancient Egypt (Breasted 1914). His first task was to consolidate his rule at home, a task that included erasing his stepmother's name (and memory) from public buildings and offices, and replacing it with his own. This probably was one of the first acts undertaken as a result of paranoia. Afterwards, he directed his own paranoia towards the subservient cities and surrounding countries, which owing to Hatshepsut's peaceful reign, were starting to test the limits and had begun forming coalitions against Egypt. Had he lacked the paranoia to help him guard against them, his empire might have fallen to surrounding enemies which envied the gift of the Nile (Herodotus 1998). Thutmosis III never lost a battle. He fought against the Syrians, the Palestinians, the Nubians, and cities such as Kadesh and Megiddo, now largely forgotten. He restored Egypt's former glory and dominance in the Mediterranean basin but also patronized and protected its cultural heritage.

What made Thutmosis such a great leader? He had correctly identified and dealt with Egypt's real and potential enemies. One such potential enemy was the Jewish populace living in Egypt at the time. His paranoia against them, and a possible rebellion, led him to issue an order that male Jewish infants be killed at birth.[7] Long-drawn-out sieges, fierce fighting, trickery and treachery, and strategic planning helped make him a successful leader. Ability as a civil magistrate, but also a healthy dose of paranoia about the intentions of Egypt's neighbours and the minorities within, composed a personality profile destined to succeed.

---

[7] The well-known Book of Exodus story about Moses having been taken from the Nile by the Pharaoh's daughter is set against this background of Jewish persecution.

Another telling Egyptian legacy, evidence for which was discovered serendipitously,[8] and illustrative of a leader's influence, is that of Amenhotep IV (1353–1336 BCE), a controversial Pharaoh who has been described by historians and archaeologists with such names as fanatic, crazy, reformer, saint (Payne 1992), romantic, scientist (Hall 2012), and the first 'individual' in history (Breasted 1939). Said to have been a bookish, sickly, and moody child (attributes that perhaps attest to proneness towards psychopathology that could account for the above descriptions), he grew up under the reign of his father, Amenhotep III, during a time of increasing strain between the king and the high priest at Amon's temple; the strain was due to a tacit competition for power (Payne 1992). A lesser god, Aten (the sun-god), began to gain popularity while traditional gods' worship withered (promoted at least partly by the king in order to curb the priests' power). Aten moreover had universal appeal to Egyptian cosmopolitan society having counterparts in foreign lands (Payne 1992). Amenhotep IV became a devoted worshipper of Aten while ignoring Amon and his priests. In an apparently surprise decision he went so far as to move his capital from Thebes, and equally unexpectedly, changed his name to Akhenaten, honouring his newfound god.[9] Thereafter, he lived with Nefertiti his wife in the new capital of Akhetaten (meaning 'Horizon of Aten') (Clayton 2006), which was to become a religious centre as well. Akhenaten was to become the only intermediary between Aten and his people (Redford 1987) to the chagrin of the priesthood.

So far this story would constitute perhaps a curiosity in Egypt's long history. However, because of his peculiar personality and psychopathology, stemming from an as yet unspecified chronic illness, he was characterized by 'abruptness and indifference to consequences in every move he made' (Payne 1992) ignoring his people's sensitivities and long-time traditions. Such behaviour eventually caused a clash between him and the Egyptian establishment so that his immediate successors, referring to Akhenaten himself as 'the enemy' in archival records (Trigger *et al.* 2001), engaged in a systematic erasing of his reign and memory. While still in power however, and using his prerogative as the leader of Egypt, he brought about revolutionary changes in the way state, religious, and everyday affairs were conducted. We already discussed the change of his name, his capital, and his god. Moreover, he introduced

---

[8] By a peasant woman in Tell el Amarna, located approximately 250 miles downriver on the Nile.

[9] The name's meaning is 'servant of the Aten'.

perspective in art and artists were instructed to follow realistic and naturalistic depictions of himself and others (as opposed to superhuman representations typical of the Pharaohs); this, however, led people to ridicule him, as they lost awe and respect towards him (Payne 1992). The most noteworthy change he brought about however was his insistence that Aten was to be viewed as the only god for the whole universe, to the exclusion of other deities. This was a radical idea that perhaps introduced monotheism in history, along with concepts such as peace and universal tolerance that Aten represented. A ban on portraying other deities' images was also decreed even though not adhered to by his people.

Let's now get to the point; even though the jury is still out on the issue, there are many scholars and Egyptologists who see the beginnings of the Jewish religion in the reforms Akhenaten tried to bring about. Starting with Freud (1964) who considered Moses as a priest of Aten – forced to leave Egypt after the death of Akhenaten, along with a crowd of followers – a score of other scientists and populists saw parallels between the two religions and subsequently with Christianity and Islam as well. The physical presence of the Jewish people in Egypt makes these theories plausible regardless of whether they were a separate nation or a religious sect (Aten's worshippers?) within Egypt. The implication is that the seeds of Judaeo-Christian-Islamic monotheism may have been planted in Egypt as a result of one leader's peculiarities. There is even a claim that Akhenaten and Moses were one and the same person (Osman 2002)! Besides parallels between Akhenaten and Moses, others have proposed a connection between Akhenaten and Christ (Redford 1987, Breasted 1933) claiming parallel teachings. Certainly the Christian Bible teaches that Christ spent part of his early life in Egypt where he may have been exposed to a secret sect that continued to honour Aten.

Whether the above theories about the Jewish origins are true or not, these people constitute yet another telling example of leader–follower interplay in the solidification and preservation of both a group's identity and cohesion. The historical existence of these people profited a great deal from the workings of the dyad prophet/king-people; from the very inception of this ethnic group, this relationship becomes manifest; Abraham is particularly remembered for his covenant, the agreement he struck with God to follow and worship him exclusively in exchange for his protection. This also seemed to imply that Abraham and his people believed in other gods during their time, but refused to worship them in preference for the one that Abraham had favoured. Thereafter, he and his tribe became the 'chosen people' of their chosen god, a distinction that would grow in importance as they attributed to him the distinctive universal and cosmic qualities of the only God, the creator, as a result of their own perception of importance and self-esteem. Thus, interplay between a god and his special people was established and set the stage for all future Israeli historical and religious experiences. It also became the pattern of their worship in God-inspired laws, covenants, and prophesies. Abraham's paranoia, (remember his auditory command hallucinations and near sacrifice of his son Isaac), and his unyielding position on matters of faith, were instrumental for the solidarity and cohesion of the nation under 'construction'. A man's psychopathology would set the stage for all succeeding generations to be inspired and codify a religion that would influence a significant part of the world in ways too numerous to count.

Unquestionably, the next great figure in Jewish history was Moses. He was destined to lead his people out of the slavery of Egypt and into the Promised Land where the nation of Israel would settle and establish its own physical territory, and develop the culture that later brought forth the man who would be considered the Messiah by millions of Christians. It also solidified the religious traditions and observances and holy days for both Jews and Christians through the events that allegedly occurred during the Exodus, the great and massive migration towards Palestine. Even though Moses was born and raised into Pharaoh's privileged nobility (remember the theories and claims about his person that were expounded as we discussed Egypt and the Pharaohs above), he maintained or regained his connections with his people and, at the ripe time, assumed their leadership. Thereafter, he led them out of Egypt. Butler (2007) writes that 'The Exodus, as this mass migration is called, is probably the most important single event in the history of the Jews, since it won them their freedom and gave them their identity as a people.' It also solidified their religion and, subsequently, determined the shape of Christianity and Islam.

Moses' personality and leadership style is shadowed by the mixture of legend, faith, and myth. A turning point in his life and conversion into a leader was the alleged sign from God of the burning bush that inspired him to lead the Jews out of Egyptian slavery into the Promised Land. Could this have been a sign of psychopathology? Psychoanalysts certainly seem to think so (Wagenknecht 1995) in their treatment of Freud's writings on the subject. Moses also displayed certain behaviours typical of paranoids; he assumed the leadership of the oppressed Jews in Egypt perhaps without an unchallenging acceptance if we consider reactions against him by quarrelling members of his group; he nevertheless solidified the Jewish identity and defined their goals; he identified the outsider who was responsible for their tribulations, personified in the face of the Pharaoh; last, he proposed the solution, which was the exodus from Egypt to the Promised Land. Thereafter, he maintained his paternalistic attitude towards his newly found followers, who transgressed from his command every chance they got.

II.

Democracy as practiced by the Greeks gave theoretical power to the demos, the people, who chose their leaders through a system of formal elections. Communicative skills and a persuasive predisposition were the determining factors to succeed; again, the importance of language becomes apparent. The rise of politics, as a communal affair, has its origin in those early societies, which for a brief historical time, adopted a system that elected its leaders. However, in order to choose a leader, people most probably went through similar mental processes and deductions as those of their modern counterparts, and, we have argued, during critical points of their history people are attuned to persons that embody, in behaviour, in attitudes, and in language, the innermost ideals, hopes, and wishes of the group. The individual who is most likely to express those ideas directly (who in other words would be more disinhibited than the average person in the group), would be the personality-disordered one, especially the paranoid, because he would lack the social skill to understand the social limits of tolerance that applied. Hampsey (1954) describes a 'paranoic' style in Pericles' speeches, especially as losses began to be sustained in the Peloponnesian war; such language, however, helped galvanize Athenian resistance and resolve. Kagan (1998) writes that 'when the occasion demanded, he informed them of the realities and advised them how to cope; he called upon them to rise above their fears and short-range self-interest, and inspired them to do so'. In times of crisis, people, including those ancient ones, are ready to accept behaviours that violate their expected norms, in order to ensure a safe transition into greener pastures. Their security would thus be assured, and that would consequently assure their survival and reproduction. The reciprocity constituency of power (Harvey 2006) would be most recognized here.

The development of democracy can also be seen as an attempt to solve the problem of inequality and power, since it would, at least theoretically, allow each member of a group to assume this role. Even Pericles 'had to stand for re-election [each year] and was constantly subjected to public scrutiny and political challenge' (Kagan 1998). The same act was repeated in 1215 CE when the feudal barons of England forced King John to sign the Magna Carta in an attempt to curtail his power and protect their own rights (Linebaugh 2008). The document was an elaboration of a precedent one, the Charter of Liberties, issued in 1100 by Henry I, limiting certain of his powers, probably in an attempt to mollify contenders to the throne and dissatisfied constituents (Hollister 2003). Hammurabi had acted similarly, likely for parallel reasons, many centuries previously. These documents influenced the rest of the English-speaking world, Europe and other areas, as they planted the seeds for the subsequent rediscovery of democracy. These democratic/freedom legacies began on the initiatives of individual leaders and law-makers (Raaflaub 2007) and spilled outside Athens as well.

Concurrently of course, other less democratic systems were alive and well both within, as well as outside Greece. Sparta, the great contender of Athens, had chosen oligarchy, strict rules, and emphasis on the well-being of the state at the expense of individuals. Even though its leaders were also characterized by a paranoid predisposition, their leadership style must have been different and more concordant to Spartan realities and expectations, most fitting with Harvey's command constituency of power. The creation of the Spartan state had resulted from their victory over and subjugation of the Helots, the original inhabitants of the area, who vastly outnumbered them (Cartledge 2002); thus, the development of a state that relied on strict military rule, paranoia about their safety, and constant guard against their serfs, was inevitable in order to ensure the continuing survival of the Spartans. Therefore, the prevailing rise of paranoid individuals, in this historical predicament, was a necessary ingredient for the success of the State. Similarly, during our times, the small State of Israel surrounded by enemies, needs leaders with enough paranoia to help avert the dangers it faces.

Spartan rearing practices have remained legendary to this day and resemble totalitarian and autocratic concentration camps with the aim of producing tough and unyielding fighters in order to defend their city. A boy could enjoy his home and parental care only up until the age of seven years. At that point he would be taken to live under strict military rule and was subsequently considered the property of the state and not his parents. Thereafter he would be trained, educated, and be taught the limits of behavioural tolerance as well as his elders' expectations of him. In adolescence he was provided with scant clothing and forced to sleep outside year-round in order to cultivate his swiftness and strength. His diet would not fare any better; a black froth prepared from pigs' legs, blood, salt, and vinegar would make contemporary boys flinch with aversion, its nutritive value notwithstanding (Butler 2007); let's not forget that blood soups are still prepared by various cultures even today. Treachery and cunning was highly valued as the means to provide necessary survival skills. Such traits came naturally in paranoid personalities, providing a 'selection bias' for their future leaders. Even stealing and foraging was thought to be a good preparation for the (unavoidable) time of battle. By today's standards the Spartans were a ruthless, uncivilized people who terrorized their children and neighbours; the reality of their predicament however, along with the necessity to be constantly on guard, enabled the most paranoid among them to draft such rules of contact so as to ensure their supremacy and dominance (Forrest 1968).

Girls in Sparta also underwent rigorous training and exercises, even though they remained at their homes of origin. Their life purpose was twofold; on the one hand they had to be strong and healthy in order to produce strong and healthy men for the next generation (we all know the unfortunate fate of sickly born Spartan babies being thrown off the cliffs of Mount Taygetus); and on the other hand, they were responsible for running the city and supervising the Helots while the men were fighting away. This arrangement produced liberated and outspoken women who at times were envied by the rest of the Greeks (Thucydides 1974). Their roles though were designed in order to serve the paranoia-laden Spartan society.

Spartan men had to serve in the army for 30 years with an additional ten being on reserve. Adult life wasn't any easier since they too had to live in barracks and only see their families during clandestine escapes, mostly at night. But to begin their service in the army, first they had to spend two years in the Krypteia, their secret service, so to speak, where they engaged in spying and bullying the Helots and other enemies of their state (Butler 2007). We see therefore that their whole system, mentality, and way of life were based on paranoid principles geared towards keeping their enemies at bay. Eventually they succumbed to the free-thinking democratic Athenians, just as their modern day counterparts the Soviets succumbed to the West (Martin 1996). Their paranoia however sustained them against their surrounding threats.

Price and Hicks (2006), echoing ideas put forth by contemporary moral philosophers, assume that leaders and followers are, in fact, equals. Therefore, any inequality visible between them constitutes an affront to justice and morality. However, as early as ancient Greece, Aristotle and his pupil Plato formulated the pragmatic terms of inequality, which by necessity, characterize leader–follower relations. They both identify a qualitative difference between them, with hints of biological determinism, which either prepares men to be philosopher-kings and lead among equals, or, if not so endowed by nature, to assume their proper sub-ordinate roles; so, for Greek philosophers,[10] inequality becomes justice and is based on real differences between leaders and followers (Aristotle 2001, Plato 2001). Moreover, there are references that echo modern concepts about the servant–leader ideal (Greenleaf 1977), in that leadership is not considered a means to enhance the well-being of the leader, but of the city as a whole. The example of Sparta especially illustrates this principle.

It is not the purpose of this book to recapitulate history or even to sketch the flow of one empire after another in order to highlight the personality disorders of great historical figures and leaders. I have offered several examples from antiquity as well as more recent history as an illustration of the thesis that great leaders are born with special and distinct characteristics that set them apart, with paranoia being at the core of their personality structure. Be that as it may, one cannot peruse through history without pausing and paying some tribute to Alexander the Great and his remarkable achievements. We will approach him of course from the angle that illustrates our argument. He was certainly born into a life of privilege; his royal descent assured him ease of goal fulfilment, and luxury. His mentor, none other than the father of Greek philosophy, Aristotle, moulded a mind with the best educational and intellectual tools of his time. And his military training turned him into a capable strategist destined to conquer the world. He displayed both an incredible physical toughness and intellectual genius (Butler 2007) providing fertile ground for shaping his powerful personality. After conquering Greece and uniting all those city states under his rule, he turned outwards and overtook the world east of Greece. Even today there are pockets of people in central Asia and Afghanistan who consider themselves his descendants (Wood 1997).

Certainly Alexander's success was not only due to his privileged upbringing, but also the result of his charismatic personality. He led by example and could rouse his troops with his enthusiasm and energy. He could put down a mutiny with a mere speech; a quality that allowed him to magnetize his followers. The importance of language and its relationship to psychiatric traits and leadership is expounded throughout this book. It is well-known that as he grew older (remember, he only lived 33 short years) his megalomania but also his paranoia increased to the point of having some of his closest friends and associates murdered. Ernst

---

[10] It has been said, perhaps not inappropriately, that all of western philosophy is a series of footnotes to Plato (Whitehead 1979).

Badian (1958) in his character study has described him as a megalo-maniac, paranoid autocrat and a ruthless killer. Even though it is always risky to analyse distant historical personalities, we do have cross-referenced information about Alexander's life to be able to make such deductions; and in any case, his character pathology descriptions re-semble those of his modern counterparts such as Mussolini and Stalin. Badian's claims can be corroborated by a contemporary biographer of Alexander, Cleitarchus (301 BCE), who described him as a cruel, para-noid alcoholic. His life and accomplishments however are strong proof for the argument that history is driven by special individuals; by uniting the ancient world and infusing it with Greek cultural and linguistic elements, he prepared the ground for the advent of two other great forces that shaped western thought and culture; we are referring of course to the Romans and their empire, and Christianity. Both were influenced, enhanced, and shaped by the Greeks through Alexander and, to use Butler's (2007) expression, 'the Greeks are still very much with us'. Alexander's personality certainly was both conducive as well as impera-tive for this cultural amalgam, the first Common Era, to be accomplished.

Rome started out as a democratic state but soon evolved into an empire that was often subject to the whimsical behaviour of its emperor. Machiavelli (2001a [1531]) succinctly states that democracy evolves into anarchy once the generation that established it passes away. Democracy frequently gives way to the rule of individuals characterized by megalo-mania, self-absorption, and tyranny. They either inherit their throne or assume it through violent means. The latter would have required them to convince enough of their subjects to follow them in order to solidify their suppressive rule. In this instance, besides coercive conviction, verbal skills (that is, language) would be of paramount importance. The advent of Christianity brought about a new political climate over the empire, but the empire itself helped shape the orthodox beliefs of the people in a way that assured the importance and role of the emperor, even if he would be, at least theoretically, under the spiritual jurisdiction of the Church. Interestingly, the role of the fallen Roman emperors was subsequently filled by the Bishops of Rome.

The amalgamation of Christianity with the Roman Empire gave rise to the first Pan-European civilization and ushered into history the Common Era, the period of shaping and rehashing of Western thought – political, religious, and philosophical. Distinct patterns of Western beliefs and practices are thus established. The Pauline version of Christianity becomes dominant and takes on the world. His fervent enthusiasm, extensive travel, copious writings, and overbearing personality helped shape the way this new religion would evolve. Paul's personality, with elements of manic psychosis on the one hand and depression on the other,[11] was certainly instrumental in the establishment of Christian orthodoxy. He remains one of the most instrumental leaders that history has known.

The time between the fall of Rome to the fall of Constantinople is traditionally considered by historians to be the boundaries of the Middle Ages, when Christianity, at least in Europe, reigned supreme. The dogma had been established and deviance (that threatened both the political as well as the religious order), was not tolerated. Leadership was established 'by the grace of God' and authority was unchallenged. Anyone different was burned at the stake, exiled, blinded, exorcized, anathematized, or simply murdered. Many psychiatrically impaired individuals lost their lives on account of their illness. Remember that schizophrenics would be found way beyond the limits of their society's tolerance and were thus persecuted. Aggression and paranoia were the rule and rulers appeared to be inbred for these conditions. Thus came centuries of senseless bloodshed over issues such as land disputes, inheritances, or religious dogma. Christianity was once divided and armies clashed over the spelling of a word, over a syllable, which according to the adherents of religious orthodoxy, altered the essence of, none other, than Christ's true nature. In the early Creed, Christ is described as being of one essence, *homoousios*, with God the Father, but some theologians could not swallow the concept; they took comfort instead in the notion of resemblance to the Father, *homoiousios*, but to the ruling class this was offensive and unacceptable heresy. Wars were launched, lives were lost, and a schism ensued among Christians that persists to this day. Quite certainly the opposing leaders of such debates were unyielding, due in part to their rigid (paranoid) personalities and suspicion of each other. An even wider divide ensued between the Eastern and the Western Church over the addition of the word *Filioque* (and from the son) to the Creed.

Therefore the Middle Ages had also their share of bloodshed. There was of course a religious flare to those wars – enter knights and crusaders – but, nonetheless, the end result was still loss of life and destruction of property. The blind devotion that medieval leaders enjoyed is worthy of admiration. In the final analysis, however, the same biological principles can explain the phenomenon that is probably not unlike what we observe today, when terrorists follow their leaders blindly.

---

[11] The Biblical quotation from Ecclesiastes 1:2;12:8 'Vanity of vanities; all is vanity' (Vanitas vanitatum et omnia vanitas) was used prominently in his epistles (Ephesians 4,17).

The legendary Joan of Arc exemplifies a person who combined a clear deviation from the 'normal' individual of her time along with leadership skills; her visions, having occurred through adolescence (Barrett 1932) were instrumental in inducing her to come forward, declare her presence, suggest a course of action, and assume the leadership of French troops against the English. Moreover, she directed and brought forth the coronation and legitimization of Charles II who in turn delegated to her the command of his army. For an illiterate peasant to achieve such prominence, she must have possessed special characteristics and qualities. Even to this day, scholars and scientists debate on what exactly was her (psycho)pathology, however the fact remains that she acted outside the limits of her society's expectations; proposed diagnoses include such diseases as epilepsy (d'Orsi and Tinuper 2006), migraine (Foote-Smith and Bayne 1991), tuberculosis (Henker 1984), and schizophreniform psychosis (Allen 1975). The latter seems unlikely given her astuteness during her trial (Mackowiak 2007) and the way she carried herself before her king and his people. Abnormal she may have been, however she appears to have escaped the ravages of schizophrenia or other severe psychopathology, and was perhaps afflicted by a lesser condition that endowed her with leadership potential and language skills; this is manifested in the way she carried herself during her trial when she used astounding language in answering her accusers; 'Asked if she knew she was in God's grace, she answered: "If I am not, may God put me there; and if I am, may God so keep me"' (Barrett 1932).

The case of Joan of Arc described above illustrates also that the timing of appearance of leaders is instrumental in their acceptance as such, but also for their success. Richey (2003) claims that 'only a regime in the final straits of desperation would pay any heed to an illiterate farm girl who claimed that the voice of God was instructing her to take charge of her country's army and lead it to victory'. Desperate conditions breed desperate decisions. Her personality and the use of persuasive language enabled her to gain followers even against the wishes and the orders of official war councils (DeVries 1999) leading France to victory against the English invaders. Her legacy continued on for centuries, eventually leading to her canonization as a saint of the Roman Catholic Church. She has remained a common point of reference for diverse factions of French society; Philippe-Alexandre Le Brun de Charmettes (1817) wrote that as a supporter of her king and country, she became an acceptable symbol to the monarchists; as the daughter of commoners, she became the prototype of many unknown volunteers of the French revolution; and as a religious martyr, she was popular among the powerful Catholic community.

III.

The Renaissance marked the rebirth of the Graeco-Roman civilization, its humanism and cultural achievements. Many factors helped bring about this transition and they are beyond the scope of this book. Suffice it to say that the leadership of the Medici family in Florence was instrumental, along with the availability of classical works brought to Western Europe by Byzantine scholars who fled Constantinople in 1453, after it was sacked by the Turks. A third important factor was the invention of printing, which enabled scores of people to read the classics, the Bible, history, and accounts of travellers. It was in this setting that the great political thinker, Machiavelli, formulated his own thoughts about leaders and followers. He also struggles with, and eventually offers justification for the apparent inequalities that are inherent in the dyad, and he also proposes some differentiating qualities that should characterize leaders. The strongest and the bravest, according to his creation story, were given the task of leadership, which however, would evolve later on and include those individuals capable of being flexible enough to handle change (the ever-present and constant imperative of our existence). His preference for a republican rather than monarchic state, even though it appears pessimistic, hints at the desirable skill of a leader to muster support, perhaps by the appropriate use of language (Machiavelli 2001a [1531]).

Rousseau (2001 [1762]) considers the emergence of leadership as problematic and counter-productive for the fulfilment of man's self-perfection. It is a necessary evil that is required to transform the 'noble savage' from a state of a 'stupid, limited animal into an intelligent being and a man'. However, social and political arrangements, according to Rousseau, do not succeed in bringing forth such qualities, but rather, they induce a condition that is 'even lower than the animal itself'. In his primitive state, man has only pain and hunger to fear, whereas his only needs are basically food, rest, and women. This is a happy, natural state of bliss, as described in the introduction of this book. Leaders need to see beyond this situation and visualize a higher state of existence for man, a state where he is transformed into perfection. In his own words:

> He who dares to undertake the establishment of a people should feel that he is, so to speak, in a position to change human nature, to transform each individual (who by himself is a perfect and solitary whole), into a part of a larger whole from which this individual receives, in a sense, his life and his being; to alter man's constitution in order to strengthen it; and to substitute a partial and moral existence for the physical and independent existence we have all received from nature.

To the extent to which men tolerate inequality, they have only themselves to blame, so long as that inequality is not instrumental in bringing them out of their natural, to a higher state of existence. Napoleon's example comes to mind. A product of the French Revolution, he ascended to power at a time when the French people were trying to hold on to their newly gained freedom and defend themselves against surrounding kingdoms; their astonishing behaviour towards their royalty and aristocracy was looked upon unfavourably because it threatened to upset established order and set unpleasant precedents. He was the right man for the job with his multitasking capabilities, his bipolar traits, and his paranoia that helped him defend his people from real and potential enemies.[12] According to Gifford (2010) he possessed:

> a piercing intellect constantly focussing on the key issues of the day; the mental stamina to analyse a problem from every perspective until a solution was decided upon; the determination to put that solution into effect; the force of personality to inspire other people to undertake the process of change; the ability to store and recall huge amounts of information needed for the implementation of the plan; the mental toughness not to be distracted from the main objective by set-backs and material changes; the mental flexibility to adapt the plan, but not the objective, in the face of changing circumstances. In administrative affairs he could not see why he should not dictate everything, as he was always right and everybody else's judgement was suspect.

Some of his paranoid traits are beginning to show up through the above description. Gemma Betros (2012) describes his childhood reputation as brusque and aloof. As a true leader however he was at least initially able to bring about such changes that helped establish him, in his subjects' mind, as a man who should be followed. 'He went on to lead France to become the pre-eminent nation in Europe and to rule an empire stretching from Italy and Spain to the borders of Russia' (Gifford 2010). Had he avoided the misjudged attack against Russia, history and the world today might have been vastly different. Part of his success was what Alexander (2001) describes as his ability to change appearance at will to adapt to his surroundings and allow others to see in him what they wanted. His means and methods have been characteristic of a personality that would employ such means as 'image, objects and the written word' (Betros 2012), to effectively communicate his status as the leader. He is reputed to have falsified army records in order to promote his image and

---

[12] His decreased need for sleep has become legendary; this is a characteristic of a bipolar person's hypomanic or manic state.

strategies. Luxurious gifts would win over followers who might otherwise oppose him such as the 'jeweled snuffboxes adorned with his
portrait and distributed to the bishops who officiated at his coronation as
Emperor' (Betros 2012). He thus promoted a cult around him that saw
him as a God-sent saviour of the French people. Paranoid individuals
frequently create an entourage of followers that are mesmerized by their
personality and leadership style.

The humanism of the Renaissance eventually gave way to industrialism,
the age of discoveries, colonialism, capitalism, and sadly, communism. We
have now entered the post-communist era with a single superpower at the
forefront of world affairs. Marx's and Engel's ideas have been expounded
already in the introduction. At some point however, even they accepted that
leadership in the form of collective effort, is dependent on circumstances
that have resulted from past historical and social events. Thus, again, the
need to allow for an individual who will fit the already existing conditions
and move his followers forward (Marx 1937 [1869]).

The fall of communism was perhaps an unavoidable event in a series
of historical successions that preceded it; it was the policy of a single
leader, however, that brought about its final collapse. Would events have
occurred as they did had Gorbachev not been elected secretary of the
Politburo? One wonders. However, his actions were the crucial factor at
that crucial moment for what followed. History was subsequently
changed forever. Gorbachev's personality certainly played a pivotal role
in the application of glasnost and perestroika and his willingness to
consider younger advisers' ideas (Ciobanu 2004). He grasped the political and economic realities of his time and foresaw the need for radical
reforms. His charisma charmed the West, however he failed to understand
the leadership needs of his own people. Perhaps he lacked enough
paranoia to defend his own interests and those of socialism, leading to
the fall of the Soviet Union, to the chagrin of Soviet hardliners, and the
joy of the free world.

Our world, however, despite its globalization, appears to be increasingly
more complex, more unmanageable and probably more hostile. Pluralism
and not uniformity is the characteristic on the New Common Era. Current
reality is a far cry from the societies that moral philosopher John Rawls
(1971) had envisioned. He claimed that the primary concern of leadership
was to create a just and fair society, based on just institutions as the basic
structure of a fair society in which everyone would have an equal
opportunity to ascend the leadership ladder. His views have been criticized
by several theorists; my own reservation is whether such a situation could
exist, given the biological determinants of leader–follower relations as
they have been explicated previously. In all fairness, however, we should

keep in mind that many of his liberal theories were formulated prior to the current state of global affairs and before the cataclysmic fall of the Soviet Union. Huntington's prediction of the clash of civilizations (2002) is therefore beginning to appear more plausible than in the Cold War era. His visions about enlightened leaders (1999) who would guide their followers beyond narrow national interests towards an international arena of fairness, is probably mere disillusionment. Given the disillusionment of *Homo economicus* following the global financial collapse in the latter part of 2008,[13] we are truly living in a transitional, confusing, and chaotic time of history; such conditions are ripe for the ascent of paranoid leaders by virtue of their apparent strength of character and unyielding personalities. That is another reason why Rawls' propositions are just too idealistic and improbable in their application.

Pinker's (2011) four motivations of empathy, self-control, morality, and reason are in line with Rawls' thinking when he proposes that they may 'orient us away from violence and towards cooperation and altruism'. He argues that violence has been declining in the world both in the long as well as in the short run. Among other factors leading to this development according to his thinking, is what he calls 'The Escalator of Reason', which he identifies as an 'intensifying application of knowledge and rationality to human affairs'. He goes on to identify trends that have enhanced this putative decline in violence and for the most part originated following the enlightenment of the eighteenth century. Unfortunately, current world events do not corroborate his claims and he himself has asserted that this decline might not be guaranteed to continue. Moreover, Pax Romana and Pax Byzantina have also produced such peace and non-violence for protracted periods of time and were finally disrupted both from within as well as from outside forces.[14] The hopes of the world in post-communist, post-Cold War New Peace (Pinker 2011) are withering rapidly.

---

[13] *Homo economicus*, or economic human, is the concept in many economic theories of humans as rational and narrowly self-interested actors who have the ability to make judgements towards their subjectively defined ends. Using these rational assessments, *Homo economicus* attempts to maximize utility as a consumer and economic profit as a producer. The term 'Economic Man' was used for the first time in the late nineteenth century by critics of John Stuart Mill's work on political economy.

[14] Ahrweiler (2012) reminds us of the little-known historical fact that during the dominance of Byzantium – roughly the period of the Middle Ages – torture was forbidden as a means of interrogation, in opposition to the practices of Western Europe (inquisition), which were dominated by the papacy.

This is the time that we will probably see the rise of messianic movements and, perhaps, new religions. Such developments will not fall out of the sky; they will be driven by those gifted individuals who, by virtue of their linguistic cunning and timely appearance, will win scores of followers. This holds true for small groups, businesses, as well as nations. Kelloway and Barling (2000) reported that in organizations facing increasingly turbulent times, the ability of potential leaders to communicate optimism is a critical factor in enhancing organizational outcomes. Therefore, anyone who projects optimism into an optimism-seeking world will succeed in leadership ascendance. Paranoid personalities are well equipped to accomplish that.

A brief word is in order about two other approaches, opposing for the most part, regarding inequality in leader–follower relations and their treatment of outsiders. Communitarianism allows for a group to turn inward and focus within itself to better its conditions of existence, even at the exclusion of outsiders. McIntyre (1994) expresses this approach in accepting that each group, under the guise of its leader, has a moral right, and a responsibility to further its own interests. Cosmopolitanism on the other hand, considers national interests to be too narrow for considering justice and fairness in the world, and that the role of leaders would be to strive towards the creation of a world community and citizenship. Singer (1972) considers the distinction among groups based on boundaries or even distance immoral. Both communitarianism as well as cosmopolitanism are critical of liberalist approaches like those proposed by Rawls.[15] What matters at the end is the timely appearance of capable leaders who can measure up to the demands of their times and guide their people in ushering in a new era. Whatever the demands and whatever the task, a true leader will tailor his policy in order to bring about the necessary changes as he sees fit. An eloquent leader will muster the emotional support of his followers as well.

I am wondering whether Obama's amazing success is ushering in this new era. Time will tell. It is in a crisis, after all, that, according to Hermann (1976), a leader is measured up and has a chance to affect outcomes; the leader's personality style plays a key role in determining the type of action to be taken and the way (foreign and domestic policy) affairs will go. As she states, 'idiosyncratic personality features can play a determinant role'. Idiosyncrasies are those personality characteristics, including language style, which set us apart. A paranoid individual will

---

[15]   For a nice discussion and comparison of their approaches and ideas, see Price and Hicks' (2006) discussion.

likely become overly cautious and eventually may act pre-emptively in order to avert a perceived threat. Personality styles and distortions will invariably affect political (that is, leadership) decisions, especially when the leader is emotionally and cognitively involved (Hartmann 1958). Obama is certainly not devoid of paranoia. Given that, he still appears not to have fallen for the paranoid cries of his grief stricken nation, nor has he given in to calls for revenge and retribution. He has not scapegoated any particular group of people and he has been steadfast in his pursuit towards a safer, more tolerant, and financially revived country. Nancy McWilliams (2010) feels that 'such a leader would have to acknowledge harsh realities, develop adaptive programs, and avoid regressive distractions that simplify and blame'. To the extent that he will manage to do so, Obama will also be deemed a great leader. In doing so, he needs to rally the support of his own electorate, convincing them that any change should come gradually and methodically, while at the same time fending off those opposing voices that would brand him as weak, ineffective, and pensive. A healthy dose of paranoia would help him fend off those malignant attacks that strive to crush his reforms.

Contrast Obama's healthy paranoia to that of Turkish Prime Minister and later President Tayyip Erdogan whose recent actions have increased tensions in the Mediterranean basin as he has taken on, for one reason or another, the Israelis, the Lebanese, the Cypriots, the European Union, his people, and others who have disagreed with his views. The way he has demonized his enemies, perceived or real, internal or external, typifies the reaction of a paranoid personality towards criticism. Of concern of course is the appeal he may have on the Turkish people who, reacting unconsciously to his admonitions and prompts, might follow him and be dragged into the violence and destabilization of the area. The potential danger for such a development becomes visible as the Turks are growing increasingly uneasy about Erdogan's domestic policies; this was demonstrated by the anti-government demonstrations that swept through many Turkish cities beginning in May 2013 and that have continued to erupt periodically since. Turkey, in that respect, may prove to be another link in the long chain of dissatisfied nations that take on their destiny at the prompting of a charismatic contender–leader.

Undeniably, most other non-Western and non-European societies have had their share in a bloody past. That tradition is of course by no means surpassed since, to this day, people continue to lose their lives over senseless issues. If we assume that average people everywhere, and throughout history, shared the same basic desires and drives, that is the security and comfort to lead their lives and raise their children in peace, how can we explain the fact that time and again hordes and scores of them leave their homes and families and go to war, especially when they know perfectly well that they might not return? This is such a constantly observed phenomenon that a significant number of sociologists and political scientists have argued that it, too, is part of human nature (Bion 1961). Like the development of culture and the evolution of language, war also appears to be a universal human characteristic. Could it somehow be related to our genetic predisposition to follow our leaders blindly? And, moreover, could it be biologically linked to our presumption that leaders are psychiatrically impaired and more likely to lead us into conflict? In other words, does our biology induce us to appoint warmonger leaders, in order to ensure that war will occur and our innate need for conflict is secured? And is Jane Austen (2005) right in stating 'how quick come the reasons for approving what we like'? If we can prove these hypotheses the apparent inconsistencies in human behaviour might be explained. In psychology, Denning (2007) reminds us, this phenomenon is called confirmation bias; he quotes Francis Bacon's saying that 'the human understanding when it has once adopted an opinion ... draws all things else to support and agree with it'.

Scores of people rise up and participate in armed conflict precisely because they ultimately link their survival, and hence reproduction, to the outcome of that very conflict. Research on group polarization has revealed that individual attitudes become more extreme and actions get riskier, when a multitude judges a given situation, than when single persons decide (Levine and Moreland 1998). Anyone who has participated in a rally or a demonstration can attest to that fact. Notions are exaggerated under the influence of a group at large. De Duve (2010) also explains:

> The need to believe, especially within the context of a group, is ingrained in human nature, probably carved into it by natural selection because those populations that believed in something had a greater chance of surviving and producing progeny under prevailing conditions, whatever the plausibility, or lack of it, of the object of the belief.

Therefore, following a leader in a group and adopting that particular group's beliefs appears to be a social phenomenon albeit with a biologically determined causation.

An effective leader is the one who manages to join these notions in his subjects' minds. Bennis (2003) also asks, 'what is it that makes us go riding unto the breach – following even those leaders who don't have

Will Shakespeare writing their speeches?'[16] He answers his own question later on by stating that the 'reasons to follow someone ... is an honest belief in the person you're following. The other is selfish. The person following has to believe that following is the best thing to do at the time.' In other words, this is the best way to increase chances of success (that is, survival and reproduction); and Price and Hicks (2006), paraphrasing Rousseau (2001 [1755]) remind us that 'it is the desire to rule that first puts people in a position to be ruled by others'. This is the socio-biological reason we form hierarchies and pecking orders. After all, to fight for territorial dominance, and therefore a better chance to reproduce, is a trait present in many species including man. Mayer *et al.* (1995) provided a model proposing that when followers believe their leaders have integrity and capability or benevolence, they will be more comfortable engaging in behaviours that put them at risk (for example, sharing sensitive information). That is, individuals who feel that their leader has, or will, demonstrate care and consideration will reciprocate this sentiment in the form of desired behaviours (Konovsky and Pugh 1994).

The destructive power of war may be our legacy from earlier days when the motto 'your death, my survival' was the rule. We see, then, that conflict is a legacy of all peoples, of all times. Add to this the findings from research on group polarization, and the stage is set for mobilization and fighting. Technological progress in the West has not, unfortunately, abolished this phenomenon. In the previous chapter we saw that pre-meditated violence is not only a human characteristic but occurs regularly in the wild among non-human primates as well (Leaky and Lewin 1992).

Neurobiological research has been shedding some light into the issue of free choice, free will, and the way decisions are made, as well as why (and how) followers put their trust in leaders who subsequently lead them into dangerous predicaments. It turns out that unconscious processes may determine or influence goal pursuits (Custers and Aarts 2010) by preparing actions well before any conscious thoughts instruct the brain to do so. In other words, motivation towards a goal can arise without

---

[16] He begins this argument by quoting from Shakespeare's *The Life of King Henry V*:

Once more unto the breach, dear friends, once more

...

Follow your spirit, and upon this charge
Cry 'God for Harry, England and Saint George'!

conscious awareness (Bargh *et al.* 2001) by taking into account information and other environmental clues in a continuous state of a brain primed for action. Even such simple motor acts as moving a finger can be initiated by unconscious brain processes before a person perceives the need for that action (Rizzolatti and Arbib 1998). If goals and actions are activated outside of conscious awareness, one could begin to explain why followers react the way they do to their leaders and follow their commands blindly. It would be intriguing to suggest, but not far-fetched given the evidence exposed above, that a leader's language and communication style sets off unconscious processes in his followers' minds who subsequently exhibit actions resulting from pre-determined decisions unbeknownst to them.

Recent research on the neurobiology of choices, including not only those between different material options, but also in terms of leader–follower choices, revealed that humans as well as animals, mostly make choices in sensorimotor tasks that are nearly optimal – in the sense of approaching maximal expected utility – or complying with principles of statistical inference (Kirk *et al.* 2007). In other words, the leaders we choose are expected to maximize our expectations whichever those might be. Monkey work that attempted to learn about decisions from rewards has honed on frontal cortex processes as the anatomical site sub-serving such decisions (Lee and Seo 2007) and also on the posterior parietal cortex, an area which is classically thought to be involved in the so-called visual processing stream (Trommershäuser 2011) that integrates incoming sensory modalities and synthesizes them into a meaningful representation of the world.

Another sociological reason to mobilize and rally for a cause is when all other alternatives seem hopeless. The desperado phenomena of South American peoples are examples of that; fighting against poverty, political oppression, at times mere hunger and disease, was the only perceived option left to those desperate individuals. Liberation movements such as the French Revolution are another such example. As Granovetter (1978) argues in his description of similar events, 'the point where the perceived benefits to an individual of doing the thing in question ... exceed the perceived costs' is when mobilization occurs. He calls those points 'threshold points' where people's cups run over, so to speak, and also, the perceived fear of retribution is suppressed by the need for change to counter intolerable conditions. Usually a leader will emerge under those circumstances who will identify the issue, target the 'guilty party', and charge the group forward. The foreseeable danger in these situations, of course, is that leaders will emerge, as previously discussed, who will likely possess a paranoid predisposition and a language style, such that groups will give them unquestionable support.

Often times, the end goal of a movement changes direction so that the result is more to the benefit of the leader than the group at large. In the 1950s, on the island of Cyprus, Archbishop Makarios, led a struggle against British rule and for political unification with Greece. That struggle ended with the granting of independence to Cyprus and the formation of a republic with Makarios as president. In the mid-1960s, another chance for union appeared but President Makarios, as a result of his own inflated self-esteem (narcissism), as well as his paranoia against Greece, America, and the Soviets, failed to grasp it. In the early 1970s he failed to embrace a political solution that was reached between the Greek and Turkish communities of the island. That led, eventually, to the tragic division between a Turkish Northern and a Greek Southern Cyprus. Remarkably, the great majority of the Greek Cypriots continued to support their charismatic leader even after several of his failures. The case of Cyprus illustrates Weber's observation (Weber *et al.* 1946) that 'the final result of political action often ... stands in completely inadequate and often even paradoxical relation to its original meaning'. A paranoid leader will gain easy assent during times of crisis. However, the same paranoia may prevent him from realizing his followers' true interests.

With post-industrialism there appeared notions of individualism in which each person is seen as a microcosmos of society. This notion led to the concept of equality among individuals but not necessarily liberty. Priority was given to relations between people as equals and between people and things.[17] Each, to the extent of his/her capabilities, had the right to alienate property from others and use it in any way seen fit.[18] In opposition to this view, and probably as a result of church dominance over worldly affairs, the world was seen as structured in a hierarchy.

Individual initiative by paranoid leaders was conducive to the development of social change and the succession of political systems in historical times. Some societies were more open than others, reflecting, up to a point, a greater or lesser degree of collective paranoia. In that respect, states could be characterized as paranoid or democratic, free or oppressed, depending on the social flavour that leaders bestowed on their political regimes. Remember twentieth-century rhetoric about the free

---

[17] Hence the designation of *Homo aequalis* in descriptions of this type of society.
[18] In this light, the rise of colonialism, capitalism, and imperialism can be understood as by-products.

world and the axis of evil. American society was undeniably freer and more individualistic than that of the USSR, which was undeniably oppressive and over-controlling; leaders of both societies however, were ironically paranoid on those opposing sides. Consider the behaviour of Richard Nixon and Ronald Reagan on the one hand, and that of Leonid Brezhnev and Nicolae Ceausescu on the other. Whereas the western leaders were pronouncing truths about the Soviets, it was their paranoia that prompted them to do so, as well as their strategy to be unyieldingly tough towards their opponents. This toughness was, during the Cold War, necessary, important, and functional, since it eventually led to the fall of the Iron Curtain. In this situation, Western paranoia, even if nurtured in a democratic environment, constituted the necessary ingredient to allow the West to deal with the intransigence of the Soviet leaders. It was critical that Nixon and Reagan had those ingredients and used such language, so as to rally the American public's support, get democratically elected, and get the job done. Their paranoia helped them see the lurking dangers to their world, real or imagined, and act accordingly. So we see at play the combination of a paranoid predisposition, a certain language (communication) style, the presence of a threatening vicissitude, and a public that is genetically programmed to follow, under such circumstances, leaders who stand confidently firm on their ground.

One issue was of paramount importance for Reagan: the threat of the Soviets. Denning (2007) writes that 'not having a clear and inspiring goal is one common failing of leadership. Another is having too many of them.' The desirable result is the rise of the unyielding personality style of leaders such as Pericles, Churchill, and Nixon, among many others. These were leaders who have saved their people at times of danger. Their timing was of course another important factor in their success story; as Shakespeare wrote, 'Ripeness is all' (Craig 1914). Perhaps a crucial reason why Jimmy Carter suffered such a humiliating defeat by Reagan (the attack on the US embassy in Teheran notwithstanding), was the very fact that he lacked an adequate dose of paranoia and could not, therefore, mobilize people behind him. The American public recognized this and turned to Reagan whose rhetoric touched their innermost beliefs and values. His charisma flowed from his personality, but was also bestowed on him by the needy public, just as Weber (1978) predicted.

The Soviets on the other hand, were so keen on holding onto their power and governing style, that not only were they hostile towards the West; they brutally suppressed every expression of individuality or the slightest disagreement from their own people. Think of the way they treated such dissidents as Aleksandr Solzhenitsyn. At the end I should suppose we should all be grateful that the West won; oppressive regimes can only last for a limited period of time. This probably occurs as not only secondary to the people's reaction, but also as a result of inter-personal conflicts between paranoid contenders themselves. The mentor-ship case of Lenin and Stalin as described by Tucker (1973) illustrates the initial camaraderie as well as eventual conflict between paranoid individuals and how they come to split off. Closely allied and fighting together for their revolution, they came to view each other as competitors when young apprentice Stalin came of political age. Their split led in part to Lenin's demise, who suffered an incapacitating stroke afterwards. Interestingly, and expectantly in psychoanalytic circles, Stalin sought to discredit his mentor when he replaced him. This is paranoid action at its fullest and reminiscent of Thutmosis' treatment of after he replaced her (see p. 63). And let's not forget that senility usually plays an important role in consolidating, as well as strengthening prior personality styles, since whichever control could be exerted on those (paranoid) styles during healthier periods of life, is irrevocably gone. Hachinski (1999) explains Stalin's last years in which his life-long suspiciousness (that is, paranoia) became florid paranoia as the result of multiple mini-strokes; 'The most plausible explanation of Stalin's late behaviour is the dimming of a superior intellect and the unleashing of a paranoid personality by a multi-infarct state.' Whichever the cause might have been, it is reasonable to assume that the process of senescence brings about a damping of the executive functioning of the brain and, consequently, the unopposed exaggeration of premorbid traits.[19]

Post (1973, 1980) agrees with the above notion and states that old age does not necessarily result in mellowing of personalities. We will see examples of this later on. That is why my patients with Alzheimer's disease become more aggressive and more unreasonable as their disease progresses, or more timid and withdrawn, depending on their personality structure when they were healthier. That is why I think Post (Post and George 2004) is off the mark when he writes 'In considering political

---

[19] Executive brain functions are the responsibility mainly of the frontal lobes. This is an area that is frequently and disproportionately affected by senescence as well as dementing processes. A physical manifestation of the consequences of dysfunction of the frontal lobes is the appearance of the so-called 'frontal release signs', which represent the re-emergence of primitive reflexes; these are present at birth and during variable periods of infancy, but are subsequently suppressed by the development of the frontal lobes. Their reappearance signifies damage or dysfunction of the frontal lobes as occurs in cases of Alzheimer's disease or multi-infarct (vascular) dementia, along with executive dysfunction, which leads to strengthening of pre-morbid characteristics.

paranoia, it is sometimes difficult to determine whether an act was an example of hard-headed prudence, simple overreaction, or a reflection of paranoia'. Any act of political paranoia, is just that; the result of paranoid thinking by a paranoid leader whose paranoia has helped him attract followers and rise up the hierarchy of leadership. His followers may have voted him into office, as happens in free democracies, or may have established him in position as the most effective leader in a revolution, or he may have stirred up the revolution and attracted others. The point here is that, as will be discussed time and again in this book, a dose of paranoia is a necessary ingredient for effective leadership, especially during periods of instability or crisis. Unfortunately, in totalitarian regimes, the degeneration of ageing leaders is not readily apparent, often gets covered up, and their replacement becomes long overdue. This fact applies to all organized groups of people who follow a strict hierarchical structure of leadership such as the military, religion, and academia.

Failure to appreciate the role of paranoia in world politics may lead to overreaction by opponents or misjudgement of crisis situations. For example, had Stalin's paranoia been understood better during the 1940s and 1950s, the West might have dealt differently and more effectively with him. The notion that he was paranoid was actually conveyed to the US State Department (Wolf 1948) but its significance was not grasped. His insistence that Western embassies such as those of the United Kingdom and the US be moved outside the Kremlin in 1953 was such an act of paranoia (Tucker 1965). Similarly, a few decades later, the US itself tore down its embassy which was under construction in Moscow on fears that it had been laden with bugging devices (Hyde 1990). US paranoia in this instance allowed detection of the covert listening devices.

A freer society, that gives the sense to its people that they too participate in the common affairs by voting on the issues, is more likely to survive and overcome its enemies. Consider here other similar examples such as that of ancient Athens (remember Pericles' skills of persuasion), and Sparta, or a more recent example, the allies against Hitler. In both situations the free societies had to collectively choose and select those leaders who embodied their own ambitions, aspirations and frustrations about their perceived enemies. The leaders themselves had to use the persuasive and seductive language of the paranoid personality to lure the public into appointing them. Again, we see the interplay between language, paranoia, and leadership, all most probably coded for on a common genetic domain. The interplay of these factors is paramount for 'good' as well as 'evil' leaders. The brutality of the Bolshevik leaders stemmed not so much from their anxiety to achieve their goals as from their own paranoia and suspicions of insurgency, and the state they created was thus based on fear, oppression, and persecution.

Perhaps a close modern counterpart of Sparta would be that of North Korea, which as Baird (2003) describes, 'remains cloaked in an aura of secrecy, xenophobia, and military preoccupation' designed so by its two father figures, Kim Il Sung and his son and successor Kim Jong Il. Unquestionably the two men's paranoia played a key role in the establishment and maintenance of such a suspicion-driven, isolated regime, reflecting their (disordered) personality style and modus operandi. The whole setup is so typical of the way a paranoid personality thinks and acts and patterns a regime, that it probably serves as the premier example of the autocratic state. As such, it remains withdrawn from the outside world to which it has progressively grown aloof. The outside world in its turn has become aloof of North Korea. There is increasing evidence, however, that the heroic figure of saviour father Kim has not developed into a lasting legacy so far as the son Kim or the grandson Kim Jong Un were concerned. The Japanese enemy has long ceased being a threat; inland insurgency is perhaps the most important issue currently but this is fended off by the identification of outside threatening states (perhaps the rest of the world), that necessitate the continuation of an oppressive regime and a mighty military establishment. Just as the Soviets would turn their people's attention towards the outside world, in order to avert insurgency within, the North Koreans turn to outside enemies to solidify their rule at home. The result could be catastrophic.

Regimes may be democratic or autocratic. In the final analysis, however, their success and survival depends on their founding fathers' initial dose of paranoia so that appropriate checks and balances are set up to see that they survive. Following stabilization and peace, however, the same dose of paranoia becomes dysfunctional and counterproductive, just as the case of North Korea. It is at this point that democracy should be given the chance to function properly and effectively. Repressive regimes almost always are crushed from within as a result of internal public dissatisfaction, but also, and most importantly, due to the appearance of a different focus of paranoia in the revolutionary leader that topples them. In the final analysis, it is best to have a chance to choose which paranoid leader will see us through our vicissitudes, so that we can replace them democratically when they are no longer needed. Autocrats are usually there to stay until they die or are violently thrown out.

Churchill and Charles de Gaulle were needed for the war, but both were replaced in peace; Stalin was not. All three had their own personality (paranoid) style and often they conflicted with each other.

Their uneasy alliance brought out many of their individual characteristics. De Gaulle's paranoia was invested in the service of France and its people, to the point where he identified himself with the country and the nation. Post (2004) believes that his narcissism was instrumental in his reactions towards the many enemies of France; the British and Americans, Anglo-Saxons as he used to called them, the Germans, his internal political opponents, and his last and final tribulation, the student uprisings of 1968. He fought them all with a never-ending zeal, unshakable determination, and self-sacrifice. A narcissist he may have been; however, his apparent aloofness and arrogance (de Launay 1968), along with his long-standing suspiciousness and mistrust of those he perceived as potential usurpers of France's legitimate power and rights, point to a hefty dose of paranoia as well.[20] Reaction by the French people was finally instrumental in replacing him when his beliefs, style, and ethos became irrelevant. Such was also the fate of his British counterpart and unwilling partner, Churchill. He was a source of inspiration to Britons and allies alike. He saw them through the crisis of German attacks and helped them prevail. He too was replaced during peaceful times.

I have argued previously that under critical and dire situations, people have the tendency to seek out strong and assuring leaders. According to Post (2004), even psychologically healthy and mature personalities would cling to such a leader and allow him excesses of power and temporary transgressions in order to overcome the crisis. In post-crisis situations, leaders tend to be more directive, autocratic, and goal oriented (Mulder *et al.* 1970, Yukl 2002), at times trying to cling onto their acquired privileges. Free societies therefore retain the option to replace their crisis-chosen leaders just as the English and the French did. Stalin on the other hand, stayed on, his paranoia worsened, and millions died as a result of his psychopathology; thus, he proved to be a hero against Hitler, but a menace to his own people. Under growing discontent leaders may become coercive in order to maintain power. This fact could be another argument for democratic procedures, examples of which were described above. And this argument brings us back to the issue of inequality, which has tried thinkers since antiquity. For Hobbes (1991 [1651]), the degree of inequality stems from the type of license that people give their leaders

---

[20] I am borrowing the description of paranoid personality here from Post (2004), the same source that describes de Gaulle as a narcissist (see page 111), to strengthen my own claim that, indeed, his actions and reactions were more the result of a paranoid than a narcissistic disposition. De Gaulle chose to step aside during France's hour of need in order to avert civil discontent and conflict; this was not the mark of a narcissist but that of a defeated and embittered man.

in order to reach a desired goal, and therefore have only themselves to blame when they receive unfair and excessively unequal treatment (Price and Hicks 2006). But provisions should exist, and usually are in place, according to Hobbes, so that a leader may be replaced, as long as his initial task of protecting his people is either not necessary, or he cannot perform it (Hobbes 1991 [1651]). That was the fate of both Churchill and de Gaulle when their policies no longer moved their people. Harvey (2006) has also reflected on this issue as shown in the following quotation:

> Leaders derive benefits (material and psychic) from effectiveness; how to be effective varies over time, and requires judgment and flexibility. Followers accept their place in the bargain as long as they perceive they are benefiting from the relationship. When followers no longer perceive these benefits, they are less likely to comply or follow. Leadership in such situations may turn increasingly into coercion, and lose legitimacy.

The fate of Soviet leadership turned into coercion as more and more Soviet citizens became disenchanted with it.

In concluding this chapter I would like to borrow Hickman and Couto's (2006) observations regarding the effectiveness of leadership in various situations, and under different social contexts and historical times.

- We can assess leadership only after some change has occurred. We can observe leaders acting to influence outcomes in the present.
- The nature of leadership in any change effort corresponds to the historical and social context in which we place it and the leader(s) through which we examine a network of change.
- The less we consider historical and cultural context, the fewer influential events and factors we take into account.
- The interaction of a leader's effort with the efforts of other leaders and participants shapes the outcome and hence the significance and nature of leadership.
- Every change effort takes place within a system of change that provides opposition and modification of other leadership.
- The more credit a particular leader is given for change, the less we credit contributions of co-actors to the outcome.

I opted to quote their complete set of conclusions, even though they are not all directly relevant to our discussion on the personality characteristics of leaders, in order to allow for some appreciation of the complexity of the issue and to remind readers that a leader always acts within a given context. Leadership and leader characteristics, therefore, are not synony-mous and studying the one may distort our perception of the other (Wheatley 1992), just as what quantum theory (Schrodinger 1944) has revealed regarding the observation of natural phenomena.

4. Social deviance and the limits of tolerance

> I cannot see that anything is involved in attributing causal efficacy to rules
> beyond the claim that these rules are constituent elements of the states
> postulated in an explanatory theory of behaviour and enter into
> our best account of this behaviour.
>
> Noam Chomsky

So far, we have considered evidence that schizophrenia is somehow related to our 'humanness' as it appears to have evolved along with language, a characteristic that is uniquely ours; moreover, if Horrobin's (1998) hypothesis proves to be sound,[1] the condition may have enhanced the introduction of such qualities in our species, as inclinations towards the arts, religion and politics. In other words, many of the attributes that set us apart from other primate species.

The price we have paid, as we previously argued, is the constant presence of schizophrenia, at a rate of about 1 per cent, across all human populations. Obviously, as it was also discussed, this illness is dysfunctional enough to preclude its bearers from meaningful participation in the social process. It is their relatives, however, who bear milder forms of psychotic conditions (such as manic-depressive illness and personality disorders characterized by paranoia), that exhibit characteristics that in certain circumstances, inspire trust in others, and who are subsequently elected into positions of leadership. This phenomenon can be observed in all branches of human activity such as politics, religion, or the military to name but a few, and beyond the traditional boundaries of leadership, such as political or religious, we find people who excel (lead) in areas such as the arts, science, and philosophy. Many studies have revealed that such excelling figures have high rates of eccentricity among them, as well as close relatives with major psychiatric disorders. Matt Ridley (2003) summarizes these findings by writing that:

---

[1] See Chapter 2.

This eccentricity may even help them achieve success. It is perhaps no accident that many scientists, leaders, and religious prophets seem to walk the crater rim of the volcano of psychosis, and to have relatives with schizophrenia. James Joyce, Albert Einstein, Carl Gustav Jung, and Bertrand Russell all had close relatives with schizophrenia. Isaac Newton and Immanuel Kant might both be described as 'schizotypal'. One absurdly precise study estimates that 28% of prominent scientists, 60 percent of composers, 73 percent of painters, and an astonishing 87 percent of poets have shown some degree of mental disturbance.

No wonder so many students of human behaviour and culture consider schizophrenia the disease of humanity, meaning that without its beneficial effects on society we might still be living in our African cradle, bearing little difference from our primate cousins. We indeed seem to pay that price in order to have language and be human. The charismatic King Abdullah of Jordan had a son with schizophrenia (to whom he bequeathed 50 per cent of his genome). Was he perhaps less affected but gifted (charismatic) enough to be an effective leader? It is a tempting if unproven hypothesis. Randolph Nesse (2004), a psychiatrist theorizes that schizophrenia may represent an evolutionary 'cliff effect'; the full-blown disease manifesting only when multiple genetic factors (mutations) combine in a person, whereas, if only one to several are expressed, the result is the appearance of a gifted individual, one that oftentimes carries leadership potential. It is also interesting that the more language is required to express one's vocation (see poets in the quotation above), the greater the affectation one has by schizophrenia (and other psychoses or personality oddities), crediting thus the claim regarding the association of the two conditions. Also, let's not forget that Albert Einstein fathered a schizophrenic son (Isaacson 2007).

A paranoid leader will likely also bear some personality disordered children whereas others might escape the ravages of mental illness. Saddam Hussein's son Uday, known as a bad boy among Iraqi circles, exhibited many characteristics of an antisocial and paranoid personality partly at least owing to the genetic makeup that his father bequeathed him; a psychiatrically impaired son of an unstable leader, with violent excesses, a bloody lifestyle, and a series of embarrassing episodes for his father. At some point, he exceeded the limits of tolerance, even for his father, who publicly humiliated him in order to distance himself from his actions.

Of course one may find several examples of individuals who have reached high achievements in their societies in such areas as the arts, religion, and even politics who either had schizophrenia or became ill afterwards. Some of these people were born into high positions or simply rose up the hierarchy due to some particularly favourable conditions. Others might have been in their prodromal phase, that is, in the period during which there are no frank psychotic symptoms but only some type of oddity, if not near normality. We are really not interested in such cases since they do not, usually, represent typical examples of chosen mad leaders. We are interested in the milder forms, as stated above, of psychiatric illness that results secondary to the presence of schizophrenia in the genetic endowment of their family histories and reflected in the general population. These individuals are not marginalized by their societies; they remain in the mainstream and, if conditions are ripe, excel in accomplishments. To reiterate, people with personality disorders have a much higher chance of having schizophrenic relatives than normal ones. This is another indication that severe mental abnormality, just as a physical one, is on a continuum with mild forms of mental illness as well as normality.

Society has tolerance, and in certain cases, even reverence of such people since, on the surface, they appear gifted, talented, or highly intelligent. Each social group sets its own, culturally defined, limits of tolerance, beyond which behaviour is deemed to be abnormal and unacceptable. The norms of each culture are those sets of rules of behaviour considered appropriate, customary, and expected of its members. People with personality disorders, for example, do tend to stand out from the majority. However, so long as they avoid going beyond their group's limits of tolerance they remain in 'good standing'. If they exceed these limits, they are labelled as deviants and sanctions will apply against them. These sanctions may take any one of several forms depending on their group; an out of tune singer in a choir will get a reprimand; a student showing up consistently late for class may have his final grade adjusted accordingly; the perpetrator of a traffic violation will get a ticket that translates into a fine and probably points on his licence; a murderer will be incarcerated or executed depending on where he lives; and, finally, a schizophrenic patient will be committed to an institution. This is by no means an exhaustive list of possibilities but, rather, an attempt to make one point clear; that each social group has rules and regulations (laws) by which deviants are excluded or punished, depending on the nature of their deviance. As Harvey (2006) reminds us, 'social reality, a shared definition of what is true, what is valuable, and how people should behave, is lodged within the group'. It goes without saying that these laws and punishments are not the same across groups or different historical times. In other words they are not constants of human behaviour; their existence alone is, however, a cultural universal. Exclusion becomes more likely if the 'deviant' group also poses a threat, perceived or real, to the dominance of the majority. The recent obsession of French legislature to abolish religious symbols, an indirect attack on the Islamic burqa,[2] is indicative of fears about the takeover of French society by Muslims. Harvey also emphasizes the role of language in the development and maintenance of such limits of tolerance:

> It is within this framework that individuals imagine and invent, and it is from the repository of the group's memory and experiences, stored in images, symbols and in language itself, that individuals express their thoughts and dreams, even if only to themselves.

Obviously, then, and in accordance with social theorists 'the leadership relationship is fundamentally rooted in language and communication' (Conger 1991, Insch *et al.* 1997).

More often than not, the group's leader becomes a leader precisely because he can express those defining determinants for his people in ways that enhance their solidarity. In addition, the leader helps define the group's role and behaviour towards other groups, and subgroups, and the limits of tolerance for their (aberrant) behaviour. In doing so, he solidifies the cohesion of the group in relation to outsiders. The problem of maintaining cohesion in contemporary, large, spread out groups may be solved by innovative mechanisms of communication, such as the recent development of social media. Specific abilities such as theory of mind, empathy, social identity, and language may have played a role in maintaining group cohesion (de Waal 1996) in the past and they remain as important in our day as well. Communications, based on language, are therefore the fundamental roots of leadership.

Punishment of free riders (individuals who benefit from group living without contributing to it) and rule enforcement provide alternative means for maintaining cohesion and are also crucial leadership functions (De Cremer and Van Vugt 2002). Human history is replete with examples of how deviants are excluded. Each group, in each and every historical time, has had to face the issue; religious wars were waged against heretics. The medieval Cathars were annihilated by the Catholic Church. Their sin was to have introduced a purer form of religious zeal, equality for women, and more tolerant behaviour. These attributes, however, clashed with the dominant dogma of their times; they had turned against

---

[2] An enveloping outer garment worn by women in some Islamic traditions and, since 2007, by probably a few ultra-orthodox Jewish women for the purpose of hiding a female's body when out in public.

religious orthodoxy. Out of their persecution the horrific institution of the Inquisition was born to protect Catholic faith against all false beliefs.

The American Indians, as well as other aborigines from newly discovered lands, were nearly exterminated by white settlers once they got labelled as different enough to be considered deviants. Their difference was defined in terms of their race, culture, language and colour, not to mention the fact that they 'interfered' with the newcomers' economic development plans. It is unfortunate that even today, in the twenty-first century, we still encounter racial and ethnic discrimination, and religious persecution is certainly alive and well. The perpetrators of such acts more often than not have leaders with personality disorders. Thus, having mentally disturbed leaders may be an advantage to the short-sighted interests of groups, but probably not for the global arena at large. The events in former Yugoslavia of the early 1990s are a bitter reminder of this fact.

One unfortunate social phenomenon that disturbed leaders often take advantage of, is what Le Bon (1969) called the process of deindividuation. What he meant by that term was the tendency of individuals in large groups to become disinhibited and act in ways that are rather out of the ordinary and certainly beyond the limits of tolerance for their societies. Thus we have witnessed, throughout history, acts of brutality of one group towards another. The social basis for this phenomenon may lie in the fact that deindividuation enhances an individual's identity and conformity to the larger beliefs and values of the group (Postmes and Spears 1998), which therefore, under the guidance of the group leader, exhibits excesses in behaviour. So, a leader's role, under such circumstances could be positive, in a way that allows the group to engage in constructive acts (think Woodrow Wilson), or negative so that the group is fired up, mesmerized, and directed towards acts of violence and destruction (think Hitler). Biologically, such transgressions may help a group attain its goals, enhance survival, and maintain territorial dominance.

People with severe psychosis exhibit such deviance from norms, that their social isolation is guaranteed. Relatives of these people have quadruple chances of getting diagnosed with odd and eccentric personality disorders, as well as manic depression and its milder expression of cyclothymia; and moreover, these people's behavioural abnormalities do not interfere with their social, professional and political climbing; in fact, as was said above, it may be that their character disorders are the very factors which help them achieve high positions in society. On the other hand, their psychopathology may be perceived by average folk as an advantage and a desirable quality for leadership. As we saw previously, these individuals are more likely to be inflexible in their beliefs, uncompromising in their positions, and intangible in their goals. Such are the qualities that attract others, especially in times of crisis or social upheaval; whenever our values and traditions are questioned, that is when we tend to cling to those who represent us (as well as our values) best. Those are the times when an otherwise strange or marginalized person might appear strong and able to assume a role of leadership.

Michael Elliot in *Time* magazine (2009) reminds us that 'Churchill spent the 1930s in the political wilderness, warning of the need to rearm against the Nazi threat, and was treated as a bit of a joke by smaller men'. His underlying paranoia, however, was instrumental in mustering the support he needed when the threat appeared real. Elliot also cites examples of other individuals who, initially considered to represent failed political agendas, eventually managed to rally enough support, assume leadership roles, and bring about such changes in their societies, to turn their fates around; Helmut Kohl who successfully reunited Germany; Ban Ki-moon, the United Nations Secretary General who builds consensus among warring parties by his skills of persuasion (and language); Manmohan Singh who ushered India into the modern family of nations; and Kevin Rudd of Australia who got enough nerve to admit and apologize for his fellow white man's wrong-doings towards their Aborigine populations. What all these leaders needed to achieve, was a gut reaction on their followers' part.

Denning (2007) argues that Al Gore failed to win the presidential campaign precisely because he failed to engage the public on an emotional level; interestingly, he also argues that the use of appropriate stories, personal or otherwise would have been an effective means to achieve that goal. In other words, the appropriate use of language is what enhances the delivery of messages and makes or breaks a potential leader. Gore's language probably lacked the inflection of paranoia and was thus unimpressive to his audience. Neuroscientific research has demonstrated novel links 'between neural activity during initial idea encoding and the enthusiasm with which the ideas are subsequently delivered' (Falk *et al.* 2012). As these mental reactions and processes occur unconsciously, what becomes apparent is the 'gut' reaction of followers, hovering on an emotional level and therefore not easily lending itself to an objective analysis.

So we have identified two basic ingredients that are conducive to the rise of behaviourally compromised leaders; social or political crisis and a feeling of despair. George W. Bush was considered by many people around the world and in America, as the lesser choice in the 2004 US presidential elections. To the majority of voters, however, the election was decided on that period's feeling of uncertainty, insecurity, and the anxiety over the questionable outcome of the war in Iraq; those were not times to experiment and to switch their focus (or, for that matter, their leader). Those were times to be steadfast, persistent, and above all, unmitigatedly patriotic; G. W. Bush embodied those ideas. He exhibited what Harvey (2006) calls 'a kind of virtual Machiavellianism' whereas his counterpart, J. F. Kerry did not. Americans needed to cling to whoever represented their basic values and instincts best. Bush was delegated the power to see the American nation through its tribulation. In that respect, Americans also conferred on him the authority that is reserved for charismatic individuals that Weber (1978) defines as the 'power to command and duty to obey'. History itself will judge whether their choice was good or bad. Remember, Hitler was also elected during a critical time in German (as well as European) history, and his prognosis was positive; history however showed otherwise.

Time and again history has confirmed that, during times of crisis, we tend to choose leaders whose paranoia helps them (as well as us), set the limits of tolerance towards threatening circumstances so that our survival is assured and high returns come our way. As Elliot (2009) also reminds us, 'When leaders understand the nature of their followers, they can get away with an awful lot.' That is why Reagan's image could not be tarnished after the Iran-Contra affair,[3] or the frequent mishaps of his statements and those of his staff. Italians, to use another example, kept forgiving Silvio Berlusconi's repeated transgressions for the same reasons. Tolerance limits can be thought of as existing on a sliding scale; depending on the circumstances, as well as the individual leader, they can widen or close up. When Margaret Thatcher of England failed to stay in synch with her citizens, she was thrown out of office (Elliot 2009); in former, better times, she rallied enough support to be able to bring about the necessary reforms in order to improve Britain's social conditions and economy.

Conferring and withdrawing support is a theme that occurs recurrently and characterizes the relationship between followers and their leaders. The ability to establish novel communicative modes is a skill most

---

[3]   The Iran-Contra affair was a political scandal which occurred in the United States during the Reagan administration and came to light in November 1986 while he was still in office. Senior administration agents secretly facilitated the sale of arms to Iran, which at the time, was the subject of an arms embargo. Some US officials also hoped that the arms sales would secure the release of American hostages held in Iran while, at the same time, allow US intelligence agencies to fund the Nicaraguan Contras who were opposing the Sandinista junta.

leaders possess and it is influenced by a combination of the communicator's ability to understand intentions and the addressee's ability to recognize patterns (Volman *et al.* 2012). Groups give something and they expect something else in return. Hollander (1993) formulated his 'exchange theory' in describing such relationships, but also went further in explaining, so to speak, why leaders, the guardians of a group's repository of traditions and knowledge, are allowed to deviate from those very norms; he proposed that once the group is satisfied that the leader is indeed their guardian and commander, he is then given licence to deviate from normative types of behaviour; this is allowed, in order to come up with more adaptive notions of behaviour, ones that will be subsequently adopted by the group at large. Harvey (2006) cites the example of President Nixon who, having demonstrated his firm anti-communist stance was subsequently given the licence to visit communist China and perhaps usher in a new era in Sino-American relations. A liberal president would probably not have fared so well. Nixon's success helped better legitimize his power (and charisma). This example also demonstrates what I have been proposing repeatedly in this book, that paranoid leaders gather those personality characteristics best suited to appear steadfast, true, and capable of carrying their followers through to their aspirations.

Obviously, one may not claim that all elected leaders are psychiatrically impaired; Franklin D. Roosevelt and J. F. Kennedy are examples of enlightened leaders that immediately come to mind. A closer look however, will usually reveal aspects of their personality that represent dormant paranoid traits; and such traits become readily manifest under politically stressful situations. Consider Roosevelt's treatment of Nazi spies. According to McCarthy (2010):

> In June 1942, the Führer dispatched teams of saboteurs to conduct a terrorist campaign on US soil. One was a 22-year-old American citizen named Herbert Hans Haupt. The Nazi infiltrators were arrested by the FBI, but President Franklin D. Roosevelt directed that they be detained as enemy combatants, tried by military commission, and put to death – that is, the executive branch acted as judge, jury, and executioner.

Such actions might be thought of as resulting from heightened paranoia about enemies operating on American soil and were accepted by the American people without question. In the 2000s, many Americans, including the administration, were perfectly happy with the creation, operation, and sustenance of Guantanamo Bay prison. As Richard

Hofstadter (1964) proposes, 'It is the use of paranoid modes of expression by more or less normal people that makes the phenomenon significant'. So a paranoid streak in a normal-appearing politician (leader) is an expected mode of behaviour and a sign of heightened alertness that potential dangers are lurking; such behaviour would set one apart and mark him as a leader. Roosevelt assumed prophetic status while delivering his second inaugural address (Willner 1984) by asking, 'Shall we pause now and turn our back upon the road that lies ahead? Shall we call this the Promised Land?' In a similar way J. F. Kennedy's paranoia prompted him to prove his leadership potential, acting under the threat of communism, in his decision to invade Cuba. The circumstances tip a leader into more or less paranoid actions. Churchill was also plagued by a paranoid personality. He was appointed Prime Minister in 1940, during the dark and uncertain times of the beginning of World War II. The structure of his paranoid personality was the key ingredient that enabled him to see his nation through the vicissitudes and dangers of what followed. He was unquestionably the right man for the job. In his case, his personality helped him take such stances against the Germans that, eventually, led to allied victory. The same cannot be said of Hitler, whose paranoid personality led to the destruction and defeat of Germany.

Two men and two countries; one rises and becomes a hero, the other loathed as a madman. Both well outside the boundaries of average, but within the limits of tolerance for their countries. In the case of England the 'oddball' proves to be a saviour, for Germany a menace. Thus, whether a leader turns out to be a blessing or a curse depends, at least in part, on circumstances beyond one's control. The question that arises, in turn, is whether the same man would, under different circumstances, turn out to confer an advantage on his people, or whether a man like Hitler would be a disaster anywhere. After all, a person's paranoia is pervasive throughout his life. Could Hitler, had he been born in England, have fulfilled Churchill's role? Such questions are doomed to remain forever unanswered. Intuitively, however, one might be inclined to think that a certain personality would fare differently under different circumstances. The 'fittest' for each job is selected by what the situation demands.

Hussein, the madman of the Middle East, had an unquestionably abnormal, paranoid, and violent personality (Makiya 1998) just as many of his counterparts in the Soviet-dominated countries, in Germany during the Second World War, Idi Amin, and so many others did. Perhaps during some periods of his rule, he achieved some unity and stability among the many tribes and religions of Iraq. His paranoid predisposition however, led to the many atrocities and ethnic cleansings that were subsequently carried out. Having had his reputation tarnished during the first Gulf War, he became hardened, more paranoid, and more violent. In addition, however, he became less efficient in calculating his moves in the international chess game and hinted about possessing weapons of mass destruction, and that kept the West on constant alert about him. This, in addition to other factors, including Western paranoia, led to his eventual downfall during the second Gulf War. So, historical circumstances and context also play a role in the enhancement or tarnishing of a leadership.

Every society devises its own laws and regulations in order to deal with those of its members that are deemed deviants. Furthermore, most societies have distinguished between those deviants who are considered mentally ill, and those who are thought to violate norms but are not mentally ill. The former are committed to psychiatric institutions; a proportion of them, those who are not severely affected, for example the personality disordered ones, may continue to dysfunction in their societies under the guise of exceptional leaders. In certain primitive societies, these individuals could assume the roles of religious functionaries, shamans, witch doctors and the like. 'Different' in such cases was given special status and roles. Epileptics also enjoyed such status among ancient people and their disorder was therefore called the 'sacred disease' (Magiorkinis *et al.* 2010). So long as their deviance was not chaotic (as in schizophrenia) they retained such special status. The legacy of this status may be, at least in part, retained by modern societies that ascribe special roles to deviants (such as leadership roles to paranoid individuals), provided they operate within certain limits; beyond these tolerance limits such persons become marginalized. The desire to lead notwithstanding, one can appreciate the social pressures on group members to avoid the label of a deviant. Studies have demonstrated that minorities often conform to majority rule in order to gain access to goods and information about the world, but also to avoid the label of deviance (Sherif and Murphy 1936). Perhaps this is why paranoid leaders emerge; they fail to conform and consistently advocate their views, so that others accept them as committed and consistent.

The second category of non-mentally ill deviants is considered to include criminals.[4] These are dealt with accordingly in prisons and correctional facilities. Some societies with less humanistic world views still apply capital punishments.

What is significant though is not the way or the degree of applied punishments, but rather the fact that a system is in place to judge and

---

[4] We are considering major deviants here such as murderers, rapists, and burglars, and not merely traffic or parking violators.

deal with deviants. Beyond the limits of tolerance, each society takes whichever actions are deemed necessary to exert control over its members. Samuel Cartwright (1851) an American psychiatrist, identified a mental disorder, drapetomania,[5] which according to him was evident only in slaves; its sole symptom was 'the desire to run away from slavery' and the only effective cure was to 'whip the devil out of them as a preventive measure'! This may appear ill-sighted to us today but in 1851, when slavery was legal and slaves routinely escaped to freedom, such a phenomenon was considered disruptive for society, and the economy, regardless of the unfortunate predicament of the slaves. It simply went beyond the limits of tolerance of (bigoted) society at the time. Thus, cohesion is maintained and deviants are removed. Depending on the social structure, the ideology, and the history of each group, its limits of tolerance are set differently. As Margaret Mead (1955) succinctly put it:

> All peoples have been concerned, inexplicitly, inarticulately, with the problem of the mental health of the members of their group. In every society we find practices and rituals designed to rear children so their original biological impulses will be channelled and patterned so that they can function within the particular culture, and we find devices for dealing with cases where this educational process has failed, with the individuals who are unable to function, who are variously prayed over, subjected to magical curing ceremonials, tolerated, or exiled, as the case may be.

It turns out that anarchy is not well tolerated in most societies. To do so would be contrary to culture's main goal, as we saw previously, to counteract entropy. Thus, strict and rigid personalities are assured an easy ride to the top so long as they appear to protect their societies from chaos. Perceived chaos, which may take many forms, such as social and political turmoil, impending conflict, economic dismay, or moral upheavals, play up the contingency tunes in people's minds who subsequently seek comfort in the reassuring predispositions of determined and uncompromising leaders. Followers will inadvertently look for more optimistic, confident leaders in times of crisis in order to receive reassurance (albeit symbolic) that the current situation can and will be overcome (Bligh *et al.* 2004). More often than not, individuals that come from the behavioural fringes of their groups will rise up to assume leadership roles.

At times of crisis our limits of tolerance may be stretched beyond their usual boundaries in order to rally our resources and accommodate our

---

[5] From the Greek δραπέτης (drapetes, 'a runaway [slave]') + μανία (mania), 'madness, frenzy'.

leaders' peculiarities. When group solidarity becomes imperative in a crisis, followers might accept a more autocratic-style leadership because the costs of being in a non-cohesive group are likely to be substantial (Van Vugt 2006). Necessity dictates justice and sub-serves the limits of tolerance. Greater allowances are typically granted in order to deal with urgent issues at hand. Crises often pave the way for directive and sometimes coercive leaders who can enforce group unity if it is needed (Samuelson *et al.* 1984, Simon and Guetzkow 1955). In turn, our leaders are instrumental in the suggestion, acceptance, and enforcement of the new limits. In post 9/11 America, many more otherwise democratic citizens were willing to follow their leaders' prompting to accept certain limitations of their rights and privacy in order to have their security enhanced. More recently, during the financial crash of 2008, people acting under duress were willing to give inordinate powers to their secretary of finance in order to ensure higher economic returns and a hastened exit from the crisis.

Porcelli *et al.* (2012) used functional magnetic resonance imaging (fMRI) to demonstrate that people under stress show decreased differential responses to reward and punishment in the areas of the brain that control and modulate decision making (the dorsal striatum and orbitofrontal cortex),[6] and have thus provided hints about the neurobiological basis of leader–follower phenomena as well as potential explanations of the inequality that followers may be willing to accept in order to maximize their rewards. Crisis situations in other words, induce a blunting of our emotional responses, as well as our standards of tolerance, in order to overcome the situation. Ethicists may take issue with arrangements which create significant inequalities between leaders and followers. However, it is generally accepted that such privileges should be used by leaders in order to attain liberty, and a greater good for themselves as well as the group (Burns 1978), and the neurocultural substrates of these phenomena are beginning to be explored by neuroscientists. The leaders' role should be re-emphasized here, since it is instrumental in defining the group's goals and needs, as well as the ways to attain them. Therefore, the leader's style, and importantly his use of language in persuading his followers are imperative. Phil Harkins (1999)

---

[6] No stress group participants exhibited a pattern of activity within the dorsal striatum and orbitofrontal cortex (OFC) consistent with past research on outcome processing – specifically, differential responses for monetary rewards over punishments. In contrast, acute stress group participants' dorsal striatum and OFC demonstrated decreased sensitivity to monetary outcomes and a lack of differential activity.

writes that 'High-Impact Leaders are Leaders [sic] not only because they themselves are focused and driven but because they are able to generate ... energy and motivation in those around them. They use Powerful Conversations [sic] that actualize strategy to do so.'

Once the crisis situation has passed, however, the same 'saviour' leaders may become dysfunctional and either they turn against their society, or the group turns against them. This ultimately depends on the personality of the leader and his willingness to 'let go', when his services are no longer imperative. To reiterate, a paranoid leader proves to be effective in times of need, danger, and a general mobilization of resources. Afterwards, however, the same leader often becomes dysfunctional because he or she continues to mobilize fighting energies to the point of depleting his society of the very useful resources that will be needed to reorganize, rebuild, and reconstitute the basic fabric of that society. Such was the case of Churchill who was idealized to the point of mystification not only by the British, during the war but also, tacitly, by the rest of struggling Europe. As the crisis came to an end, the same qualities that deified Churchill were instrumental in his replacement. Shakespeare (Craig 1914), in *Coriolanus*, struggles with similar ideas through the dilemmas of Roman citizens about how to treat a former war hero who desires civil authority. Michael Harvey uses that play to make this point clear:

> The citizens' quandary is whether to trust a man who would be their leader – and beyond him, how to understand, use, and safeguard their power. What allegiance do they owe a hero for his past service to the city? Does his valor suit him to peaceful rule? What of his evident contempt for them? If they defy him, what damage will they do to the city's fabric?

To recapitulate, leaders have traditionally been 'allowed' to stretch the limits of tolerance for their societies and deviate from normative behaviour in order to achieve their followers' goals as well as protect, guide, and at times, save them. John Locke (1988 [1690]) understood this need quite well when he wrote '[leaders] do several things of their own free choice, where the Law was silent, and sometimes too against the direct letter of the Law, for the publick [sic] good'. In turn, the leader may induce the need for his leadership by demonstrating the dangers, goals, and priorities of his followers. He achieves this by skilful use of language, an attribute that is enhanced by his paranoid predisposition. That is why Rousseau (2001 [1755]), explains that 'the most eloquent became the most highly regarded'. As a proponent of natural existence, he is very careful not to allow too much inequality between leaders and followers, except to the degree that the former could help the latter reach a better state of being. Another cause of such inequality is attributed to 'the petulant activity of our egocentrism', a theme that is also taken up by Plato in his *Republic* when discussing how the leaders of a state should be chosen. Plato also states 'that the man who is deranged and not right in his mind will fancy that he is able to rule, not only over men, but also over the gods'!

5. The role of language in defining normal behaviour

> Language powerfully conditions all our thinking about social problems and processes ... No two languages are ever sufficiently similar to be considered as representing the same social reality. The worlds in which different societies live are distinct worlds, not merely the same worlds with different labels attached.
>
> Edward Sapir

It was argued that psychiatric traits fall on a continuum with normal or non-psychiatric ones, being perhaps an extreme expression of human behaviour. Using such concepts as those of statistical rarity and norm violation, we will consider a set of behaviours as abnormal when they fall outside defined limits such as two standard deviations from the average (in either direction), or if, for example, they clearly break a given group's rules.

We must, however, define what is normal in order to be able to differentiate it from that we consider abnormal. Each society agrees upon a set of behaviours (norms), that it considers acceptable, expected, and appropriate on the part of its members. History, the environment, and the group's specific needs and vicissitudes dictate how its norms evolve through time. Humans are basically conservative at heart; centuries may come to pass without obliterating such norms. These are handed down to posterity from one generation to the next strengthening their hold on those who uphold them dearly.

Religious ritual probably falls in this category as well. At times people defend these norms by going to holy war. Moreover, these norms come to form a great part of, if not totally define, a group's identity to the point of their taking on their own life and existence, from that point onwards, for their own sake. People tend to cling to the norms long after their initial function, their *raison d'être*, has ceased to exist. Like biological traits, they linger on even when they become dysfunctional. The human intestinal appendix no longer serves any useful function either but it lingers on from generation to generation like a ghost from the past; it occasionally becomes inflamed, causing dire suffering to its bearer and a handsome fee to the surgeon who removes it; in extreme cases, it may burst causing peritonitis, a medical emergency.[1] Attempts to deviate from norms, alter them in the slightest, or modify them to fit current realities, are deemed as heresy and are often suppressed.

Cultural relativity has taught us that normal behaviour is not necessarily a universal phenomenon. What is normal for one culture is not also normal for another. Like biological evolution leading to diversity, cultural norms and traits also evolve and develop from common 'ancestral' behaviours. Think of the many Jewish, Christian, and Islamic denominations that exist today as branches of a single initial ideology and practice. One wonders what Moses, Jesus, or Muhammad would think if they returned today. The end result usually carries little resemblance to its progenitor, and this fact often leads to fierce conflict. Norms change to aid cultures adapt to changing circumstances. In that respect culture, like the human brain, can be thought to possess what Franz Boas (1912) called the plasticity to change and adapt, so that it can help people combat entropy as well as liberate them from their nature.[2] Other notable anthropologists such as Margaret Mead (1955) proposed that human nature is a constant, and put in any kind of environment, will eventually produce a culture. She came to this conclusion after studying people in the South Seas. Culture, then, is the end result of a long evolutionary process, and an ever-evolving set of rules, that has endowed humans with the unique characteristic to develop it. Ridley believes:

> The human capacity for culture comes not from some genes that co-evolved with human culture, but from a fortuitous set of preadaptations that suddenly endowed the human mind with an almost limitless capacity to accumulate and transmit ideas. Those preadaptations are underpinned by genes.

In that respect, every culture is a product of its environment and must be understood within the context of that environment (Butler 2007) and the latter's interplay with our culture-enhancing genes. This is what we refer to when we speak of the geopolitical characteristics of a nation or culture; it is an account of an area's geographical characteristics (that is, physical and climactic) and the effects of that geography on the area's history, politics, and achievements (paraphrased from Butler 2007). Geopolitics in turn influences the kind of behaviour, which within each

---

[1] Peritonitis results from inflammation-infection of the peritoneum, a thin membrane in the cavity that houses the gut that lines the abdominal wall and covers the organs within.

[2] See the exposure of entropy in the Introduction.

culture, may be considered normal whereas in a different culture, the same behaviour may be abhorrent. This fact is stated succinctly by Dalrymple (2007) who writes:

> Is it not a fact, both historical and anthropological, that what is and has been considered well-mannered behaviour has varied or does vary according to time and place, and that what is or has been considered obligatory on one time and place is or has been viewed with absolute horror in others?

Kluckhohn and Murray (1953) put it nicely in stating that 'every person is in certain respects (1) like all other persons, (2) like some other persons, (3) like no other persons'. Runyan (1988) applies this idea to the historical dimension stating that '[some] generalizations can be expected to hold across all historical periods; others within limited historical periods; and others, perhaps only within specific historical circumstances'.

When American slaves escaped to freedom at the end of the nineteenth century, they were considered mentally ill, and diagnosed as suffering from drapetomania (Cartwright 1851); similarly, Soviet dissidents who chose to speak according to their conscience were confined to psychiatric institutions (Knapp 2007).

Cultures, we argue, are the constant generalizations that hold across all historical times. The genetically determined enabler of culture of course is language. Ideas, experiences, and thoughts of the living as well as long deceased individuals, are preserved by the functions of language. Lev Semenovich Vygotsky, a Russian anthropologist (1986) insists that language, closely linked with the use of tools, and co-determined by evolution, is the human characteristic that makes us social as well as enabling our collective and our individual experiences. Consider the sequence:

Brain→Tools→More brain (enhanced structure and function)→Language→Culture

The sequence is clearly an oversimplification since culture is bigger than language itself and language is constantly modified by culture as well. All human groups, in every historic, pre-historic or modern time, and in any type of environment on this planet, has produced a culture, complete with norms, myths, songs and dance, and the necessary tools for survival. Throughout the millennia, the critical ideas and information were handed down to subsequent generations, in order to ensure their survival. Language made this phenomenon possible. Small bands of people broke off a main stem, moved to a different locale, and following the passage of many generations, produced a new culture and a different language, just like the example of the Abrahamic religions above. Like the formation of new species, new social groups can bear little resemblance to their progenitors. They may even be in direct conflict with one another. The concept is explained in a succinct manner by John Reader in his introduction to the book *Man on Earth* (1988) where he writes:

> All mankind shares a unique ability to adapt to circumstances and resolve the problems of survival. It was this talent which carried successive generations of people into the many niches of environmental opportunity that the world has to offer – from forest, to grassland, desert, seashore, and icecap. And in each case, people developed ways of life appropriate to the particular habitats and circumstances they encountered. A variety of distinctive physical, social and cultural characteristics evolved among groups isolated from one another, so that eventually the common inheritance of mankind was obscured by the bewildering diversity of looks, lifestyles, cultures and beliefs that divides and creates problems among people.

The division or unification of distinct cultural groups depends to a large extend, on the leadership of these people. A paranoid leader will tend to isolate and separate his people, whereas a non-paranoid (or one with a low dose of paranoia) may be more willing to accommodate outsider groups as well. In other words, groups need a capable leader to help them shape their ideas and their identity. Under the leadership of Abraham, the early Israelites moved from Ur to the Promised Land of Palestine. That move, and the guidance of Patriarch Abraham, whose visions and leadership were instrumental, induced the separation of his clan and the formation of its new identity in relation to themselves, others, and God. Their 'chosen people' status came about through the leadership of Abraham. Some centuries later, Moses, another accomplished leader, redefined the Israelite consciousness, gave them their Law, direct from the hands of God, and guided them back to the Promised Land of Palestine in perhaps the most celebrated exodus in human history. Whether these stories have actually occurred or represent the repository of Jewish mythology is beside the point. What's important here is the enormous influence and ability of both Abraham and Moses, as leadership figures, to take on their peoples' fates, define who they *should* be, and how they should behave. In short, they recreated Jewish culture and religion. In achieving this, they created a group of people that perseveres to this very day but still looks back to those early identity-defining stories.

One cannot avoid the temptation to speculate on the personalities of those figures. Certainly Abraham may have had a proclivity to a schizotypal personality structure with paranoid and hallucinatory features. Moses certainly must have possessed narcissistic, paranoid, and delusional features. Such personality traits would have been imperative in order to control the inadequacies and transgressions of early Israelites. Freud (1921) wrote extensively on group psychology and the tendencies of humans to regress to primitive, illogical, and violent behaviours, unless a leader redirects them towards proper conduct.[3] Moses had to do this on several occasions during the long years of his people's wandering as they were returning to the Promised Land.

Let's consider, again, the example of language. We can divide languages into several major families such as, for example, the Indo-European family that encompasses such apparently diverse tongues as Sanskrit, Latin, English, and Greek. All appear to have evolved from a common ancestral stem but over the millennia they diverged to the point where they bear little apparent resemblance to each other. Speakers of one cannot understand those of another, may consider them strange, and often may end up fighting each other. Language in this sense becomes a distinctive and characteristic behavioural norm that defines the boundaries of a group. Whoever speaks it, in other words whoever behaves according to that norm, is included into the group; whoever does not speak it is excluded. Consider the way people react towards foreigners who utter a tongue with an accent; that 'abnormal' behaviour automatically sets them apart. On the other hand, subgroups within a culture maintain their identity by using (behaving) a dialect of the officially accepted form of language. This identity forms solidarity within the subgroup but also defines it as such for the dominant culture as well. Successful leaders are aware of the significance of the dialect and oftentimes will code switch (that is, change from the formal dialect to the dialect of the group they are trying to influence) in order to show allegiance and create emotional response by the target group. Aristotle echoed the notion more than two millennia ago when he stated in his *Politics*:

> It is by speech that we are enabled to express what is useful for us, and what is hurtful, and of course what is just and what is unjust: for in this particular man differs from other animals, that he alone has a perception of good and evil, of just and unjust, and it is a participation of these common sentiments which forms a family and a city.

---

[3] Freud quoted extensively from previous writers, especially Gustave Le Bon's work, 1895.

That language shapes thought is an accepted theoretical framework for anthropologists, most linguists, and communications specialists (Boroditsky 2001). It is therefore an important, if not *the* important determinant of a group's identity in terms of both the culture at large, as well as the subdivision within. A Londoner with a cockney accent, for example, is automatically identified both as a Briton from London, but in addition, a Londoner from the East End of that city. His language defines who he is but also shapes his way of thinking in subtle ways that set him apart from the rest of his co-citizens. Moreover, a fellow cockney speaker becomes normal within that context and slightly abnormal in the larger culture of London. As Hickman and Couto (2006) put it:

> Humans make sense of their world and seek meaning through processes of imagination and interpretation, which are situated within social constructions of reality and affirmed through language and inter-subjective encounters. These processes enable humans to conceptualize space, time, and conditions beyond their immediate context and to employ linguistic discourses such as narrative to express and communicate those alternative realities. As social beings, humans depend on others not only for survival but also in the construction of frames of social reality through which people understand their everyday experiences, collaborations, and conflicts ... Through ... language, humans organize and assign value to some attributes (for example, along lines of sex, skin pigmentation, or age) and construct systems of social relations in order to distinguish among individuals of the group and among groups.

The greater the diversity that exists between languages and by extension between thinking and behaving, the greater is the perceived abnormality regarding a particular group. Having been defined as the characteristic that empowered our speciation event, language also helps define who we are socially, culturally but also sub-culturally. In that respect, language also determines our mating choices and, in the end, may help pick our descendants' genetic makeup. As Cavalli-Sforza (2001) puts it, 'If there's any interaction between genes and languages, it is often languages that influence genes, since linguistic differences between populations lessen the chance of genetic exchange between them.' Leaders, especially those who have the ability to play into the subtleties of their fellows' language, will gain access into their hearts as well as their minds. They will be able to lead them onward in directions they choose. History has proven this on innumerable occasions, and the successful leader should be astute and flexible enough to be able to adjust his behaviour in order to suit the needs of the circumstances (Machiavelli 2001a [1531]).

Language, then, also defines and borders the type of thoughts that are considered appropriate. Language, by shaping thought, also recreates culture; this is accomplished both by providing the vehicle of expression of the ideas of a specific culture (or any other group for that manner), but also by forming the substrate upon which the culture will sustain itself and develop. This is why it is so difficult to break away from the ideas that have nourished the development of a group (after all, the language does not provide alternatives for thought), and the group's norms appear so 'natural' to their adherents. Whorf and Carroll (1956) expressed these notions as follows:

> We dissect nature along lines laid down by our native languages ... The world is presented in a kaleidoscopic flux of impressions which has to be organized by our minds – and this means largely by the linguistic systems in our minds ... No individual is free to describe nature with absolute impartiality but is constrained to certain modes of interpretation even while he thinks himself most free.

Like creatures that live in a three-dimensional world cannot conceive of a fourth or fifth dimension, groups that have been created by a certain language and thinking mode, cannot easily break away from the boundaries imposed by that linguistic–thought enclosure; those who do are oftentimes labelled as deviants and are persecuted. Think of great religious leaders who managed to see their world through a different language and attribute new meanings to their exigencies; so many of them suffered ostracism or were thought of as mentally impaired. Mentally impaired they might have been, or at least, they had closely related individuals with major mental compromise; this in itself, would have conferred a different thought process and the linguistic vehicle to express it. This is another reason we claim that schizophrenia is the disease that perpetually makes and sustains us as human. Remember what John Nash, the Princeton mathematician, said after recovering from 30 years of schizophrenia and accepting a Nobel Prize for his work on game theory (Nasar 1998): 'the interludes of rationality between my psychotic episodes were not welcome at all. Rational thought imposes a limit on a person's concept of his relation to the cosmos.' Rational interludes were none other than the standard, accepted, and expected ways of thinking, imposed by a subsisting language, the boundaries of which could only be superseded by the 'mentally ill'!

So, language produces a kind of imprinting on its native speakers and thus it colours all their thoughts, perceptions, and views. Michael Harvey (2006) also considers language, communication, and storytelling to be of paramount importance in consolidating a group's identity:

One way that humans construct their reality is through storytelling. Narratives fulfil many purposes: to motivate, to reassure, to challenge, to provoke, to define identities, to unite, to divide, to scapegoat, to set goals or limits, to teach lessons, to inspire wonder, and to establish particular uses of power as legitimate or illegitimate. Stories connect reason, emotion, intuition, and the subconscious; they help us see feelingly in Shakespeare's words. A story offers an account of reality that seeks either to affirm or contest an existing terrain of meaning.

Storytelling – in other words a 'good' use of language – is at the core of culture as we defined it previously. A leader who masters this skill has moved half way to achieving the approval and support of his constituency. Research has been revealing dramatic inter-individual differences in the implementation of human competence for communicative innovation, storytelling and effective use of language, based on a special type of complex collaborative activity (Volman *et al.* 2012). A paranoid personality, as discussed elsewhere, possesses such competencies as a result of their psychopathology, to enable just enough uncouthness to go the extra step in the use of language, so that they get the attention of others. Underlying paranoia helps define the issues at hand, and propose appropriate solutions.

There is a critical period, as discussed elsewhere that is of paramount importance for the imprinting of language to produce its permanent results. In humans, this period lasts up to about eight years; afterwards, even though a child may learn to speak a language like a native, it begins to lose its instinctive, natural feel. This is the reason that the age of eight years is considered critical when contemplating epilepsy surgery in a child whose fits aren't well controlled with medications; the brain, before this critical period is over, retains its capacity to switch sides, so that if the language centres are affected by the surgical procedure, the homologous opposite side of the brain can take over. Ducklings imprint on their mothers early on and internalize her distinguishing vocal features. Douglas Spalding (1873) and Konrad Lorenz (Nisbett 1976) were the pioneers in our awareness of this critical period during which animals respond to external (nurturing) cues and modify their behavioural patterns immutably.[4] Ridley (2003) insists that 'language does not just develop according

---

[4] The critical period is tied to language universals, which are divided into five segments: semantics (lexicon and meanings of concepts), phonology (sounds), morphology (words with grammatical meaning), syntax (combination of words based on language rules), and pragmatics (the social use of language). While these basic principles are mastered by the time a child enters school and even earlier, they continue to develop through formal education. In addition to

to a genetic program. Nor is it just absorbed from the outside world. Instead, it is imprinted. It is a temporary innate ability to learn by experience from the environment, a natural instinct for acquiring nurture.'

Language helps determine the actualities of a given culture as it shapes human thought. It is at the very core of both and makes both possible, and it is that characteristic that enables understanding, empathy, and communication between humans, attributes that, having been mustered by talented individuals, help them become attractive leaders. Michael Tomasello (1999) concluded from a series of experiments that only humans can place themselves in other humans' mental processes, thus enabling ideas, and culture, to evolve. This fact gives leaders the capacity to play into the minds of their followers, but also it allows followers to gain access into their leaders' minds as well; this two-way process is made possible by language. Other primates have probably developed such abilities, albeit in rudimentary form (Mineka *et al.* 1984). Humans however have excelled in this respect to points beyond reach for all other species of primates, including our closest relatives, the chimpanzees. This finding forms the basis of social influence tactics as practiced in a two-way exchange between leaders and followers. Consciously or un-consciously, effective leaders have, according to Hoyt *et al.* (2006), mastered these tactics and are thus able to affect their followers' behaviour (Kipnis *et al.* 1980, Yukle and Falbe 1990). In turn, followers respond to their leaders' style and exert their own influence in a reciprocal way (Ansari and Kapoor 1987). In that respect, Smircich and Morgan (1982) defined leadership as a socially constructed, interactionist phenomenon through which certain individuals attempt to frame and define the reality of other individuals.

That is why a common language and thus common understanding of major world issues is so difficult to achieve, and this is why it is so easy for paranoid leaders to tap into the nuances of their own language and use them to their own advantage. Jesse Helms Jr., the five-term US Republican senator from North Carolina, won his first term over his Democratic opponent Nick Galifianakis, by using the slogan 'Vote for Helms – He's one of us'; that slogan's manifest message was a benign designation of another guy from the neighbourhood bunch; its hidden meaning (the nuance) was the message that *he* was the real American, while his opponent was a foreigner. That type of language would drive a message

---

the above, suprasegmentals contribute to effective public speaking and are part of effective leadership. Leaders use suprasegmentals such as emotional register, rhythm, and intonation extremely effectively in order to manipulate the audience.

right through his conservative audience's hearts. His paranoid disposition was instrumental in enabling him to vehemently oppose anyone who strayed from his conservative views (Holmes 2008). He was the reification of the political paranoid; his unyielding positions were directed against anyone who was not a white, Anglo-Saxon protestant. His political views were extreme, however his words fell on fertile ground in the Southern United States of his time because, using the right language nuances, he echoed what many whites felt; fear of blacks, homosexuals, Catholics, and immigrants. The steadfastness of his convictions predictably armed him to oppose such ideas as affirmative action, gay rights, civil rights, feminism, tax hikes, foreign aid, communism, and nudity in art (Barnes 2008). His style, his beliefs, and his language were probably abnormal for most Americans except his voting constituents who admired him for voicing what they felt deeply, but could not openly express.

All of these functions are of course possible due to the evolutionary advantages that were conferred on our brains by natural selection. The last two decades or so have been very exciting for neuroscientists trying to tie together the unique phenomena of culture, language, and human speciation. The Italian neuroscientist Giacomo Rizzolatti (Rizzolatti and Arbib 1998), a Parma-based researcher, and his colleagues (Iacobini *et al.* 2001), have discovered the presence of what they have called mirror neurons; these neurons have the capacity to become activated when a monkey (and therefore a human being), both perceives an action as well as upon initiating it motorically; hence the designation 'mirror' neuron since it mirrors the observation of and the actual performance of an action. Interestingly, these neurons are located in areas of the brain controlling motor and sensory, as well as hearing, activities (Kohler *et al.* 2002); they are also associated closely with functions such as language and imitation, creating a system that Lionel Tiger and Robin Fox (1971) have named the 'culture acquisition device', because of the importance it has in the creation of culture. Imitation here becomes important both as a mechanism through which language is learned but also because this was how it was probably transmitted originally, through gestures (Iacobini 1999, Vicario 2013).

More credence for this theory emerges from studies of repetitive transcranial magnetic stimulation of Broca's brain area, which produce an alteration of the verbal responses to gesture observation (Gentilucci *et al.* 2006).[5] This result suggests that Broca's area is somehow involved in

---

[5] This is the part of the brain located in the inferior-anterior area of the frontal lobe, which is traditionally considered to be involved in and to control the motor aspects of speech.

the simultaneous control of gestures and word pronunciation (Vicario 2013). Hence the enhanced degree of gesturing that people exhibit when they become excited and animated about a topic they discuss. This fact may prove important as a fine characteristic of leaders who possess the ability to combine speech and gesture in getting their audiences' attention. In other words, evolution may have separated out certain individuals capable of tapping into the very core of the human psyche. These individuals, if my theory is correct, must possess the ability to get into their followers' mind, speak in a way that arouses the core of their wishes, and engage in such mannerisms that portrays their messages perfectly.[6]

In fact, Ridley feels that Broca's area, that part of the brain responsible for motor aspects of speech, and where Rizzolatti's mirror neurons are found – those that are responsible for hand gestures, hand movement observation, and oddly, hearing that action – is where it *all* comes together in the creation of a human being. As he puts it, 'To imitate, to manipulate, and to speak are three things that human beings are peculiarly good at. They are not just central to culture: they are culture.' Hence the reader may appreciate the importance I have been placing on the role of language, in determining cultural norms and leadership expectations.

Paranoid individuals possess superb language skills to lead others who share their culture. This, they effect by cultivating, in a charismatic way, a strong emotional linkage to followers, which they use for their own (and, hopefully, their followers') purposes (Harvey 2006, Lindholm 1990). Makarios was quite canny in his use, and manipulation, of Greek Cypriots during his terms as their president. The same leader changed goal and focus from union with Greece in the 1950s, to independence for Cyprus in the 1960s, to a bi-zonal federation in the 1970s, all with the applause of his magnetized followers. As Harkins (1999) tells us, 'it is the way great leaders communicate that sets them apart'; this way may make or break a leader whose core goal is to achieve a powerful enough communication which Harkins defines as:

> an interaction between two or more people that progresses from shared feelings, beliefs and ideas to an exchange of wants and needs to clear action steps and mutual commitments ... [it] produces three outputs: an advanced agenda, shared learning, and a strengthened relationship.

---

[6] Mirror neurons are thought to be limited in children and adults with autism, a condition characterized by lack of social competence.

Such a skill is conferred by heredity. Discipline and learning may improve upon it but cannot develop it in a person from scratch. In this respect I take issue with Harkins when he claims (1999) that 'natural communication skills have nothing to do with it'.

A common language may not be possible, however common modes of thinking and explaining the world do exist as a result of painstaking human advancement; science might turn out to be the common medium for understanding each other and its language is probably going to prove immune to the paranoid's parlance. Science is a rather late evolutionary development in the history of cultures, and is proving to be a haven for people of diverse ideologies and backgrounds. It is perhaps the only system of knowledge that strives to disprove itself. With its principles of observation, null hypothesis testing (and rejection), and relentless modification of its creeds, it guarantees an ever-increasing approach towards universal truths. Based on mathematics as its universal modus operandi, it goes beyond historical, social, and culture-bound prejudices and sensitivities. A Bolshevik scientist can find common ground with an American counterpart; where their spies fight each other, scientists can, if they so wish, meet eye to eye and work together.

Science has the capacity, when used constructively, to overcome regional and international conflicts (often, as we saw, driven by paranoid leaders), and solve common existential problems, such as survival, in a user-friendly environment and reproduction. As such, it can safeguard against those disordered individuals who would lead us into conflict and strife. Obviously, paranoid individuals can be high scientific achievers as well, and science can be used to do harm rather than good. However, the very fabric of scientific thought is more likely to shut out dogmatic and erratic behaviours as well as isolate paranoid people who would find the task of forming cults exceedingly difficult. Its underlying rational (mathematical) language might eventually be established as the measure of all things and truly reunite all people under its aegis. This, of course, would presuppose its acceptance by all people, a rather unrealistic wish. Unfortunately, more often than not, madness prevails over reason just as entropy (discussed in the Introduction), overcomes the order of the day. Be that as it may, only science possesses the intrinsic qualities needed to ensure normality of thought and action and behavioural orthodoxy. The scientific method may be used to discover intricate biological truths about human behaviour, just as we are attempting to achieve in this book. It can also dispel non-truths, especially those that result in bigotry and persecution. As the famous Polish anthropologist Bronislaw Malinowski (1961) wrote, 'The time when we could tolerate accounts presenting us the native as a distorted, childish caricature of a human being are gone. This picture is false, and like many other falsehoods, it has been killed by Science.'

Science, then, which perhaps represents the colophon of human culture, may be in the unique position not only to bring us together, but also to humble us so that we seek the answers to our existential questions in a more contrite way. As Leakey (Leakey and Lewin 1993) admits in his prologue to *Origins Reconsidered* – as compared to the original work *Origins* – science keeps building on new evidence and new discoveries so that what is held to be true today may be radically different from the truth of the future:

> More in the scientific realm, I see a range of anthropological ideas and interpretations presented in *Origins* that have turned out to be wrong. As philosophers constantly tell us, and we keep finding out the hard way, science is tentative; existing perceptions are constantly replaced by new ones. And so it will be in the future, because this is the way of scientific progress. But I hope, too, that fifteen years of experience have helped me to be less inclined than I once was vigorously to defend conclusions, to insist that what we think we know now is the Truth. Absolute truth is like a mirage: it tends to disappear when you approach it. One of the most important lessons for me during these years is my learning that, passionately though I may seek certain answers, some will remain, like the mirage, forever beyond my reach.

If this passage sounds too anti-paranoid-leader, it was meant to be. Science, at the end of the day, may qualify as that guarantee that will act as reality testing in reorienting societies and other groups of people to judge and choose leaders correctly. This may be our ultimate salvation as envisioned by philosophers, religious leaders, and politicians throughout history. Natural selection has probably endowed us with the capability of counteracting it through reason, culture, and science as an ultimate tool for survival. De Duve (2010) claims that 'we enjoy the unique faculty of being able to act against natural selection.' Of course, to overcome our biology we need to arm ourselves with as strong an education as possible, free of biases, prejudices, and preconceptions; Don Ray (2011) reminds us that 'education exorcises belief' producing an open mind that can help us rid ourselves from the mistakes of the past. It will not be easy because 'in order to do this, we must actively oppose some of our key genetic traits [which] surmount our own nature' (de Duve 2010). Difficult it may be, but not impossible. We know today facts that even a decade ago were scientific anathema; epigenetic processes, once delineated more accurately, may guide us into shaping the leadership personality that could see us through the difficult issues we collectively face as humanity.

We may now begin to create such possibilities through visionary leadership. Thus a careful and well-thought-of educational system can lead us into the next step in our own evolution and into a true Common Era. Carl Sagan (1977) suggested as much when he wrote 'while our behaviour is still significantly controlled by our genetic inheritance, we have, through our brains, a much richer opportunity to blaze new behavioural and cultural pathways on short timescales'.

Neurobiology is opening for us new avenues of research in education, behaviour, politics, and social organization. 'Genes can be overruled by education ... so that some among our most decisive traits are epigenetic – acquired later in life, under genetic control but in response to outside factors' (de Duve 2010). A key question that arises immediately of course is which type of education we should choose and who will decide that. Here again science can help point to the right direction, but scientists cannot do it alone. We need to (epigenetically?) recruit the aid and cooperation of people (leaders) who can influence their followers into morphing this world to a place of higher quality of life where each and every one of us can reach his or her true potential. De Duve has some good ideas on the matter:

> Philosophers and, especially, religious leaders have managed to influence huge masses across national boundaries. They, more than anybody else, are in a position to help spread the epigenetic changes needed to save the world. Invention of the myth of the original sin, with its attendant need for salvation, may well represent the earliest human appreciation of our fundamental, inborn behavioural defects and the necessity that they be corrected.

After all, the declared role of religious leaders, at least so far as the Abrahamic religions are concerned, is to counteract the original epigenetic change (sin) that entered the human race early on and continues to hassle us to this day. Ancient holy books may have thus proclaimed truths about our existence that science is yet to discover, despite Dawkins' (2006) proclamations to the contrary! So the 'original sin' may be 'reinterpreted in the light of knowledge, namely the genetic flaw imprinted into human nature by natural selection (de Duve 2010)'. Our path to salvation may have just begun to be delineated by neuroscience. Future theologians will thus have to be conversant in the biological sciences in order to put forth their messages; inspired ancient ones foretold the message by the means they possessed at the time; 'Men have the power of thinking that they may avoid sin' (St John Chrysostom). The true Common Era for humanity should be born out of scientific achievements.

6. Abnormal behaviour

> Justice is a political virtue, by the rules of it the state is regulated, and these rules are the criterion of what is right.
>
> Aristotle, *Politics*

Abnormal behaviour can be defined in various ways and from different perspectives. As we saw previously, society determines the limits of tolerance regarding the way it expects its members to act. It sets the boundaries of what is normal and what is abnormal. Each social group, be it a whole culture, a kindergarten class, a monastic order, a church choir, or a terrorist organization has its own set of rules that members are expected to observe. Hunter and gatherer culture expects men to hunt animals, and women to gather fruits and vegetables; pre-school children are taught and expected to sit quietly in class while the teacher is talking; monks are expected to gather for evensong, pray in solitude, and harvest their fields at the set schedule of their specific order; a choir member is expected to sing in unison according to his/her assigned place and not be out of tune; and a terrorist is obliged to accept his group's manifesto. A temporarily sick hunter may be allowed to gather for a while, but a female gatherer cannot go hunting; a kindergarten child may get up and go to the bathroom, but he is not allowed to be disruptive in class; a monk may modify his personal order for praying, but he cannot awaken at his own leisure; a choir member may skip rehearsal once in a while, but she may not sing loudly and out of tune; and a terrorist, sadly, is expected to forgo his own consciousness in favour of his leader's. The social group sets up the norms, which are the rules of what is right and what is wrong in the behaviour of its members. Abnormal behaviour according to this concept, then, is seen as a violation of cultural and social norms. The social group is also responsible for deciding the ways by which it gets its rules obeyed, as well as the types of responses and the kinds of punishments it would inflict on deviants.

The concept of statistical rarity is a common way to define abnormal behaviour that is seen as a deviation from the statistical average of a set of behaviours. Normal behaviour here is that which falls around the average and (usually) within two standard deviations from it. This is a mathematical construct that is referred to as a normal distribution of (a set of) values. In regards to our discussion, the values pertain to observable behaviours. Most drivers stop at a red light; a few might run through it, and these fall outside the mean and standard deviations of the way most people drive. Their way of driving (their driving behaviour) is abnormal and society has decided and delegated to policemen their arrest and to judges their punishment.[1] This is the concept that I have used frequently in this book to define disease and abnormal behaviour. Ethical behaviour in this respect is also that which is expected, acceptable, and normal. The word *ethics* etymologically means habitual or frequently occurring behaviour, and therefore refers to statistically observed behaviours that, by definition, approach the average. Ethical in this sense, means customary. A limitation of this method, obviously, is that not all rarities should be identified as abnormal. An individual with an IQ score that is above two standard deviations from the mean would probably be considered gifted and not abnormal, at least up to a point, and these individuals may also become effective leaders. An ethical leader, even if paranoid, will keep his followers' interests at heart whereas an unethical one will have self-interest and personal gains as a goal. Paranoia may be an added extra for effective leadership; coupled with ethics, it becomes benevolent. Unfortunately, and contrary to what Joanne Ciulla (2004) hopes, ethics is not always at 'the heart of leadership', even though it should be. Numerous mentions of malignant leaders in this book attest to this reality.

Psychosis, personality disorders, and schizophrenia can be considered to be at the extremes of normal behaviour, certainly greater than two standard deviations from the mean of observable behaviours, but on a continuum with what is considered normal. The main theses that are presented in this book claim just that, in a way that humanizes these disorders rather than categorizing them as qualitatively different.

A more vague way to assess abnormality in one's behaviour is the concept of personal discomfort, where people are their own judges; abnormality, in this case, stems from what they consider to be distressing thoughts or behaviours. They seek help on their own and these individuals constitute the majority of patients undergoing psychotherapy. The limitation here is that, frequently, behaviour may not be distressing to a

---

[1]   The concept of statistical rarity is used to – sometimes arbitrarily – separate normal from abnormal in sciences including biology and health and disease. For example, mental retardation is defined according to statistics as follows: a score of 100 on an IQ test is considered average; two standard deviations below this average, or a score of 79 or less, is considered mental retardation.

person, but may still be (very) abnormal. Someone with extremely narcissistic attitudes or with delusions of grandeur may not be distressed by his/her psychopathology, which is still abnormal and frequently in need of treatment. If these individuals can continue to function adequately within their groups in other areas of life, and assuming they can persuade enough people that their peculiar ideas hold true, they may rise to higher echelons of society and attain leadership roles.

Maladaptive behaviour exists when the abnormality pattern prevents the demands of life from being met. This again is related to norm violation and to life circumstances. Successful leaders on the other hand may be maladaptive within certain societal norms but still able to bring about cohesion and awareness in their followers in terms of necessities and life demands that must be met. That is why these people cannot be expected to fall within the average of their societies nor can they be considered representative; as Runyan (1988), in discussing leaders puts it, 'this issue of representativeness is irrelevant because one is often interested in studying individuals who are *not* representative, who because of position, chance, or personal characteristics have unusual interest for us or had an unusually great influence on the course of history. Questions about the representativeness of an Alexander the Great, a Joan of Arc, a Vincent Van Gogh, or an Adolph Hitler are not to the point.'

We see, therefore, that defining abnormal behaviour is no simple task and in most instances a combined standard is used. Despite cultural diversity, most societies accept similar categories of behaviour as abnormal; these include behaviour that is out of contact with reality (as in schizophrenia), emotional responses that are grossly inappropriate to a specific situation (for example, laughing at a funeral), and unpredictable, or erratic reactions. Such behaviours would be separated out from that set of behaviours most groups consider normal, and the individuals exhibiting them would be marginalized. Their chances to lead their people would be minimized unless they exhibited their abnormality in very subtle ways or came into a position of leadership as the result of a birth right. The latter, if unopposed, may in times of crisis annihilate their societies. This situation has borne many historical examples of deranged leaders: Nero, Hitler, and Slobodan Milosevic were such cases.

Disordered personalities at times possess such exquisite skills in detecting other people's sensitivities, and expressing them in a succinct way, that they project an image of uncompromising adherence to principles, values, and deontology. What may, in fact, constitute lack of tact on their part, is taken to mean integrity, honesty, and courage. Their inflexibility is translated into stability of character whereas, in reality, it is only a reflection of the fact that they are crazy. What, in fact, becomes highly instrumental in such cases is the use of language. Hitler used to mesmerize his followers by the idiosyncratic use of language and his use of what Post (2004) called the 'all-or-nothing absolutism'. It constitutes the 'we against them' slogan, good versus evil, angels against Satan struggle, where all positive qualities are, of course, being embodied by the rising (paranoid) leader. We all remember George Bush's rhetoric in the aftermath of the tragic 9/11 events and his attempts to rally the support of the free world in his fight against terrorism: 'You are either with us or against us' he proclaimed, leaving no room for doubt that he embodied the *good* whereas the other side was evil. Some years previously the same argument was turned around by the Ayatollah Khomeini's rhetoric, in post-revolutionary Iran, with his 'We (God's people) against them (USA-Satan)' proclamations. Similarly, Saddam Hussein proclaimed that 'He who is not totally with me is my enemy' (Post 2004). The dichotomous 'us versus them' argument continues from historical times, on to current times but with different players. The Crusaders fighting against Islamic domination of the Holy Land, and Bin Laden fighting against the US and its allies are illustrative examples.

According to Post, such 'either/or' categorizations are characteristic of charismatic leaders' use of language. Because the German nation was good, according to Hitler, and the Jewish nation evil, there was but one option: crush and destroy the Jews. Anti-Semitism was the defining characteristic of his personality as well as his political agenda; it was 'central to his ideology and an *inflexible* part of his political program and rhetoric ... [it] was of a psychotic quality ... [Hitler] remained pure, good and righteous' (Loewenberg 1988, emphasis added).

Purity versus contamination, strength versus weakness, God versus Satan are themes that reoccur from time immemorial. The rhetoric becomes more dramatic as the degree of a leader's paranoia increases. Robins (1984) observes that when paranoia is associated with charisma (qualities he considers to be independent of each other), the result is a most malicious and atrocious personality. I am of the opinion that, as Phyllis Greenacre asserts,[2] the two qualities occur together in order to have effective (by whichever measure) leadership, and language serves as their common denominator. This is how Post (2004) describes the phenomenon.

> There is a quality of mutual intoxication in the leader's reassuring his followers who in turn reassure him ... To watch the films of Hitler's rallies

---

[2] Quoted by Post 2006, as a personal communication.

and focus on his hypnotic use of language – the repetition of simple phrases, building to a crescendo, the crowd echoing his phrases – is to watch hypnosis on a large scale ... [he] placed his entire audience into a trance ... And most striking of all, it was also autohypnosis, as Hitler apparently entered a trance state, mesmerized by the enraptured responses of his mesmerized followers.

Mass hysteria brought about by a psychopath. This phenomenon is probably the outmost example of the fulfilment of a biological need to form hierarchies and pecking orders; one may theorize that gene activation occurs in response to psychosocial and environmental pressures and acts as the expression of this biological legacy. Nature can be guided by nurture, as previously discussed, to produce behavioural phenotypes that either conform with or are antithetical to social norms. According to Harkins (1999) 'High-Impact Leaders are the ones who take charge wherever they are. They are the ones others *want* to follow.' Besides the leader's endowment, potential followers are also biologically inclined to assume such roles in response to the same environmental pressures.

Such a process induces in followers a magnification of an underlying belief such as a prejudice, especially under the influence of a group they belong to, and the prompting of a like-minded leader (Myers and Bishop 1971, Myers and Kaplan 1976, Levine and Moreland 1998). Moreover Hoyt and his co-workers (2006) argue that 'as individuals identify with the group, they feel pressure to conform to the extreme norm of the group'. That norm often reaches, under the guidance of paranoid leadership, dangerous positions. This may be one of the basic processes that underlie fanaticism and fundamental extremism.

What, however, might be abnormal in terms of those followers who choose disordered people to lead them? After all, in a rational and democratic society, one would expect that logic and reason prevail and that such checks and balances are operating, that ensure the rise of the most capable. The issue here is twofold; on the one hand, the most capable may actually be those individuals who, by virtue of their unique qualities, fall into the realm of the abnormal. Thus, they would somehow manage to project their qualities towards their fellow men, who would as a consequence, accept them as leaders. On the other hand, it may be that at times of crisis people turn to the most steadfast and uncompromising individuals among them, precisely because they appear to embody the desirable qualities to guide them through their vicissitudes. George Bush's re-election in the United States in 2004 may have come about exactly due to this situation. When Americans were under attack at home and at war abroad, Bush embodied and reified their deepest fears, hopes, and desires. That won him his second term in office. He capitalized on the 'either/or' categorization in a way that implied divine guidance. In fact, invocation of biblical figures and hinting at special relationships with the Almighty is a commonly observed tactic among leaders whose followers have religious inclinations. It is a recurrent theme in American politics, and even non-religious leaders would not dare ignore its impact, let alone ridicule it. Constantine used the symbol of the Cross on his banner in order to rally the fighting stamina of the Christian soldiers among his troops. In cases where the leader is himself religiously inclined (and paranoid), the unmistakable message put forth stems out of his conviction that the Hand of God is guiding his actions. Hammurabi claimed divine guidance in drafting his laws for the Babylonian citizens (Roth 2000).

As argued previously, severe abnormalities may carry an evolutionary advantage if they are associated with the continuous supply of individuals who are mildly affected but possess additional attributes that somehow enhance survival. Such attributes we argued, include the appearance of language and the advent of culture. Galton (1869) wrote 'I have been surprised at finding how often insanity has appeared among the near relatives of exceptionally able men.' Examples of this fact are mentioned throughout this book. The limits of societal tolerance appear to allow such disordered personalities to assume charge under circumstances of threat and danger. Those same characteristics, as we saw previously, enhance a leader's removal from power when the crisis ends.

The North Koreans tolerated the iron-fist rule of Kim Il Sung in order to avert the imminent threats of the Japanese empire. The paranoid disposition that characterized him at that time was seen as a saving grace for the nation. His son, Kim Jong Il, continued to rule his people in an ever-increasing flair of paranoia, mysticism, and mythology as he gradually displaced his own father in power and control, even though he introduced many principles of government in his name. Central to his control was the demand (as befits a paranoid) for total submission and obedience on the part of his entourage and of his subjects. These have been codified as the 'Ten Principles' to aid his people exhibit proper conduct (Baird 2003). He, of course, like scores of other paranoid leaders, remained outside the bounds of such limitations as evidenced by his preoccupation with special preparations of his meals, his hedonist lifestyle, his notorious alcoholism, and his well-described complete lack of empathy (Oh and Hassig 2000). These attributes combined with a volatile personality, indeed synthesized a dangerous and unpredictable leader. Post (2004) called him a malignant narcissist even though in his breakdown of his personality components he included a paranoid orientation that saw himself as surrounded by enemies, a characterization that corroborates my own thesis. Other components included grandiosity and self-absorption, no constraint of conscience, and unconstrained aggression. Whereas a narcissist would exhibit the above qualities, I feel that a paranoid befits them to a greater extend.

Following Kim Jong Il's unexpected death in 2011, his young and largely inexperienced son Kim Jong Un assumed the leadership of North Korea. The West and Asia watched in anticipation of a milder personality, influenced perhaps by years spent in Western boarding schools. Everyone hoped for better days in North Korea, which Powell (2012) characterized as 'a cocktail of poisonous elements: autocratic, repressive, isolated and poor'. Such conditions create thriving circumstances for paranoid leaders to emerge and act. As the last remnant of the Cold War in Asia, North Korea keeps raising the nuclear ante in order to gain benefits and bargain deals from the West and China. A paranoid predisposition however may easily go over the edge and bring about a catastrophe, as history has shown repeatedly. Disappointment about the new leader soon set in. Young Kim Jong Un has been described as 'competitive, encouraging or scolding' (Powell 2012), but like his predecessors, ruthless, revengeful, and isolationist. His treatment of what he considered dissent from officers of his armed forces is telling: 'several tanks rumbled forward and ran back and forth over the officers crushing them to death' (Powell 2012). Moreover, he has recently taken on the world by threatening the United States with nuclear Armageddon, declaring a 'state of war' with South Korea, announcing the restart of a nuclear reactor, and setting off a nuclear test (*The Economist* 2013). Thus he fits Robins and Post's (1987) assertion that a paranoid political actor creates his own self-fulfilling prophesies:

> The individual who believes he is endangered by a conspiracy and acts aggressively so as to protect himself (and his followers) from those he believes are conspiring against him will inevitably produce a defensive response from his designated persecutors, which in turn will confirm his fears (or hopes) … The designated enemy … must necessarily react against the delusively defensive aggression of the paranoid political actor, and in so doing provide confirmation of the dangerous reality he perceives.

Kim Jong Un's own people do not fare much better; they are brutalized and terrorized 'with some 150,000–200,000 individuals exiled in a vast gulag; farmers are herded into collectives and forced into gruelling manual labour; he is thought to have ordered the sinking of a South Korean naval corvette in 2010, with the deaths of 46 crewmen, and the shelling of a South Korean island later that year' (*The Economist* 2013). *The Economist* (2013) wonders whether such actions might represent 'a rite of passage to prove his leadership credentials' or whether 'he gets a thrill from orchestrating the chaos – as if he were playing a video game, or whether he is out of his depth and therefore more prone to miscalculation'. Or perhaps he is off the deep end like his father and grandfather before him (see the argument below about the biological basis of paranoia), and acts in the only (abnormal) way he knows in order to preserve his rule. The further removed from the needs of its people a regime is, the greater are the chances for it to miscalculate its hold on them and crumble unexpectedly after a popular uprising. My prediction is that North Korea will collapse from within allowing outside forces to deliver the final blow.

Abnormal behaviour, including paranoid ideation, can be thought of as a biological aberration. Similar examples may be found in all other life forms. Biology teaches us that what appears to be a disadvantageous characteristic, or a disordered behaviour may, in reality, result in the possession of traits that enhance survival. Let's see a relevant example.

Many people of Mediterranean and North African extraction are afflicted with a disease known as thalassaemia A. This is a terrible disease associated with abnormalities in the blood, which are frequently, and have until recently been, incompatible with life.[3] It is related to another frequently fatal blood disorder, affecting Africans, and known as sickle-cell disease.[4] Their geographic predilection suggests that their high prevalence in these areas resulted from evolutionary pressures. But what on earth, one might wonder, were those evolutionary pressures, and what kind of advantage did they confer on those people by such a heavy price?

It turns out that the price Mediterranean and African people pay is well compensated for; malaria, a febrile illness transmitted by mosquito bites that resulted in many deaths prior to the advent of antibiotics, was once endemic in that whole area.[5] Individuals who are heterozygous for

---

[3] Thalassaemia is a disorder caused by weakening and destruction of red blood cells, which carry haemoglobin, the protein that binds and delivers oxygen to the body. It results from genetic mutations that affect how the body synthesizes haemoglobin.

[4] Sickle-cell disease or sickle-cell anaemia is a blood disorder, in which red blood cells assume an abnormal, sickle-shaped form. This results in 'stiffening' of the cell, which affects its circulation through blood vessels and leads to multiple medical complications; this occurs due to a mutation in the haemoglobin gene.

[5] The term is used by epidemiologists to indicate high prevalence rates of a certain disease in a population to the extent that it becomes part of its defining characteristics.

thalassaemia and sickle-cell disease,[6] turn out to be resistant to malaria; in other words, the many more individuals who carried the trait for these blood diseases, also carried a better chance of surviving in a malaria-ridden environment. The price these populations paid was that a fraction of them died of thalassemia A or sickle cell disease. This may have been an unfair deal for those few individuals with a fully blown disease, but the population at large survived. This mechanism explains why, over the years, the frequency of carriers for the two diseases increased. The evolutionary pressure was to generate as many carriers as possible. When two such carriers have children, each child has a 25 per cent chance of being normal, a 25 per cent chance of developing thalassemia A, or sickle cell disease depending on which mutation their parents carried, and a 50 per cent chance of being carriers themselves; the latter, along with normal individuals (that is, 75 per cent of the population) will survive and reproduce. However, the ones considered normal in this case, may succumb to malaria, since they do not possess natural resistance against it. Their numbers will gradually decline.

Another example of evolutionary adaptation is visible in the effectiveness of antibiotics on microbial organisms that carry infective potential towards human beings. As a result of antibiotics being used widely and perhaps not always wisely, we are finding the appearance of increasing proportions of resistance from susceptible organisms, leading to progressively greater difficulty in dealing with them; in other words, as the bugs are exposed to antibiotics, a number of them develop resistance and they thus survive whereas the susceptible ones die off. Over time this process results in more and more bugs with resistance to antibiotics and greater difficulty in controlling the infections they cause. This is why the pharmaceutical companies, along with pharmacologists, are on a never-ending race to stay ahead of the evolution of drug-resistant organisms.

The analogy with schizophrenia becomes, I should hope, evident. The price we as humans are paying to have individuals who excel in the arts, literature, religion, and leadership, is the constant affliction of 1 per cent of us with this disease. Their close but unaffected relatives enrich our lives by their many contributions. Language and culture, as we have seen, are the evolutionary advantages we derive at the price of schizophrenia and other related disorders.

Being closely related to mad people, our leaders carry a partially manifest abnormality in the form of paranoia and other milder mental

---

[6] Carriers who do not develop a fully blown illness but can pass on its genetic trait to their progeny.

affectations. Abnormality in biological phenomena, including behaviour, can be thought of as extreme expressions of traits that are found in smaller doses in other individuals along a continuum. As we approach the opposite end of this continuum, the frequency of these traits becomes less and less, to the point where it disappears. In thalassaemia, to belabour our familiar example, severely affected individuals would be found on the left hand side of the continuum, carriers would cluster around the mean, and unaffected ones at the right hand side. In psychosis the same scheme could apply; schizophrenia, manic depression, and schizo-affective disorders would be found over on the left end. Personality disorders would come next, but well before the middle: depression, anxiety, and various other ailments just around the mean; and to the opposite right hand side, those without manifest psychiatric disability. This is another way to conceptualize the gradation from normal to abnormal and to explain that, indeed, we all share the same humanity.

Mental illness then, like all biological phenomena, probably represents an extreme adaptation of milder forms of behavioural abnormalities that convey advantages for survival. It is not our purpose to survey such phenomena in a comprehensive manner. Rather, we used some examples to illustrate as well as to explain the social phenomenon of putting into high offices individuals who, behaviourally, come from the left side of our behavioural continuum. In other words, 'evolutionary plasticity can be purchased only at the ruthlessly dear price of continuously sacrificing some individuals to death from unfavorable mutations' (Dobzhansky 1937).

Pecking orders are evolutionarily determined, and thus carry advantages for the survival of species. A biological programming helps determine the order so that the fittest one for the top usually gets there. Humans most likely have retained such programmes, albeit in rudimentary forms, that influence or even determine how *we* order our societies and who our leaders are, especially when our survival is threatened. This threat may be either real or imagined but it affects, nonetheless, our choices. Hard times require hard individuals and who is better equipped to assume that role than the uncompromising, rigid, and intransigent personality of the paranoid individual? All one would need to rise up in such circumstances, is to align with the multitude's innermost fears, wishes, and desires. George Bush Jr. was re-elected as a defence against the threat of terrorism, real or imagined. Desperate people make desperate choices, and these choices, in turn, enhance the rise of individuals with rigid personalities.

Galanter (1980) has offered, over several years and multiple studies dealing with charismatic religious groups, a psychoanalytic model of leader–follower relationships, in what is called the ideal-hungry personality. What this model proposes is that narcissistically wounded individuals are attracted and make ideal followers of charismatic leaders. The more wounded an individual is, the more uncritically attracted he would be to an idealized leader, and this holds especially true in those followers in whom their self-concept was injured early in life. The theory offers an explanation of the apparent inconsistency between the unquestionable acceptance of a leader's far-fetched claims and the follower's prior background and beliefs. The process supposedly includes the merging of the incomplete, ideal-hungry personality, with the idealized charismatic leader. In this way, the leader's success becomes the follower's success as well.

Kohut echoes similar notions but from the aspect of the omnipotent leader who, according to his theories, is a narcissistically-fixated person bordering on *the paranoid* who also possesses many of the other qualities we have been considering so far, such as a distinctive voice, unshakable self-confidence, and a judgemental attitude towards others' deficiencies, whose only logical choice would be the unquestioning reverence of their leader's authority. This becomes even more relevant at times of threat.

The perceived threat, we need to re-emphasize, can be either real, as during armed conflict, or imagined, as during social upheavals, economic depressions, and political flux. Such uncertain times and conditions provide ample breeding ground for people to come out of the fringes to preach, convert, and persuade others about what needs to be done. As a given group's vulnerability magnifies, so does its tendency to seek quick, simple, and clear-cut solutions. These are the times for prophets and messianic movements, and these are the conditions to bring about significant historical and socio-political changes. If the leaders guide their societies into a better milieu, they become great and are baptized heroes; if, on the other hand, they lead people to make wrong choices, they are forever despised and deemed unworthy. So the same type of personality may, depending on the outcome, be glorified or doomed. Current world events, in this New Common Era, could prove to be a fertile ground for harvesting such personalities.

Psychoanalysis, of course, has gained important insights into the workings of dyadic relationships, including those of leaders and followers. Recent and better understanding of the biological determinants of behaviour however, have come to supersede the uncontrolled findings that are gathered on an analyst's couch, even though those insights are still, by and large, relevant.

There probably exists a gene in our genetic endowment that gets activated during times of stress, as when survival is threatened, to help us overcome the danger in self-defence, self-preservation, and protection of offspring. This is clearly shown in the animal kingdom where instincts rule the day. Anyone who has a female and unspayed pet cat knows this from the way she reacts around her kittens. During dangerous times there's no time for cool, unemotional, or rational consideration of options; that would be a recipe for disaster. Those are times for quick, reflexive, and effective action; shoot first, ask questions later. These are thriving times for persons with paranoid disorders who tend to see the world in terms of black and white, leaving little room for shades of grey. Add the multitude's perceived state of helplessness, and conditions become ripe for misjudged actions.

Another type of reflexive reaction that is observed during times of danger is the well-known phenomenon of 'fight or flight'. This is a neurophysiological response controlled largely by the autonomic nervous system in close collaboration with the endocrine system.[7] When the perceived danger is overwhelming, the economical response would be flight. If the situation is more manageable, or there is no room to escape, autonomic over-activity occurs, steroid hormones are released into the bloodstream (which cause increased production of glucose in the muscles to prepare them for the fight), and the organism is readied for fight. Such arousal is often observed in crowds as they delegate the fight to their leader. This is a fight by proxy that will, however, eventually involve the crowd as well. Mesmerized crowds like the German nation described above, exhibit the fighting neurophysiology in response to their leaders' hypnotic prompting.

When the leader, having gained the unquestionable support of his followers, manages to deliver them from their tribulations, he becomes idealized to the point of having god-like features attributed to him. At that state, any behavioural, personality, or medical shortcomings might be ignored to the point of pathological denial. Such was the case regarding the terminal illness of Mustafa Kemal Ataturk,[8] the father of modern Turkey (Volkan 1982). Having managed to unite the withering pieces of the former mighty Ottoman Empire into a cohesive nation,[9] he was elevated to an immortal status by his inner circle as well as the Turkish nation, so that his terminal liver failure was utterly ignored by his own

---

[7]   The autonomic nervous system is a part of the brain and its projections that is outside the direct control of the conscious mind and deals with functions that are vital for survival such as, for example, our heartbeat, our breathing, and of course the 'fight or flight' response.

[8]   Meaning 'Father of Turks', a title granted to him later on.

[9]   Ethnic cleansing of minorities and the Armenian genocide notwithstanding.

doctors until non-Turkish physicians examined him objectively (Volkan and Itzkowitz 1984). The 'dear leader' of North Korea, Kim Jong Il, is another example of idealization, at least for his close associates, as far as we can discern for that isolated and paranoid regime. Ailing leaders of the former Soviet Union were thus artificially idealized to rally the support (or at least the tolerance) of the people, in their 'good' struggle against the evil and decadent West. Unsuccessful but unrelenting fighting leaders are also idealized in similar ways, a process that is necessary for the continuation of their struggles. Perhaps a notable example of this situation would be that of the Palestinian leader Yasser Arafat who did not see his struggle to full fruition; however he managed to make the world aware of his people's plight and achieved the recognition for the need of a Palestinian state as the culmination of the Palestinian Authority.

Paranoia may be a pathologic state when it is present, however a healthy dose of it is necessary, as we saw, to help leaders maintain control and cohesiveness of their followers. According to Kelman (1958), there are three ways a leader can manipulate his followers' attitudes and compliance in order to maintain cohesiveness of rule. The first is pure coercion, a method not truly representative of effective leadership as we have defined it here; it is usually short-lived and precarious since it creates discontent and reaction at the first opportunity the subjects get. Leadership happens without participation from unwilling followers; the fall of Eastern European states in the 1990s attests to this fact. The second and third ways, namely identification and internalization respec-tively, are characterized by some degree of willingness to follow a leader. In these situations, 'leadership happens when people go along with an influence attempt with some degree of volition' (Hoyt *et al.* 2006). Subjects identify themselves with attractive aspects of a leader's style, or internalize his attitudes into their belief and value systems. Such psycho-logical processes produce enduring attitudinal changes. It is the rhetoric and language style of a paranoid and unyielding personality that's most effective in inducing such changes, and according to Hogg's social identity theory of leadership (2001), the more representative of a group's attitudes a leader appears to be, the more his followers will identify with him as well as with each other. American presidential elections in the recent past have demonstrated this rule well; consider the duels between Reagan versus Carter, and Bush versus Kerry. The winners' advantage was the perception by the public that they represented them the most, and also that camaraderie between each other would be strengthened.

Women leaders-to-be face a double whammy when it comes to assuming leadership roles in many societies; on the one hand, they are expected to be nurturing, tender, submissive, and sensitive (Eagly and

Karau 2002), but on the other hand, as leaders, they are expected to be aggressive, assertive, and decisive (Heilman 2001). Therefore, they exhibit an incongruity of roles that compromises their potential, even though they probably make as good (or bad) leaders as men (Eagly and Karau 2002). For these reasons women leaders belong to a social phenomenon that is viewed as outside of 'normal' expectations. But of course, many women assume such roles even with the blessing of the opposite sex. What qualities might they possess to aid them in such endeavours? I would propose similar ones to those of their male counterparts; that is, abiding to their beliefs, a paranoid outlook, and the language skills to bring forth their ideas. These women would be more predisposed to fight for a leadership position, perhaps as a reaction to negative stereotyping (Stoddard *et al.* 2003) on the part of males. Thus, a paranoid personality would be more likely to induce a woman to take action at a time of crisis, just as it would in a man. The examples of such women as Indira Gandhi, Golda Meir, Margaret Thatcher, and Angela Merkel, illustrate the point well. In a sense, women in leadership roles represent a deviation from stereotype expectations and may thus be thought of as abnormal by many 'mainstream' thinkers.

7. Politics and mental illness

> Man is naturally a political animal.
>
> Aristotle, *Politics*

Aristotle said that man is a political animal, and as such, he requires the social medium in order to function in roles of leadership. To achieve that, 'leaders can persuade followers by good arguments' (Gardner 1995). But are these good stories people tell one another enough to gain an entourage, let alone a multitude of followers? Certainly not, since the leader's personality traits and behaviour also play a significant role. As Hoyt *et al.* (2006) state 'other elements matter greatly'. They continue:

> Is the leader someone with whom followers might identify, or trust and believe? Has the leader presented his or her message in a manner that encourages receptivity and credulity? Personal characteristics are important here, but so are contextual features, such as illustration, easily remembered slogans and impressive-looking documentation.

It is imperative that the leader at least appears to care for his subjects. Whereas the psychological literature often assumes that the goals of leaders and followers are the same (Hogg 2001), an evolutionary perspective suggests that this may be an unfounded assumption (Van Vugt 2006).

Ray (2011) says that, 'The basic definition of leadership is the person who rises above the crowd and gets something done.' A successful leader must be willing to pay a price in order to succeed. Just as the alpha male in a herd invariably must fight its way to the top, similarly an aspiring leader must be ready to face resistances that more often than not will result in antipathies. Paradoxically leadership in humans is often determined by whoever has the greatest incentive to move (to take action), and is least concerned about the interests of others. Indeed, leadership correlates strongly with ambition and autonomy traits (Van Vugt 2006). Ironically, followers are drawn to such persons as they recognize leadership potential in them. The ability to communicate effectively, that is, the appropriate use of language, in congruency with the followers-to-be, is at the core of successful leadership and, hence, politics. This has

133

Madness and leadership

been demonstrated since antiquity, a time when direct, face-to-face contact with constituents was the way to get the message through. Communication is crucial in coordinating group action, especially when there are goal conflicts, and leaders who possess such skills are at an advantage (Dunbar 2004). Holladay and Coombs's (1993, 1994) research demonstrated that delivery is an important component of charismatic leadership, and suggested that although both content and delivery contribute to attributions of charisma, the effect of delivery is more powerful indicating that the style of language is the critical factor to get a group's attention. Similarly, quantity of communication is a better predictor of leadership emergence, whereas the quality of what one says is a better predictor of leadership effectiveness (Van Vugt 2006).

Nowadays, mass media communications have largely replaced direct contact, even though a charismatic leader should invent ways to appear as if he is in direct contact with followers. Reagan was successful on television. More recently, Obama reached people through electronic means, just as an old friend would. Social media are thus replacing personal contact but in a way that preserves the personal touch. Consider the following message, which could have also been from my brother:

Savvas –

I keep a to-do list in my desk.

It's ambitious, but you and I didn't set out to do easy things.

As long as I can count on you to be a part of this, we will find a way to make progress on all of it – continuing to create good-paying jobs, fixing our broken immigration system, finding a common-sense way to reduce gun violence in this country, and more.

No president can do it alone.

Say you're in:

http://my.barackobama.com/Are-You-In

There's a lot of work to do – thanks for doing your part.

Barack

The common denominator of successful communication does not depend on the medium used, but on the personality of the leader. The message above first and foremost, creates a partnership between Barack and the recipient. It is short, urgent, to the point, and states the issues clearly. The solution, any solution, will depend on the President as well as his followers. The success will be shared. Such language mobilizes the masses.

In studies conducted by social scientists, one common trait emerges consistently regarding the ability to lead, and that is extraversion (Judge *et al.* 2002). By a leap of faith we can deduce that paranoia and other related psychic states must be underlying extraversion. Clearly a vocal and outspoken person (that is, extraverted), would get the attention of would-be followers and such a person would be more up to be extraverted. Extraversion correlates highest with leadership emergence, and this trait – an indication of boldness – has a substantial heritable component (Judge and Bono 2000), another indication of its biological basis. It is also a trait that many paranoid, outspoken persons possess, one that makes them intolerant of 'mediocrity', wishy-washiness, and beating around the bush. It is a trait that would-be leaders will depend on in order to get their own, often opposing, points across.

From time immemorial, world literature and folk stories are replete with examples of what popular belief held to be true regarding leaders; that, indeed, leaders are kind of crazy. Mythology and religion provide us with many such cases when, either as an act of nemesis, or due to individual hubris, a leader goes mad. Thus folk culture explained this phenomenon, which appears to occur time and again in all societies and places. The bigger question of course is why it is such a constant theme and what factors, psychological, social, genetic or other, contribute to its appearance. Could it be that the pressures of leadership at times of crisis drive a leader to madness, or is it that those very pressures, coupled with an underlying personality trait predispose one first towards action, and second, to go over the limit? Clearly there are qualitative differences between leaders and followers, between political activists and constituents. King *et al.* (2009) propose the possibility that personality differences (and hence different propensities towards political activism) are maintained in populations because they foster social coordination. As we saw previously, such an arrangement carries evolutionary advantages with respect to solving problems and surviving. The differences in question most probably constitute what folk beliefs have constructed and perceived as the 'craziness' of leaders. In addition, Ghaemi (2011) claims that depressed leaders have heightened attributes such as empathy, realism, resilience, and tenacity and are therefore not only crazy but also more effective at times of crisis. Affective (mood) disorders (depression and mania) as we argue elsewhere, can also be characterized by paranoia, especially if they are severe enough or protracted. Perhaps, then, it is paranoia that underlies such effectiveness and not the mood disturbance itself.

Van Vugt *et al.* (2008) inform us that selection pressures that gave rise to leadership in non-human social species resemble those that evolve in humans, a fact that points towards the biological determinism of the phenomenon. Thus, leadership in social animals (including humans) is important. According to Van Vugt *et al.* (2008):

> During times of peace and prosperity, it seems not to matter. However, when politicians start wars, when business leaders gamble with our life savings, and when religious leaders create violent sectarian divides, leadership becomes a matter of life and death.

As we have argued, there appear to be genetic factors that determine who will lead and who will follow, and there are clear individual differences in the propensity to lead (Van Vugt 2006). Twin studies reveal substantial heritability coefficients of traits predicting leadership such as intelligence, empathy, extraversion, and ambition (Ilies *et al.* 2004, Rushton *et al.* 1986). Extroversion was mentioned previously as the most consistent trait. Leadership along with other complex social characteristics is thought to be influenced by multiple genes and each plays its role in producing differences in a particular trait (Plomin and Colledge 2001); the makeup of a personality therefore is polygenic and multifactorial. On the other hand Van Vugt *et al.* (2008) discuss followership as having emerged in response to specific ancestral problems that were best solved through collective effort coordinated by a leader–follower structure. Such an arrangement enhanced individual and group survival. This implies that leader–follower patterns will emerge more quickly and effectively in circumstances that mirror adaptive problems (for example, internal group conflict and external threats) (Van Vugt *et al.* 2008). The above notions were echoed long ago by Aristotle in *Politics*:

> It is also from natural causes that some beings command and others obey, that each may obtain their mutual safety; for a being who is endowed with a mind capable of reflection and forethought is by nature the superior and governor, whereas he whose excellence is merely corporeal is formed to be a slave.

Behavioural characteristics evolve in response to particular environments through natural selection. Therefore, 'the ancestral environment may have shaped our leadership prototypes' (Lord *et al.* 1984) and has bestowed on us a tendency towards a natural preference for leaders who reify these (unconscious) prototypic traits. These prototypes 'can be inferred from characteristics that are both prominent among hunter–gatherer Big Men and endorsed across industrial societies' (Van Vugt *et al.* 2008). Evolution has thus assured that 'humans easily recognize leadership potential in others' (Lord *et al.* 1986).

We have also seen that a significant number of leaders (especially those who induce others into recognizing them as such), possess some sort of oddity about them that sets them apart from the average or 'typical' character in their groups. Moreover, we proposed that culture is that product of human evolution that has enhanced and assured our survival and expansion over the globe. It reasonably follows then, that in order to understand, let alone explain, why leaders go crazy, we must consider the issue from all of its aspects, namely the biological (genetic), the psychological (or psychopathological), and the socio-cultural. All three aspects are intertwined and interwoven, and, in fact, probably represent different forms of the same thing. To consider all forms of this tripartite phenomenon enables one to comprehend it better. The issue was dealt with separately by sociologists, biologists (including geneticists, physicians, and psychiatrists), and anthropologists. Each considered the matter from his or her unique perspective, often ignoring the other points of view. Moreover, even within the social sciences, different camps have developed that took different approaches, and often ceased to communicate with each other.

Thomas Wren (2006), has tabulated many of these approaches in a manner analogous to the periodic table of elements that chemists use, and called it, *periodic table of leadership studies*.[1] What we are attempting in this chapter is to synthesize the various parts into a unified theory that adequately explains the psychologically compromised political leader phenomenon. I am using the model by King *et al.* (2009) that utilizes biological, social, and psychological approaches to leadership in order to achieve 'an integrated evolutionary perspective [and] a more complete picture as well as a scientific grounding'. We are also told that 'across species, individuals are more likely to emerge as leaders if they have a particular morphological, physiological, or behavioural trait increasing their propensity to act first in coordination problems' (King *et al.* 2009).

---

[1] Wren has also summarized the work done by J. Ciulla (2004) and C. P. Snow (2001). According to their views, there was an initial split between the natural sciences and the humanities. The later have subsequently split into the humanities and the social sciences, which even though they were represented by equally intelligent and trained people, somehow ignored each other. Ciulla has provided an interesting exegesis of the various camps: 'Description is generally done by social scientists, explanation by historians, anthropologists, religious scholars etc., and critical analysis by philosophers.'

Paranoia may very well be the common denominator trait that confers these tendencies on would-be leaders.

Leadership can be studied in various settings and situations. Religious and political leadership is where a leader's role can be dissected and assessed with some degree of precision since these individuals are subject to public criticism and their style is manifest in the public arena. An early contributor to such studies was Harold Lasswell (1930) who proposed a formula by which leaders were predisposed to act politically. In a psychodynamic interplay between feelings of general inferiority, their displacement onto a public object (that is, followers), and the rationalization of a need to serve that (inadequate) public, a leader seizes power and uses it to restore his fragmented self.[2]

Many psychobiologies have been attempted using this scheme in an effort to explain problematic political leaderships from a psychodynamic point of view. A notable one is that of George and George's (1956) treatise on the presidency of Woodrow Wilson, in which they use the characteristics proposed by Lasswell to explain the way his decisions and political actions were conducted. More recently however, the paranoid predisposition of Woodrow Wilson was proposed as an adequate explanation of his leadership style (Hampton and Schroeder Burnham 1990). Malignant narcissism is the preferred pathology used by psychoanalysts to interpret vicious political acts. Thus, Post and Robins (1995), apply the scheme above to explain Idi Amin's despicable record of suppression, violence, terror, and murder; his self-proclaimed super-grandiose title as 'His Excellency President for Life Field Marshal Al Hadji Dr. Idi Amin Dada, VC, DSO, MC, Lord of the Beasts of the Earth, and Fishes of the Sea, and Conqueror of the British Empire in Africa in General and Uganda in Particular', is offered as a convincing example of the power seeker who projects his inferiority feelings onto his people and rationalizes his brutal acts as necessary in order to save, protect, and guide them. Certainly no one would doubt the narcissistic nature of Amin's personality in explaining his actions. This however, is coupled with a severe state of paranoia to compose such an abnormal power seeker. His brutal vindictiveness against betrayers is unquestionably the result of his injured low self-esteem. His brutality against the intelligentsia, however, is more fitting to his paranoia, and in any case Idi Amin was not a successful leader.

---

[2]   Lasswell uses an equation p}d}r}=P to define such leaders; P is *Homo politicus* who results by the interplay of p=the power seeker, d=personal needs (as they stem from inferiority feelings), and r=rationalization regarding further action.

Ronson (2011) feels that 'many of our political and business leaders suffer from Antisocial or Narcissistic Personality Disorder and they do the harmful, exploitive things they do because of some mad striving for unlimited success and excessive admiration'. Couple such personality traits with paranoia, which frequently accompanies these disorders, and the ingredients are gathered for the formation of a malignant leader. On the other hand, couple paranoia with dignity and respect for others, and the recipe for a benevolent leader is produced.

Anthropological evidence suggests that there are no known human societies without some form of leadership (Boehm 1999, Diamond 1998, Lewis 1974). Political behaviour, like its encompassing culture, results as an adaptive phenomenon that helps organize a social group in order to improve its subsistence. This has been recognized since antiquity along with the fact 'that some should govern, and others be governed, is not only necessary but useful, and from the hour of their birth some are marked out for those purposes, and others for the other, and there are many species of both sorts' (Aristotle, *Politics*). Biology, in other words, has the final say as to who can lead and who should follow. Upbringing, education, and coaching notwithstanding, our genes take the lion's share in the formation of our personality and behavioural patterns.

Experimental research on social dilemmas shows that leaders enhance group cooperation, thereby producing outcomes that everyone in the group can enjoy (Van Vugt and De Cremer 1999). As such, leadership evolved to utilize those 'politicians' who could apparently maximize the group's chances to achieve their specific goals. Consequently, a system of hierarchical stratification develops to maintain that organization; automatically, this arrangement leads to the acceptance, up to a limit, of inequality and differential access to power. As Harvey (2006) puts it, 'leadership originates with inequality', but this is necessary in order to solve the three basic 'problems' of the human condition, which always, according to Harvey, are 'how to survive in the world, how to make sense of the world, and how to wield power'. Depending on the particular situation faced by a group of people, a leader is licensed to provide guidance. The common underlying trait of such persons, if they are to succeed, is the presence of a sturdy, unyielding, and somewhat paranoid personality that will enhance aloofness and determination in order to stay the course. Other qualities are utilized to fit specific needs and may include, among others, 'physical strength and boldness ... cleverness, empathy, memory, imagination, vision, humor, and artistry. In addition, the IQ component most strongly associated with leadership is verbal ability' (Korman 1968), attesting to the role of language. Group leaders, such as priests, politicians, soldiers, or conductors, use a variety of signals to foster group coordination (McNeill 1995). Even in non-human primates, there is an abundance of vocal and visual signals used by aspiring leaders to initiate group movement (Boinski 1993). Global communication signals are very well developed in humans, with facial expressions, gestures, rituals, and complex language serving to synchronize group activity and transmit desires or demands (Hauser *et al.* 2002). To the extent that a leader can harness and use these signals he will gain a devoted followership. The most eloquent, having gained that advantage from a biological association with psychopathology, will secure a place at the top. The increase in human group size selected for powerful social-cognitive mechanisms, such as theory of mind,[3] and language, providing new opportunities for leaders to attract followers through manipulation and persuasion (Dunbar 1993, Trivers 2000).

Power, according to Nye (2004) is 'the ability to influence the behaviour of others and to get the outcomes one wants'. 'And of course, a person may play a leader's role in one setting, and a follower's role in another. Moreover, the crowd to be ruled has potentially a great deal of power available that can be harnessed at a moment's notice and upset the balance of power unexpectedly. Leaders do well to keep that in mind. Foucault said that much when he wrote that 'in a certain way, one is always the ruler and the ruled' (1978). Moreover, he defined power as not only manifesting in the ability to control others and things, but also, a phenomenon that colours and shapes our personality.

In order to maintain power, a leader must also capitalize on the trust that his followers bestow on him; the issue of trust is central to the leader–follower relationship if non-coercive means are to sustain it. Rousseau *et al.* (1998) proposed the following definition of trust as it has been conceptualized and studied across numerous disciplines: 'A psychological state comprising the intention to accept vulnerability based upon positive expectations of the intentions or behaviour of another'. There are several processes through which trust forms.

One perspective focuses on the nature of the leader–follower relationship (or more precisely, how the follower understands the nature of the relationship) and is called the relationship-based perspective (Dirks and Ferrin 2002). For instance, some researchers describe trust in leadership as operating according to a social exchange process (Konovsky and Pugh 1994, Whitener *et al.* 1998). A second perspective focuses on the

---

[3]   The ability to attribute mental states, beliefs, interests, desires, pretending, knowledge, etc. to oneself and to others and to understand that others have beliefs, desires, and intentions that are different from one's own (Premack and Woodruff 1978).

perception of the leader's character and how it influences a follower's sense of vulnerability in a hierarchical relationship (Mayer *et al.* 1995). Dirks and Ferrin (2002) refer to this as the character-based perspective. In both of these two perspectives, trust is a belief or perception held by the follower and is measured accordingly; it is not a property of the relationship or the leader per se (Dirks and Ferrin 2002) and, given the necessary conditions, it can be withdrawn accordingly.

McAllister (1995) suggested that interpersonal trust can be categorized into two different dimensions: cognitive and affective. Cognitive forms of trust reflect issues such as the reliability, integrity, honesty and fairness of a referent. Affective forms of trust reflect a special relationship with the referent that may cause the latter to demonstrate concern about one's welfare. Other definitions have implicitly combined these two dimensions into an overall measure of trust – that is, a blending of affective and cognitive forms – or have implicitly or explicitly focused on one of them (Dirks and Ferrin 2002). Successful leaders combine both dimensions naturally and the basic tool they possess to that end is the use of a distinctive language, which sets them apart on the one hand and on the other, it enhances delivery of critical messages that drill down to the core of followers' cognitive and affective demands. Followers in turn 'allow' their leaders to harness power in order to use it for the greatest good.

Machiavelli ushered in an era of modern political thinking that has influenced political thinkers ever since (2001a [1531]). For him, as well as his followers – such as Nietzsche – effective politicians must harness force and violence in order to maintain power and protect the interests of their people. As his disciple Guicciardini put it 'all political power is rooted in violence' (Ridolfi 1968). Echoing Hindu beliefs in Siva and Vishnu – the Destroyer God and the Preserver God respectively – he considers power and force a necessary (great hope), as well as an evil (destroyer) impera-tive. The duty of a leader (the prince in his theories), is to properly balance the two and maintain order in his society. In that respect he accepts Aristotle's notion that 'power cannot be founded in justice, but in force' (2001). To that end, sheer power must be balanced with other skills such as cunning and the avoidance of resentment on the part of the people. A typical way to achieve this is for a leader to deflect his followers' resentment and fear of his power towards an outsider group, or a minority within. History has provided many examples of this phenomenon, and scapegoating may often be rooted in such a dynamic. Against the back-ground of degenerating Italian city states, and the ominous threat posed by non-Italians such as the French, or the advancing Muslim Turks, Harvey (2006) regards the development of Machiavelli's thinking as reflecting the harsh realities of his times.[4] Such were the vicissitudes that gave rise to many leaders throughout history.

Harvey (2006) applies the term 'virtuous Machiavellianism' to leaders that correctly perceive outside threats and decisively act on them. In turn, followers will license their leader with transgressions in conduct that further enhance his power (often with an egotistical ulterior motive and the anticipation of greater returns). This may result in resentment on their part, especially if, in addition to power, leaders develop a double standard; whereas power makes people stricter in moral judgement of others they have a tendency to go easier on themselves (Lammers *et al.* 2010). This in turn can cause a severe disconnect between public judgement and private behaviour, with greater impact among people who are legitimately powerful, and it's up to the skill of the leader to diffuse negative feelings in order to maintain power and influence. Paranoids are also known to be strict on others while slacking off themselves so the connection of this aspect of their psychopathology with leadership becomes ostensible. Moreover, it is the paranoid personality that usually equips a leader to balance these two opposing trends in order to maintain power and control; on the one hand he needs to be sufficiently aloof regarding the resentment that his followers develop towards him, and on the other hand he must harvest and exhibit enough charm in order to mesmerize them and keep them tamed. Paranoids do both quite well.

As much as Machiavelli emphasized the power of the individual, he dared suggest that, perhaps, democracy might be a better state of affairs, provided that the basic issues of inequality and trust were dealt with (2001a [1531]). This had been accomplished in ancient Athens when Pericles, with the aid of his legendary 'Olympian aloofness' had gathered persuasive power with the 'blessing' of the Athenian demos. In doing that 'he confronted the problem that faces any free and democratic society: How can the citizens be persuaded to make sacrifices necessary for its success?' asks Kagan (1998). Subsequently he provides the answer:

> Pericles sought to teach the Athenians that their own interests were inextricably tied together with those of their community that they could not be secure and prosper unless their state was secure and prosperous, that the ordinary man could achieve greatness only through the greatness of his society ... Pericles tried to shape a new kind of society, and a new kind of citizen, not by the use of force or terror but by the power of his ideas, the strength of his personality, the use of reason, and his genius as a uniquely persuasive rhetorician.

---

[4] See also the quotation in Chapter 2, p. 29.

Therefore, we return again to the skill of the individual leader to sway his followers' opinion while at the same time abiding (or appearing to) by the ideals of democracy. Unfortunately, more often than not, the leader mesmerizes his crowd and strips from it every chance of making intelligent decisions, or even worse, he suppresses it beyond basic freedoms of expression. In all cases, the paranoid personality of the leader underscores the circumstances; if the leader also has integrity and empathy, he strives for good outcomes; if not, he strives for self-fulfilment. Machiavelli most likely did not consider that any kind of psychopathology was enhancing a leader's ascent.

Thomas Hobbes, even though he was a Machiavellian by tradition, reached the conclusion that only a totalitarian regime would be able to safeguard against the insecurity of the world's reality and the state of 'every man against every man' (1991 [1651]). Down to this very day, political power is considered by many to rely on violence and the use of force, and this is due, in part, to the fact that once power is attained by a person, he only wants to increase it in order to secure it even more. This however creates a double bind, a state of ever-increasing competition and anarchy; thus, the need for a strong centralized government (Hobbes 1991 [1651]). Furthermore, however, other methods must be recruited in order to make power acceptable to others, if not appealing. Such other methods would include, among others, the ability to form social relationships and coalitions to solidify one's rule; these relationships could be mutually beneficial, symbiotic, persuasive or byzantine in their approach; again, the skill of the leader, his communicative style and the use of power once attained, will enable him to maintain his command over his followers. To use Hobbes's (1991) terminology, a leader must use both 'original' (meaning intrinsic and personality derived), as well as 'instrumental' (meaning social relation derived) power. The appropriate proportional contribution of these two kinds of power, in the fitting circumstances, is the recipe for good leadership. The maintenance of power by force is for Plato and Aristotle (2001) a sign not of the state but of the state's failure.

Besides the power that is bestowed by force, Harvey (2006) discusses two other kinds of power that are clearly less malignant: soft power and the power of knowledge.

Soft power is more legitimate as it derives from interplay between a leader and a follower and obedience is voluntary. It is characterized by charismatic qualities of the leader that, according to Weber (1978), are bestowed on him or her by the followers and thus a trusting, mutually satisfying relationship develops. We will return to charisma later on in this chapter. Nye (2004) also uses the term 'soft power' to describe contractual agreements of leadership and command between willing partners and relies heavily on making followers want what the leader wants; thus it depends a great deal on the leader's skill, personality and style, context in which he arises, as well as the ability to impress others with words (language). Modern democracies, just like ancient ones – for example Athens – depend heavily on soft power to conduct their affairs, and in this context, skilful leaders have the greatest chance to put forth their ideas. In times of crisis, as we saw, the most steadfast will win the crowd, especially if they express, or appear to express, their followers' inner wishes. Mary Parker Follet (1951) calls this ability 'power with' and opposes it to 'power over' or, what Nye terms 'command power', and considers it the way to attain lasting authority in leadership. From Pericles in ancient Athens, to Kennedy and Obama in America, we see that this kind of power, seen as legitimate by the leader's subjects, creates the potential to bring about lasting and beneficial changes in a society (Greenleaf 1977). Mahatma Gandhi was such a leader. Used malignantly of course, as in the case of the narcissists and the extreme paranoids, it may bring about disaster and misfortune. Unfortunately, the latter have an equal opportunity to access people's hearts and can be masters in the use of soft power. Unfortunately Hitler was an example of such a leader. Command power (Nye 2004) is akin to Harvey's forceful and violent power, and in addition, it includes bribery.

Knowledge also imparts a kind of power on individuals who, by virtue of their privileged access to 'special' kinds of knowledge, are considered to be in a position to exert authority. This last type of knowledge creates elite groups that, by using their special knowledge (or skills), climb up social hierarchies. Such specially endowed groups include, among others, religious functionaries, financial and business administrators, education-alists and scientists. Consider the influence a white-jacketed individual has in advertising a new medicinal product. Marcus Welby MD, the popular TV character of the 1970s, could not muster great armies or angry multitudes, however the power he exerted on his patients, stem-ming from charisma and respect, was as effective as that of an army general.[5]

Successful politics leads to power. Power can be mostly endowed by force, or knowledge or charisma, but it will inevitably lead to a hierarchical differentiation of a leader from his followers that eventually commands authority. Weber (1978) dealt extensively with the kinds of

---

[5]   This series was created by David Victor and the character of the MD was played by Robert Young. It originally aired on the ABC network in America.

authority bestowed on leaders and it was summarized nicely by Harvey (2006) as consisting historically of three distinct types: charisma that 'is associated with individuals' who arise at critical times and bring about changes in the traditions and customs of their followers, which is why it is described as 'revolutionary' by Webber; tradition, which represents 'the routinization or institutionalization of power' such as that seen in church and military organizations; and legal-bureaucratic, which is so prevalent with modern-day technocrats. Harvey uses the 'nightmarish' example of Kafka's, *The Trial* (2011 [1925]) to illustrate this last type; Josef K. a civic employee is arrested by unknown men and brought to trial for an unknown offence, is hassled and harassed by a faceless bureaucracy and ends up being executed 'like a dog' without ever finding out what he did wrong.

Our modern world has experienced the rise of different types of power as governments, people, and multitudes of organizations strive to control our actions, our minds, and our choices. Due also in part to an increasing level of paranoia as a result of a recent resurgence in world terrorism, surveillance methods have invaded every aspect of our lives and our living rooms. This situation has brought forth an enormous power to monitor our lives, in a big brother kind of way, that is influencing our decisions and the way we express ourselves. The final result of this 'new societal order' is yet to declare itself. Hopefully it will not become a defining characteristic of the New Common Era.

8. Psychotic disorders and paranoia

> I remember those psychologists who said psychopaths made the world go
> around. They meant it: society was, they claimed, an expression of that
> particular sort of madness.
>
> Jon Ronson, *The Psychopath Test*

In previous chapters we reviewed evidence about the common biological
origins of psychosis and language, and how these characteristics may
have determined our human nature. Moreover, since only the human
species possesses these attributes, they may be related to other activities
such as creativity, religion, high achievement, and leadership, all of
which constitute unique human characteristics. In this chapter we will
describe the psychotic and paranoid disorders in some detail in order to
gain a better understanding of them, as well as their putative relationship
to leadership. The psychologically accomplished readers may skip over
this section even though there are useful references to, and examples of
'mad leaders' that are useful in illustrating the book's theses. I recom-
mend at least that it be skimmed over.

Psychosis is defined as that state in which there is loss of touch with
reality. The prototypical affectation of psychosis is schizophrenia a
psychiatric condition that is characterized by the following:

1.   Delusions, which are simply defined as fixed false beliefs. We all
     have, on one occasion or another, a belief that does not correspond
     to reality; for example most kids accept the idea that Santa Claus
     exists and visits their homes on Christmas Eve, bearing gifts and
     descending through chimneys. It is a false belief but it is not fixed;
     at some point during their childhood, either through persuasion or
     by their own logical deduction, they realize that this is a fairy tale,
     and their false belief is modified accordingly. If, on the other hand,
     and despite all evidence and arguments to the contrary, they
     continue to maintain that the story of Santa Claus is actually true,
     even into adolescence and adulthood, then their belief becomes a
     delusion. A person who believes that the moon is made of cheese,
     or that he is dead despite evidence to the contrary, is delusional.

Delusions of grandeur is a well-known symptom among psychotic people who may believe that they are Christ, Napoleon, or other famous persons. A cautionary note is in order here; these false beliefs must fall outside of what a particular social group considers normal. Believing in the resurrection of Christ would not qualify as a delusion among faithful Christians but might do so among agnostics and atheists. Similarly, the creationist dogma might be thought of as a delusion by adherents to the theory of evolution. In other words, one man's religion (or ideology) would be considered to be a delusion by someone else. So, one should be careful when assessing the mental health of another person, in order that cultural beliefs and social background are taken into account. Psychiatrists especially, as well as other mental health professionals, would do well to remember this fact.

2. Hallucinations, which may be defined as sensory perceptions and experiences, in the absence of an actual stimulus that explains them. Simply put, what we refer to here is hearing voices and seeing things that do not exist. All types of sensations can be perceived by a schizophrenic such as tactile ones (referring to the sense of touch), gustatory (taste), and so forth. These experiences, as one might expect, are quite distressing to the person. In that respect, either the sufferer or his close associates and relatives, will seek help. Abnormality in this case is defined in terms of the personal discomfort theory.

3. Disorganized behaviour in that the patient cannot function in a proper and effective way, cannot conform to the norms and standards of his group, and may appear withdrawn, apathetic, aggressive, or silly.[1] At times they may assume bizarre postures for extended periods of time. There are various subcategories that we need not go into for the purposes of this book.[2]

4. Disorganized thinking and language (or thought disorder as it is formally known), refers to the person's inability to engage in clear, logical, and rational thoughts. In addition, the language sounds bizarre, with no respect to correct grammar, syntax, or context. New words may be formed or old words used in a different inappropriate meaning rendering it incoherent.

---

[1] The term hebephrenic is used in conjunction with silly, disorganized behaviour to depict the situation of such a person; Hebe-puberty, and phrenic-mind, are Greek terms denoting a pubertal, and thus disorganized, mind!

[2] The reader is referred to other sources for more information that are listed at the end of the book.

5.   Negative symptoms are those behavioural aberrations that consist of
        blunted emotional responses, withdrawal from normal/expected
        social activities, anhedonia (lack of capacity to experience pleas-
        ure), and lack of initiative. It is a state in which there is turning
        away from society and neglecting oneself to the point of
        emaciation.

A host of other conditions besides schizophrenia may also exhibit
psychotic symptomatology. Severely depressed individuals may at times
be also psychotic, even though in these cases (of the so-called psychotic
depression), the illness may be curable with proper treatment. Brief
psychotic disorder is another transient illness that develops in response to
a significant psychosocial stressor and resolves with appropriate therapy.
Schizoaffective disorder is a condition that simultaneously combines
symptomatology of both affective (that is, emotional) illness such as
depression or mania (see below), and schizophrenia. Schizophreniform
disorder is one that resembles typical schizophrenia but is briefer in
duration and longer than brief psychotic disorder. Last, delusional
disorder is a condition of a specific and persistent delusion, not accompanied by the marked deterioration and social dysfunction that characterizes schizophrenia. According to the diagnostic and statistical manual for
mental disorders published by the American Psychiatric Association
(1994), 'the prevalence of these disorders is probably much higher than
commonly recognized, since the delusions often remain concealed for
years and may be manifested only in non-medical situations, where they
can go unrecognized as a medical condition'. Individuals with these
conditions may be thought of by others as odd, eccentric, strange, or
weird and may be laughed at behind their backs. However, if their
particular delusion goes unchallenged, they function quite normally and
can attain high positions at work and in society. In other words, they too
can become leaders. This condition illustrates some of the limitations of
defining abnormal behaviour as was discussed previously; a person may
have, say, delusional disorder but still function well in society. They
would be considered abnormal according to the statistical rarity concept
but may escape detection due to their otherwise high functioning. And
there would be no personal discomfort resulting from their delusion, so
they would be unlikely to seek help. An acute manic episode may at
times be indistinguishable from acute psychosis. This is described later
on in this chapter.
    The most debilitating, chronic, and dysfunctional condition from the
list above is schizophrenia. Even when some of its more florid symptoms
such as hallucinations and delusions are controlled with medicines or

other types of interventions, there remains a qualitative oddness about the schizophrenic's behaviour and overall predisposition. These are characteristics that easily set such people apart from 'normals' in their social context, and are related perhaps more to the persistent disorganization of behaviour and thinking that are much more resistant to treatment.[3]

It is obvious, therefore, judging from the above criteria, that a schizophrenic/psychotic person cannot function properly in a society, nor can he/she assume any leadership roles. These individuals are simply marginalized and excluded from active participation in group activities. Between about one-third to one-half of homeless people in America are thought to be afflicted by the disorder (Carlson 2001), and certainly they exist on the fringes of society where they play no role in common affairs, other perhaps than arousing our sympathy or contempt, depending on our point of view. It is estimated that the prevalence of schizophrenia alone is about one per cent worldwide and that this percentage remains constant across cultures. This is taken by most scientists as evidence of the biologic/genetic nature of schizophrenia.[4] In addition, there is evidence of its heritable nature, in that it appears to cluster in certain families. Moreover, some other relatives of schizophrenics appear to carry oddness about them and their behaviour in general can be described as strange. They constitute the peculiar personalities that are much acclaimed in the arts, literature, and gossiping social gatherings. They may function adequately enough in a society and can sometimes be quite successful professionally. Their persistence among populations is explained by the presence of schizophrenia, which induces the appearance of milder forms of psychosis, including paranoia. It is to these people that we will turn our attention next as they may fulfil some of the putative characteristics that we seek in our leaders. We will describe them below.

Collectively, they are classified under the category of the personality disorders. The reader should keep in mind that some of these disorders share or have similar symptoms, and that sometimes the differentiation between them becomes rather difficult to make. An experienced mental-health professional should be making these diagnoses and not every person on the street. What every person on the street can do, however, is to identify the oddness or strangeness about certain individuals in

---

[3] Delusions and hallucinations are known as positive symptoms because they represent an added or abnormally exaggerated sensation, whereas abnormal behaviour and thinking are known as negative symptoms as they represent a deficit or something lacking.

[4] Most modern concepts about schizophrenia consider it as an organic/brain disorder.

hierarchical positions and be wary about the soundness of their claims and goals. Watch out for grandiose claims about righting everything that is wrong; watch for inconsistencies between proclaimed beliefs and practices; and for a lack of sensitivity to the needs and feelings of others. Leadership implies power, and power promotes hypocrisy according to a study by Lammers *et al.* (2010) who concluded that it makes people stricter in moral judgements of others while going easier on themselves. This phenomenon may result, partly, due to licensure that followers give their leaders. We will deal again with this issue in subsequent parts of this and the following chapter.

Robins and Post (1987) have given us a succinct summary of the paranoid state, its occurrence and its functional significance:

> A paranoid state of mind can be looked on as an organized system of coherent beliefs which, while distorting reality, may serve adaptive needs. Hyper-alertness to the environment is characteristic of the paranoid. There is a readiness, indeed almost an eagerness, to find evidence of a hostile inter-personal environment. In this hostile world, there is no such thing as a coincidence. If there is a possibility of providing a negative or hostile explanation for an otherwise innocent event, the paranoid will do so. The umbrella term 'paranoid' subsumes a spectrum of disorders, ranging from transient episodes of exaggerated suspiciousness, to which we are all subject, through the paranoid personality to severe psychopathological paranoid states characterized by loss of contact with reality and delusion formation.

Most of the disorders to be described below may also occur during the course of some of the major disorders with psychotic features such as schizophrenia, psychotic depression, and others that were described above. In addition, they may occur as a direct physiological effect of a medical condition or substance abuse.[5] Therefore, in their own right alone these disorders may or may not represent bona fide psychiatric illnesses; co-operation between mental health and medical professionals is necessary to arrive at a correct, final, diagnosis. Descriptions of these conditions follow.

PARANOID PERSONALITY DISORDER

According to the DSM-IV the typical features of this disorder include:

---

[5] For more details and information about these disorders the reader should consult the DSM-IV, published by the American Psychiatric Association in 1994.

A.   A pervasive distrust and suspiciousness of others such that their motives are interpreted as malevolent, beginning by early adulthood and present in a variety of contexts, as indicated by four (or more) of the following:

1.   Suspects, without efficient basis, that others are exploiting, harming, or deceiving him or her;
2.   Is preoccupied with unjustified doubts about the loyalty or trustworthiness of friends or associates;
3.   Is reluctant to confide in others because of unwarranted fears that the information will be used maliciously against him or her;
4.   Reads hidden demeaning or threatening meanings into benign remarks or events;
5.   Persistently bears grudges, that is, is unforgiving of insults, injuries, or slights;
6.   Perceives attacks on his or her character or reputation that are not apparent to others and is quick to react angrily or to counterattack;
7.   Has recurrent suspicions, without justification, regarding fidelity of spouse or sexual partner.

B.   The condition does not occur exclusively during the course of schizophrenia, a mood disorder, with psychotic features, or another psychotic disorder and is not due to the direct physiological effects of a general medical condition.[6]

Such individuals, as may be expected, form few lasting relationships and trusting friendships. They are easily involved in frivolous law suits without a substantial case, or fixate on righting what is wrong with their society. Few people can meet their standards and in any case most confidants that they may have often become identified as traitors and are so victimized. Often enough they may join fringe social groups in order to advance their ideas and easily become leaders in such settings. They frequently write letters accusing others (usually former colleagues), with whom they have fallen out, of conspiracy, injustice, or unethical/illegal behaviour. They are usually quick to pass unfavourable judgement and easily advocate severe punishments. Yet, they may reach high positions in society, politics, science, and academics. From such positions they may attempt to institute their world ideology and may drive their fellow men

---

[6]   Reprinted with permission from the *Diagnostic and Statistical Manual of Mental Disorders*, Fourth Edition, (Copyright © 2000). American Psychiatric Association. All Rights Reserved.

into dangerous predicaments. The protagonists of the anti-abortion movement in the United States exhibit many of the behavioural patterns of the paranoid personality.[7] Niebuhr (1994) describes the case of David C. Trosch, a fundamentalist Alabaman minister, who not only had vehemently defended murder acts against abortionists, but went so far as to write to the US Congress, as well as the Vatican, and warn them of impending catastrophes should they continue to tolerate the killing of innocent unborn babies. Killing such killers, according to him, is an act of grace, likened to the resistance fighters against the Third Reich during World War II. Well-meaning people are found on either side of that divide. In order to have their views expressed, or imposed, however, they need to line up with intransigent (paranoid) personalities to whom they delegate the roles of leadership.

Another characteristic they have is that whereas they are quite intolerant of any deviations of their followers from their belief systems, they frequently allow themselves to 'fall off the wagon,' so to speak, because they consider themselves above the rules and regulations, that they demand others impeccably observe. In other words, whereas they strive to control others in order to attain full control and safety, they cannot accept even the minutest criticism; to them any sign of disagreement is interpreted as rejection, betrayal and disloyalty. Consequently, these signs only serve to intensify their paranoia further. And, as a result, they 'allow' themselves the luxury of breaking their own rules in order to protect those very rules. According to Hampton and Schroeder Burnham (1990), 'In the paranoid mind, control equals safety. Paranoia doesn't let you accept criticism, yet lets you criticize others. The only way to get along with a paranoid is to agree with her'. One may consider Popes who fathered children or kept mistresses while at the same time 'upholding' the dogma of celibacy; the notorious Russian cleric Rasputin and his escapades illustrate the point as well. Because they expect betrayal they constantly scan their environment for such signs. The Soviet leaders felt safe so long as they suppressed and oppressed every deviation of their peoples from the communist dogma. And of course they frequently found insurgency since they tended to misunderstand cues they received. Hampton and Schroeder Burnham (1990) see the paranoid trait as an evolutionary advantageous development in that:

---

[7] This statement is not an attempt to line up with either the right-to-life or the pro-choice movements; it is used as an illustration of the characteristics many leaders possess.

Paranoia has promoted and yet restricted our evolution in the development of the family, communities and nations. It was part of the process by which human beings progressed from a primitive to a cultured civilized state. Paranoia is also responsible for the evolution of politics, religions, war, science, and technology.

These same authors identify three levels of paranoia, which they call high, moderate and low. Those who possess high amounts of paranoia tend to be aggressive and domineering towards others. They 'are the least comfortable to be with because of their demanding and controlling natures. Yet often others turn to them for advice and support, because of their confident and overbearing manner.' Therefore genetic programming allows them to reach the top of their groups' hierarchies since they may ensure their survival and reproduction. Those with moderate amounts, while they subject themselves to the high-amount paranoids, usually lead safe, productive, and satisfying lives. The third category, those with low amounts of paranoia, is seen as naive, easily taken advantage of, and submissive. Many famous leaders, political, religious, or military, have exhibited behaviour stemming from high-level paranoia and this was precisely the reason of their success; their uncompromising demand for loyalty while, at the same time, their own behaviour was erratic and unpredictable. Many tended to deteriorate with advancing age as their paranoia worsened. Alexander murdered his childhood friends in a frenzy of paranoia, while Constantine's wife and children had a similar fate. The case of Stalin, an example of our own recent historical times, is illustrative of this point. As he advanced in age, his paranoia increased and his rational decision-making process deteriorated. His psychopathology caused the perception of enemies everywhere, which in itself, probably created more actual political rivals. Additional scores of individuals might have lost their lives, had he not have suffered a haemorrhagic stroke and died (Conquest 1973).

Schizophrenia begets paranoid personalities, which in turn, beget leaders. Successful novelists and other writers have understood this trait and describe it well in their works. Many heroes of popular literature are portrayed as paranoid, or their personalities are described in such ways that the readers can tease out many paranoid traits. The well-known fiction author Tom Clancy (1991) describes an imaginary Israeli brigadier general thus, 'He was not a man who often had difficulty in defining his thoughts. That was a luxury accorded him by paranoia, he knew.' Israel, a state surrounded by real and perceived enemies, cannot afford to have leaders and protectors who are not paranoid. Let's consider a related example, that of former Israeli Prime Minister Benjamin Netanyahu. In his attempt to profile his personality from a distance, Kimhi (2002) has used media information as well as others' perceptions of the man. Egocentricity is considered to be his political style, which combined with Markus' designation as 'a charismatic, driven … lone wolf, the kind of person you might say has no God' (1996), has produced a personality type destined to reach the top of Israeli politics, a feat that he certainly accomplished. Kimhi, of course, was attempting to portray his narcissistic traits but in so doing he described typical paranoid tendencies as well, in addition to whichever narcissistic ones he might possess:

> A narcissistic personality … Netanyahu's suspiciousness (bordering sometimes on a paranoid tendency) displayed itself from an early age … and saw conspiracy everywhere. His character traits – ambition, determination, excellent media skills, *superb rhetoric*, and personal charm were highly suited to the achievement of his goal of reaching the top government office. (Kimhi 2002, emphasis added)

Reading between the lines of his descriptions, one can see paranoia crying to come forth. Shavit (1996) is quoted in claiming that 'Netanyahu is convinced that he discerns the historical processes that others do not, and believes that it is his heroic task to rescue his homeland'. Moreover, he is described as lacking the ability 'to see things from a perspective other than his own' (Benziman 1993), crushing anyone who might pose a threat to him (Verter 1996), and forming no close relationships. Verter (1997) even gives us this example of Netanyahu's own words:

> I receive a lot of support from all areas of the nation. They tell me to be strong and steadfast. 'We are with you; don't give up. Stand strong; truth will win.' Because this is what the success of the Jewish people, the success of the State of Israel, depends on, and they will never be defeated.

These are the words of 'a megalomaniac trapped by feelings of persecution (Ashri 1997) and suspicion that 'the entire world is against him' (Markus 1997). Kimhi also describes him as 'an attractive and impressive man [who] has great rhetoric ability and explains his views logically'. This is an allusion to his superb use of language, another characteristic of the paranoid leader. As an 'electrifying performer' (Markus 1992), he uses 'a simple message expressed briefly, clearly, and repeatedly' (Galili 1995). *Yedioth Ahronoth* (1996) asserted that 'his appearance and rhetoric abilities are part of his charm, and they served him well during his race for head of the Likud and afterwards, for prime minister'. Kimhi calls him 'a man of words [with] the ability to enthuse people into following him'. Such are the traits that we claimed make a successful leader. These are the traits Netanyahu possessed to rise to the top, but perhaps, also contributing to his fall in 1999. Of course, his downfall came at a time when the Israeli people were hoping for peace and co-existence with the Palestinians. With the dramatic turnaround of the Near and Middle East situation, the recent advent of Islamic State, and the uncertainty about Israel's security, Netanyahu was gloriously reinstated in order to deal effectively with the threats. The occurrence of paranoia in certain families, and its relationship to schizophrenia, a genetic disorder, supports the ideas that it is also genetically controlled. Moreover, it likely falls on a continuum with the more severe psychoses to which it is biologically related.

We have so far seen many world leaders who were reputed to have suffered from paranoid personality disorder including, in recent times, Indira Gandhi of India, Churchill of England, and Stalin of Russia, and all were discussed in various sections of this book. A word of caution is necessary here. Most people may, at one time or another, exhibit a bit of paranoia (sometimes justifiably so, especially when they live in totalitarian regimes), but that does not mean they have paranoid personality disorder. Unless the symptoms described earlier are persistent and colour the person's life in a pervasive way, the diagnosis should not be made. On the other hand, if a truly disordered person can play to the tune of his or her society's collective hysteria about a specific issue (say, for example, the threat of communism or terrorism), many may easily follow and accept his paranoia as in fact, a reasonable forewarning of imminent danger, especially if current local or international events give credence to their claims. For example, it is far easier to convince people that a pan-Islamic plot is underway to take over the world after the tragic 9/11 events when sensitivities and fears are heightened. And many more may identify a pragmatic leader in such a person. Therefore, as with most life issues, it is the degree of paranoia that makes an individual dysfunctional whereas its primary evolutionary function was probably to help us control our lives as well as, under proper circumstances, have enough gusto to assume leadership, effect change, and ensure adaptation and survival in a hostile environment. Paranoia carried to extremism becomes irrational, as was the state of P.W. Botha's resistance to let go of his power in South Africa in 1989. Machiavelli (2001a [1531]) in his proverbial pessimism about individual leaders, explains this recurring phenomenon thus:

> There are two reasons why we are unable to change when we need to: In the
> first place, we cannot help being what nature has made us; in the second, if
> one style of behaviour has worked well for us in the past, we cannot be

persuaded we would be better off acting differently. The consequence is that one's fortune changes, for the times change, and one's behaviour does not.

Post (2004) describes the threatening feelings that possess authoritarian personalities when they lose control, or when they are criticized by subordinates in a hierarchy. This picture of stubbornness, rigidity, and inflexibility does not allow them, according to Post, to change positions easily. The paranoid leader at times faces criticism and responds in predictable ways. That's when the legitimacy of a leader's power is sustained by force. The amazing events of the Arab Spring of 2011 have aptly demonstrated this fact.[8] One after another, leaders brought about havoc in their countries before they were toppled. President Bashar al-Assad, the leader of Syria was once described as a mild-mannered ophthalmologist, running a private medical practice in London. When his rule was threatened however, he did not hesitate to turn his weapons against his own people and bring about a bloody civil war. Before he reacted so ruthlessly he had gradually morphed into a younger version of his father, Hafez. He almost certainly reached that state as he epigenetically activated latent paranoia-producing genes. Personality profiling by Landis (2009) sketched Bashar's style as one dominated by the need to control his environment, an obsession with order, working within a rigid framework and stubbornness in his views. Similar descriptions are given in this chapter in delineating the personality of a paranoid individual, even before it manifests in action. His brother Majd al-Assad, an electrical engineer, is rumoured to suffer from a mental illness, adding credence to our assertion that leadership and madness are genetically linked.

Hampton and Schroeder Burnham (1990) claim that living with a paranoid individual is not easy:

> What do you do if you have to live with a paranoid? It's not easy and the key is to agree with him unconditionally in everything he says and does, otherwise there will be constant friction. There is no middle ground, and there is no flexibility or compromise. Everything is black or white. So if you have to live

---

[8] Beginning with Tunisia, one Arab state after another toppled their leaders during popular uprisings and replaced them with supposedly better ones. At the time of the writing of this book, the subsequent deterioration of relations in the Middle East, the emergence of ISIS, the Russian–Ukraine crisis and the reordering of alliances were only beginning to occur and were therefore not discussed. Subsequent events unfortunately vindicate the prevalence of paranoia in the theatre of world events.

with one, be careful, and to keep peace allow him to control your actions and thoughts, dictate your opinions and options. It's not a happy situation.

Spouses are stuck. Democratic societies may, in time, vote these people out. Totalitarian regimes must live with them, accommodate them, or organize a revolution. In this case, another paranoid leader needs to rise up, rally his people, and topple the tyrant. Initially there may be attempts to reason with the paranoid leader, to sway him away from harmful and destructive decisions. As the pressures mount, however, the paranoid leader will more often than not become even more rigid and see disloyalty and betrayal. Campaigns against traitors may ensue, leading to massacres and cleansings. Eventually, the leader is toppled by a dissatisfied group.

We discussed this disorder extensively in order to gain a good grasp on its characteristics because it has been a central point in our argument about paranoia and leadership. We will now discuss other related conditions.

SCHIZOID PERSONALITY DISORDER

We turn again to the DSM-IV for a synoptic and widely accepted description of this disorder. According to its diagnostic criteria, an individual is said to have schizoid personality disorder when there is:

a pervasive pattern of detachment from social relationships and a restricted range of expression of emotions in interpersonal settings, beginning in early adulthood and present in a variety of contexts, as indicated by four (or more) of the following:

1. Neither desires nor enjoys close relationships, including being part of a family;
2. Almost always chooses solitary activities;
3. Has little, if any, interest in having sexual experiences with another person;
4. Takes pleasure in few, if any, activities;
5. Lacks close friends or confidants other than first degree relatives;
6. Appears indifferent to the praise or criticism of others;
7. Shows emotional coldness, detachment, or flattened affectivity.[9]

---

[9] Reprinted with permission from the *Diagnostic and Statistical Manual of Mental Disorders*, Fourth Edition, (Copyright © 2000). American Psychiatric Association. All Rights Reserved.

These are the odd people in our midst who seem unapproachable and distant. They are loners who shy away from attempts by others to get close to them. They seek jobs such as night watchmen, morgue assistants, or foresters, where there is little contact with co-workers. One wonders whether some of the more ambitious ascetics had manifested some of these personality traits. They seldom marry and rarely form any meaningful friendships. In contrast to the paranoid personality, who seeks the company of like-minded people, and is exquisitely sensitive to the way others behave towards him, the schizoid person neither seeks the company of others, nor cares about what they think. Consequently, these persons do not seek high offices unless of course they are born into them. Nor do they mind being replaced by more energetic relatives. They are included in this discussion for the sake of completeness regarding these disorders and to contrast them with the paranoids with whom they are occasionally confused. If, as happens occasionally, they are promoted at work to a higher position that requires frequent and close contact with other people, and consequently carries more stress, they may decompensate and go into a psychotic state.

SCHIZOTYPAL PERSONALITY DISORDER

This disorder is thought to be related to schizophrenia to the greatest extend. It is defined as:

a pervasive pattern of social and interpersonal deficits marked by acute discomfort with, and reduced capacity for, close relationships as well as by cognitive or perceptual distortions and eccentricities of behaviour, beginning by early adulthood and present in a variety of contexts, as indicated by five (or more) of the following:

1. Ideas of reference[10] (excluding delusions of reference);
2. Odd beliefs or magical thinking that influences behaviour and is inconsistent with subcultural norms (for example, superstitiousness, belief in clairvoyance, telepathy, or a 'sixth sense'; in children and adolescents, bizarre fantasies or preoccupations);
3. Unusual perceptual experiences, including bodily illusions[11];

---

[10] These are beliefs that one receives special messages from the media, that plots on TV and other mass communication devices refer specifically to him or her, or that others are talking about them.
[11] Illusions are misinterpretations of an actual experience. For example, one may misinterpret a curtain blowing in the wind at night as an intruder. In this

4. Odd thinking and speech (for example, vague, circumstantial, meta-phorical, over-elaborate, or stereotyped);
5. Suspiciousness or paranoid ideation;
6. Inappropriate or constricted affect;
7. Behaviour or appearance that is odd, eccentric or peculiar;
8. Lack of close friends or confidants other than first degree relatives;
9. Excessive social anxiety that does not diminish with familiarity and tends to be associated with paranoid fears rather than negative judgments about self.[12]

This is another one of the odd disorders that shares features with both schizophrenia and paranoid personality disorder. The criteria listed above help make the distinctions. One should remember that there are overlaps with one another, but also there are exclusions. People with schizotypal personality disorder are odd but may function in society and even assume leadership positions. They may attain leadership positions due to their personality traits when they fit certain roles. For the same reason, they may rise in corporate positions, academics etc. and if their specific delusion/oddity fulfils a shared wish of the group they may easily influence others to follow them.

NARCISSISTIC PERSONALITY DISORDER

This personality disorder is included here because it is often proposed by psychoanalytically bent authors to be the major mental affectation of political leaders, especially dysfunctional ones. I will take issue with this proposition but I am describing it here in order to help the reader draw his or her own conclusions regarding its centrality in leadership. According to the DSM-IV, this personality disorder is characterized by:

a pervasive pattern of grandiosity, need for admiration, and lack of empathy that begins by early adulthood and is present in a variety of contexts, as indicated by five (or more) of the following:

1. A grandiose sense of self-importance (for example, exaggerates achieve-ments and talents, expects to be recognized as superior without commen-surate achievements);

---

situation, a physiologic bodily sensation is perceived as a pathological one or as evidence of tampering with one's self.

[12] Reprinted with permission from the *Diagnostic and Statistical Manual of Mental Disorders*, Fourth Edition, (Copyright © 2000). American Psychiatric Association. All Rights Reserved.

2. Preoccupation with fantasies of unlimited success, power, brilliance, beauty, or ideal love;
3. Belief in being special and unique, and can only be understood by, or should associate with, other special or high status people or institutions;
4. Requirements for excessive admiration;
5. Sense of entitlement, that is, unreasonable expectations of favorable treatment or automatic compliance with his/her expectations;
6. Interpersonal exploitation, that is, taking advantage of others to achieve expectations;
7. Lack of empathy and unwillingness to recognize or identify with the feelings and needs of others;
8. Often being envious of others, or belief that others are envious of them;
9. Arrogance and haughty behaviour or attitudes.[13]

This is the person who ceaselessly talks about himself and demands the undivided attention and admiration of others. This usually occurs to the point of irritating listeners who invariably turn, eventually, a deaf ear. In contrast to the paranoid who is directing his psychopathology outward, the narcissist turns it inward toward himself and thus assumes the flair of self-importance. A narcissist's vulnerability under the grandiose facade makes for an ineffective leader, unless these elements are weak, which allows the formation of select relationships with advisors who may subsequently steer the leader towards appropriate decisions.

Many Hollywood success stories stem out of the second characteristic whereas social climbers and 'busy bodies' who will just not go away, exhibit the qualities described in the third one and observing the way political candidates speak of themselves, and their opponents, often reveals such feelings. The requirements for excessive admiration mentioned above reminds us of the Barbie syndrome of self-indulgence, so prevalent in modern society and which has a narcissistic flavour at its root.

A paranoid individual will turn the attention of others toward an external threat and in this way rally their support in achieving goals. Followers in this case assume a feeling of accomplishment and participation in the success attained whereas, in fact, they play into the narcissist's interpersonal exploitation.

Lack of empathy, point seven above, is where these individuals 'go wrong' and are abandoned by followers, unless they are also paranoid, in which case they project their suspiciousness onto some external 'other'

---

[13] Reprinted with permission from the *Diagnostic and Statistical Manual of Mental Disorders*, Fourth Edition, (Copyright © 2000). American Psychiatric Association. All Rights Reserved.

and solidify support around them. Identifying a common enemy with their followers keeps them in charge. This characteristic goes hand-in-hand with their envy of others and their beliefs that others envy them, and these feelings are a frequent source of friction and resentment. This is why narcissists seldom create true, warm relationships. As Volkan (1980) asserts, the narcissist 'lives a glorious albeit lonely life in such isolation that he could be said to dwell within a plastic or glass bubble'. Their arrogance and haughty behaviour and attitudes carry them to the point where their concern is not about the general well-being, but their own reputation.

In and of themselves, these characteristics seldom allow a leader to rise and maintain unity. The sense of entitlement will help such a person assume a leader's role; however, unless some paranoid predisposition also accompanies these features, the leader is more often than not deserted. Even Post (2004) who insists, along with other analytically bent psychiatrists, that a narcissistic personality is imperative to be an effective leader, often mentions and admits that 'the personality patterns as described are rarely found isolated from other personality traits'. The key question then, is which traits or combination of traits is needed to form a leader with the right ingredients. Hitler, Stalin, and Deng Xiaoping may very well have had narcissistic personalities; it was their paranoia, however, that created the leadership profiles they exhibited. For Fidel Castro, a most effective leader of the twentieth century and beyond, Post (ibid.) writes the following:

> Destructive charismatic leadership is associated with a particularly dangerous kind of narcissistic personality-malignant narcissism. Combining extreme grandiosity with a paranoid outlook, an absence of conscience, and a willingness to use whatever aggression is necessary in the service of his own needs, Castro is a prime example of a malignant narcissist.

The term malignant narcissist is applied by Post to leaders such as Castro, Saddam Hussein, and others. He also describes them as paranoid. Does he, perhaps, mean to equate paranoids with malignant narcissists? A paranoid outlook is *not* a criterion for the diagnosis of narcissistic personality. It is, nonetheless, a key ingredient for the formation of an effective and captivating leader. Post (2004) considers three personality styles as dominating leadership ranks, with the compulsive and the narcissistic styles dominating, whereas the third one, the paranoid personality, is seen only infrequently. I maintain that the paranoid individual is to be found on top of the list, as manifested by the many examples of leaders mentioned, and the other two are certainly significant, but less so in forming the personality of a potential leader. Brunell *et al.* (2008) suggest as much when they claim that 'Narcissists have an inflated view of their talents and abilities and are all about themselves'.

To recapitulate, a narcissist's point of reference (consciously or unconsciously) is himself, whereas a paranoid's is the crowd and that, partly, is the reason behind their success as leaders. Narcissists on the other hand, when their character pathology becomes extreme, are ineffective leaders who cannot accept advice, let alone criticism (Kernberg 1975). Only sycophants, according to Post (2004), thrive around them. Paranoids can be rigid and uncompromising but are capable of forming some close, albeit often temporary, relationships.

THE AFFECTIVE DISORDERS

A related but distinct group of disorders is that which comprises the so-called *affective disorders*. Affect in simple terms refers to a person's emotional state and the way it is expressed; it is similar to the word 'mood'. We may speak of a sad, or a depressed, or a constricted affect with regards to the person's emotional condition. Therefore, when a person's emotional behaviour falls outside the expected range of modulation we say that he/she suffers from an affective (in other words emotional) illness. On one extreme we have the depressive affective disorders, while on the other we have the manic affective disorders. In a way these are opposite of one another but in some individuals both of these two conditions are found and they usually alternate in the appearance of their symptomatology. Even though depression and its related disorders are not considered to be a major player in the psychopathology of leadership,[14] it is necessary to briefly go over their basic characteristics for several reasons: first and foremost, they can have paranoia as one

---

[14] With this statement I am, by no means, implying that depression does not affect leaders. The examples one may put forth are countless. Depression is common enough to be encountered in all types of individuals which hold distinction in their societies including politics, religion, the arts, and the military among others. In its severe form however, it is readily recognized and frequently treated. Even though it may be recurrent, it seldom spans a person's lifetime, unlike the psychotic and personality disorders, and therefore, may not impinge on the style of one's leadership. It does of course play an important role if it manifests during a leader's period in office. It is of greater interest, however, when it appears as part of a cyclic disorder in which it alternates with manic situations.

of their symptoms and thus affect leadership; second, some students of leadership consider depression and mania to be the conditions that make leaders effective; third, we need to understand their manic counterparts, since it often alternates with them. The most well-known of these conditions is manic-depressive illness, which is medically called bipolar disorder. A related condition but with milder and less debilitating symptoms, is known as cyclothymic disorder. It, too, is characterized by alternating sadness and euphoria, but not to the extremes of a fully blown bipolar disorder.

As we did with the psychotic and personality disorders, let us now turn to the medical definitions of the affective disorders.

As per the DSM-IV, depression (or major depressive episode as it is formally called), is present when a person has at least five of the following nine symptoms and which must include at least either depressed mood or loss of interest in pleasurable activities:

1. Depressed mood most of the day, nearly every day, as indicated by either subjective report (for example, feels sad or empty) or observation made by others (for example, appears tearful);
2. Markedly diminished interest or pleasure in all, or almost all activities most of the day, nearly every day (as indicated by either subjective account or observation made by others);
3. Significant weight loss when not dieting or weight gain (for example, a change of more than 5 percent of body weight in a month), or increase or decrease in appetite nearly every day;
4. Insomnia or hypersomnia (excessive sleep) nearly every day;
5. Psychomotor retardation or agitation nearly every day;
6. Fatigue or loss of energy nearly every day;
7. Feelings of worthlessness or excessive or inappropriate guilt (which may be delusional) nearly every day;
8. Difficulty concentrating or indecisiveness nearly every day;
9. Recurrent thoughts of death, recurrent suicidal ideation without a specific plan, or a suicide attempt or a specific plan for committing suicide.[15]

In addition to the above criteria, there must be dysfunction in the patient's life, present for two or more weeks, or more than two months if due to bereavement. In other words, behaviour must be undeniably abnormal. Usually such a person is easily recognized even by non-professionals who frequently direct him/her to seek help. The patient appears sad, often crying, overactive or underactive, unable to make

[15]   Reprinted with permission from the *Diagnostic and Statistical Manual of Mental Disorders*, Fourth Edition, (Copyright © 2000). American Psychiatric Association. All Rights Reserved.

decisions, emaciated, anxious, expressing the wish to die. There are often guilty feelings about the condition and a tendency towards self-depreciation.

Either subjectively or objectively, the depressed person cannot get much satisfaction out of their life; nor can any attempts by well-meaning friends and relatives help them break out of their situation. Moreover, these persons do not appear to be able to get themselves to enjoy activities such as hobbies, going out, or travel that used to give them pleasure. They become withdrawn and secluded, even to the point of self-neglect. Significant changes of their sleeping habits may occur as well as psychomotor retardation which refers to a state of apathy accompanied by stillness or motionlessness. Conversely they may exhibit agitation, the opposite of psychomotor retardation, and which pertains to a state of hyperalertness, anxiety, and hyperactivity.

The depressed person tires easily and feels as if he or she had no strength to accomplish simple chores. Not only does the person feel sad, tired, anxious, and unable to sleep, he feels responsible for the condition, thinks he deserves to be like that, and considers himself a burden on others; consequently they are at a loss as to the next action in their life. The most dangerous and serious diagnostic criterion however, as it can be surmised, is suicidality because it can be fatal. Often enough, depressed people manage to commit suicide (Hayman 1993) and it is very important that they are prevented from doing so. This is a common reason why these people get admitted in psychiatric hospitals.

Shakespeare (Craig 1914), that astute observer and exposé of human behaviour, gave us one of the most eloquent descriptions of the disorder in his play *Hamlet*:

> To be, or not to be, that is the question
> Whether 'tis nobler in the mind to suffer
> The slings and arrows of outrageous fortune,
> Or to take arms against a sea of troubles,
> And by opposing, end them? To die: to sleep
> No more; and by a sleep, to say we end
> The heart-ache and the thousand natural shocks
> That flesh is heir to?

This perhaps represents one of the most astute descriptions of depression, suicidality, and the ambivalence of the depressed person regarding life and death. Unfortunately, often enough, suicide wins over.

Whereas depression can be easily spotted by others, it is frequently more difficult to identify manic people even though their behaviour is perceived as abnormal. According to the DSM-IV it is defined as a period of at least one week which is characterized by an abnormally and persistently elevated, expansive or irritable mood, during which any three of the following nine criteria can be present:[16]

1. Inflated self-esteem or grandiosity;
2. Decreased need for sleep;
3. More talkative than usual or inability to stop talking;
4. Lack of sleep nearly every day;
5. Agitation or slowed down motor behaviour;
6. Feeling that one's thoughts and ideas are racing through their heads to the point that they cannot keep up with them;
7. Distractibility and inability to stay focused;
8. Increase in goal-directed activities (either socially, at work or school, or sexually) or agitation;
9. Excessive involvement in pleasurable activities that have a high potential for painful consequences (for example, engaging in unrestrained buying sprees, sexual indiscretions, or foolish business investments).[17]

As with depression, there must be sufficient functional disability. This is almost the opposite of major depression; during a manic episode the patient is usually overactive, talks excessively and becomes easily irritable, sleepless, and overbearing. He may engage in sexual escapades, close shaky deals, or undergo distant travel at the spur of a moment. An acute manic episode may at times be indistinguishable from acute psychosis. This was described earlier in this chapter.

For both depression and mania the diagnosis should not be made if their symptoms can be explained by another medical condition. There appear to be many mimickers of these disorders; however they are beyond the scope of our discussion. Suffice it to re-emphasize that the most appropriate individuals to diagnose and treat them are the mental health professionals. Another word of caution is, again, necessary here. Medical students are frequently advised to resist diagnosing themselves as suffering from every malady they study. This is a well-known phenomenon that is called the medical student syndrome.[18] Everyone, at one point or another, experiences either sadness or elation. This does not mean that they exhibit signs of psychiatric illness. Such feelings are part

---

[16] Some medical terms have been simplified where necessary or appropriate, to facilitate their understanding by non-professional readers. For example, criterion 6 has been simplified from 'flight of ideas'.

[17] Reprinted with permission from the *Diagnostic and Statistical Manual of Mental Disorders*, Fourth Edition, (Copyright © 2000). American Psychiatric Association. All Rights Reserved.

[18] This syndrome can apply equally to students of psychology as well.

and parcel of the human condition and experience, and as such, they are shared by all. By the same token, the readers must refrain from self-diagnosing the conditions described above. If some are totally convinced that they suffer from one of these conditions, I suggest they seek medical advice.

It was stated above that in certain individuals there is a tendency to alternate from depression to mania. These people are called, appropriately, manic-depressives or bipolar patients. There are various types of combinations that may appear in a certain patient; one may only have recurrent depression or recurrent mania; or alternation between the two, either with or without an intervening period of normal behaviour; and various others. Depression alone is less debilitating than either mania alone or bipolar disorder and its variants. However, many great historical figures are reputed to have suffered from bipolar illness along with a score of other individuals in the fields of religion, literature, the arts, and science. I would like to quote a scientist whose bipolar disorder both inhibited as well as enhanced his career. E.S. Copeland had a family history of bipolar illness and exhibited his first symptoms as he was beginning a medical education (Copeland 2009). He was advised to switch field and became a radiation biologist working at the National Institute of Health in Maryland, US. Several times his life was disrupted due to hospitalization. At other times, he formulated astrophysical and medical hypotheses that his mentors and colleagues found most unusual but plausible. He states:

> A source of encouragement in this struggle is that numerous giants in human history are reputed to have had manic-depressive illness. These include Handel, Poe, Coleridge, Galileo, Michelangelo, DaVinci, Beethoven, Bach, Tchaikovsky, Lincoln and Churchill. It is said that society without bipolars would be rather dull and unproductive.

> Bipolar affective disorder, like no other phenomenon, gives one the chance to look at oneself, to see what one has done. Coming to the end of a wave gives a chance to look back at the crest, a chance to see what one has accomplished. 'Normal' people with smooth, less fractured lives rarely get this chance. Manics get the opportunity to ponder their great ideas and yet to realize that despite these fractures and these ideas, they are like everyone else.

Langer and Roth's (1975) research showed that 'normal people have an illusionary sense of control' especially when their lives appear to run uneventfully. People like Galileo, who were persecuted for their beliefs, may have enough disinhibition to stand up to the establishment and effect change. As Copeland says, these people are like everyone else, their condition differing in degree and not in kind from others. The full expression of these illnesses is severe enough to render the sufferer dysfunctional, and consequently marginalized just like their psychotic and schizophrenic counterparts. There are, however, people whose symptomatology is far less severe than the bipolars' or the depressives'. As expected, the latter are shown by research to have relatives who are afflicted with more severe affective disorders, again just like their psychotic counterparts. These individuals show tendencies towards the severe forms of affective disorders but their symptoms are milder and do not result in significant dysfunction and marginalization.

Those who exhibit mild forms of depression are known as *dysthymic* people; they never appear quite happy with themselves and the world, and always complain about this or the other issue, but do not, usually, become severely depressed or suicidal; then we have the *hypomanic* individuals who exhibit mild forms of mania; and if they tend to alternate between the two conditions, they are known as *cyclothymics*. It is to the last two (hypomanics and cyclothymics) that we turn our attention now as they, too, may fulfil the requirements to become leaders of their social groups. Their afflictions are not severe enough to bring about marginalization, yet they confer on them a difference of degree as well as kind, that enables them to be noticed by others. Hypomanic individuals, especially, project vibrancy and energy onto their followers, who in turn, look up to them in great admiration; part one of the leadership ingredients – admiration by others – is thus fulfilled. St Paul's astounding energy and lack of fatigue was instrumental in spreading the gospel of Christ to the world of antiquity; this he achieved by means of extensive travel (personal contact) and epistles (letters). One could suppose that hypomania was a constituent of his personality.

Ghaemi (2011) believes that 'depression makes leaders more realistic and empathic, and mania makes them more creative and resilient', and therefore better leaders in times of tumult. He describes various historical leaders who had been known to have suffered from affective disorders in order to prove his position. What, however, may be underlying these disorders, and this has been argued elsewhere as well, is paranoia, which can be part of their symptomatology. For instance, he argues that General William Tecumseh Sherman's depressive breakdown in Kentucky helped him muster the resilience he needed to win battles during the civil war. He is quoted to have written 'I am afraid of my own shadow', and goes on to describe how he suddenly became convinced that he was surrounded by spies and that his troops were in imminent danger (Sherman 1889). Depressed he may have been, however it was his underlying paranoia that influenced his decisions and actions. His psychiatric condition, depression with paranoid delusions (psychotic depression) was also corroborated by his brother who wrote to him 'You are not only in error but are laboring under some strange delusions' (Ghaemi 2011).

In the field of arts and creativity, as we have seen previously, there is an over-representation of psychopathology, not only among artists but also especially among their close biological relatives. George Frideric Handel for example is reputed to have composed his masterpiece *The Messiah* during the span of 24 days! He is reputed to have been in a hypomanic state during that time of outpouring creativity. Van Gogh's various attacks of psychotic delusions (and probably epilepsy) are also well known; his symptoms undoubtedly influenced his artistic style and output. Salvador Dali and Joan Miró immediately come to mind as artists who danced to a different tune than most 'normal' people. In discussing the relationship between schizophrenia and language I expounded on the effect of mental illness on the arts and creativity and I will therefore not be repeating the discussion here.

Creativity, artistic inclinations, and other achievements are certainly part and parcel of the mildly affected bipolars. The question that arises is whether such personality types are also conducive to a leadership potential. Certainly many world leaders have been described as having bipolar disorder. These include such persons as Napoleon, Churchill, Lincoln, Theodore Roosevelt, Papandreou, and Alexander Hamilton among a multitude of others. If paranoia plays an important role into the making of these people's personality, then malignant behaviour will result. Lieb (2008) makes the point clear when he writes that:

> We uncover manic depressive disorder as a hidden cause of dictatorship, mass killing, and war, and ... the psychopathology of the disorder can be a key factor in the political pathology of tyranny ... Thus manic depressive disorder is variable to the extreme of paradox. Key to the destroyer is an indifference to the suffering of others, a need to control everyone and everything, a resistance to reason, and grandiose and paranoid delusions.

Paranoia in other words makes all the difference in the disposition of a leader as it characterizes many of the psychiatric states, both in the affective and the psychotic spectrum as the common denominator of leadership. Various students of leadership identify different personality styles as conducive to leadership. Invariably however, and often without overtly recognizing it, they describe paranoia as a constituent part of these personalities.

These statistically abnormal individuals may have been favoured by natural selection to fulfil certain guidance and leadership roles in society and hence improve their group's chances of survival. The price to pay is the steady appearance of more severely afflicted individuals with frank psychosis. In other words, they were selected out through the process of evolution precisely because their mutations resulted in such personality characteristics that allowed them to assume leadership roles. As leaders, they would have a better chance to reproduce and pass on their genes to posterity. Like the analogy we discussed earlier regarding the evolutionary advantage of the thalassaemia trait, and the protection it confers on carriers against malaria, but with the price of several members of the group dying out from major thalassaemia, the ultimate pressure is on the survival of the majority. Anything that enhances that will be selected into the gene pool.

In Chapter 2 we argued that schizophrenia is not only the price we pay for the faculty of language, but also the disease that made us human. The psychotic disorders in general probably help supply us with individuals possessing attributes and talents that enrich our lives. It so happens that, in doing so, they frequently bring about strife and discontent between themselves and other people. This is where society must intervene to keep order and justice. And this is where non-paranoid individuals should have insight and recognize the paranoid personality in action, and take defence. Whereas in times of conflict and strife the paranoid can help mobilize our resources, in times of peace the same personality becomes dysfunctional (the fighting never quite ends), and uncooperative. This is why great leaders and heroes frequently end up in jail or become marginalized towards the end of their careers. Their character pathology is part of what Maddi (1986) defines as personality; 'a stable set of tendencies and characteristics that determine those commonalities and differences in people's psychological behaviour (thoughts, feelings, and actions) that have continuity in time and that may not be easily understood as the sole result of the social and biological pressures of the moment'. That is why leaders such as Churchill, de Gaulle and Thatcher were apotheosized for their leadership during times of crisis but were nonetheless deposed when the tumult passed. Their character pathology was only useful for the rough times. In this spirit, *The Economist* (1990) asks 'How many men can you think of who led a revolution and then made a success of leading their country?' They come up only with George Washington, and quickly move on to the twentieth century to point out all the peacetime 'failures' of successful revolutionaries. They state; 'Kwame Nkrumah led his country from colonial Gold Coast to independent Ghana, and then to economic ruin … . Communism's revolutionaries had bad ideas (Lenin, Ortega, Pol Pot), and given the chance (Castro, Enver Hoxha, Mao Zedong) have made a habit of imposing them for a horribly long time'. Ghaemi (2011) expresses this phenomenon succinctly when he writes that 'when times are good, when peace reigns, and the ship of state only needs to sail straight, mentally healthy people function well as our leaders. When our world is in tumult, mentally ill leaders function best'. A prime example according to *The Economist* is Churchill, an 'impeccable democrat' whose wartime record was not matched by his peacetime performance. Society needs to have appropriate checks and balances in place in order to appoint the best leaders for each situation, but be able to remove them peacefully when their services are no longer necessary.

9. Society and its leaders

> The voyage of discovery lies not in seeking new horizons,
> but in seeing with new eyes.
>
> Marcel Proust

I.

Time and again in this book we dealt with hierarchies and pecking orders
in describing social organization. In the animal kingdom, as well as in
human groups, there are systems in place that ensure the smooth running
of their affairs; to accomplish this, individuals must be ranked according
to certain criteria that determine their station in life. It was argued
previously that the emergence of leaders and the tendency to form
hierarchies is to a large extent genetically preconditioned and is therefore
biologically determined. That this is the case in social animals is
accepted easily; when we attempt to apply the same way of thinking to
humans, however, all bets are off. The nature versus nurture business
re-emerges and people have difficulty accepting that their behaviour can
be explained better in terms of genetics rather than learning. People
intuitively prefer social phenomena to be considered as events resulting
from specific time-and-place-locked factors producing such outcomes as
leadership and followership independent of biological determinants.
Along these lines of thought, various authors have proposed that adaptations for leadership and followership do not exist as such, and that
behaviours associated with such roles are simply by-products of adaptations for dominance and submission (Alexander 1987, Hollander 1985,
Nicholson 2000, Wilson 1975). Part of the reason of course, is that if we
were to accept the genetic basis of our behaviour, we could do away with
all responsibility for our actions: a murderer would claim that murdering
is part of his genetic predisposition; and so would a rapist and a thief;
and great achievements would be explained away in terms of a particular
genetic endowment.

If however we accept that language and culture are products of
biological evolution, then we should also accept that their outcomes are

171

determined by evolution, which ultimately is driven by genetics. The issue to be concerned with is the extent to which subsequent factors (that is, epigenetic processes) play a role in determining behaviour (including the emergence of leadership) and how they can be potentially manipulated for the benefit of society.

Obviously, the attempt here is not to downplay either nature or nurture. Rather, we strive to place each in its rightful position. From antiquity down to modern times, hierarchies have been justified on natural grounds as well as other necessities. In human societies, as we saw previously, inequality was tolerated as a necessary condition to enhance the group's interests *vis-à-vis* other groups; thus, the necessity for leaders arises. Price (2006) mentions that, 'without this kind of unequal consideration, leadership would not be recognizable to us'. It is obvious that, at times, one group's interests come in to conflict with outsiders' and create moral and deontological dilemmas.[1] Reality however dictates that 'leaders and followers must be willing to put the interests and projects of group members ahead of the interests and projects of outsiders' (Price and Hicks 2006). Therefore, there is a need to have the right individual rise in the right circumstances, in order to see the group through its interests, troubles, and needs. Such individuals are the product of their genetic endowment and the imprints of history as well as personal experience. Environmental and developmental factors are likely to determine the phenotypic expression of genetic traits associated with leadership (West-Eberhard 2003).

Initial efforts to delineate the personality correlates of leadership, an approach that attempted to define its critical characteristics, resulted in a laundry list of traits, needs, and motives that supposedly distinguish leaders from non-leaders reliably; such traits included attributes such as power, ambition, extraversion, self-confidence, and intelligence (Van Vugt 2006). In the majority of these reviews only one trait emerged as related to leadership and that was self-confidence (Judge *et al.* 2002). Two other traits, dominance and masculinity-femininity, achieved a statistically significant association with leadership emergence (Lord *et al.* 1986).

An overall consensus has recently emerged about a five-factor model of personality (often termed the Big Five) that can be used to describe the most salient aspects of personality (Tupes and Christal 1961, Goldberg

---

[1] These dilemmas are expressed by moral and utilitarian philosophers, starting with John Stuart Mill who holds that an action should be judged on the degree of happiness it brings to the largest number of people possible. For a discussion, see Price and Hicks's review (2006), p. 133.

1990, Norman 1963). It has been validated cross-culturally through research in many countries (McCrae and Costa 1997). Evidence indicates that the constituents of the Big Five model are heritable and stable over time (Costa and McCrae 1988, Digman 1989) lending credence to the biological basis of the phenomenon. The dimensions comprising the five-factor model are neuroticism, extraversion, openness to experience, agreeableness, and conscientiousness (Judge *et al.* 2002).[2] Of the five factors, extraversion is strongly related to social leadership (Costa and McCrae 1988) and, according to Watson and Clark (1997), to leader emergence in groups. Hogan *et al.* (1994) noted that extraversion is related to the perception of appearing as leader-like. Extraverts are known to be energetic, lively, and confident people.

Kirkpatrick and Locke (1991) commented, that 'leaders are more likely than non-leaders to have a high level of energy and stamina and to be generally active, lively, and often restless'. Such characteristics will result from and confer self-confidence in emerging leaders. FDR's sociability and therefore extraversion, was described as his strongest asset, one that certainly helped him climb to the top (Jackson 2003). Adjectives used to describe individuals who emerged as leaders in leaderless group discussions included among others, active, assertive, and energetic (Gough 1988). Such traits, as we saw earlier, can also be seen in paranoid and hypomanic people; they are substantial in inducing the perception of leadership among potential followers. In later research, the emphasis shifted towards the study of leader functions and styles in view of task demands and the needs of followers, and this is known as the situational or state approach (Bass and Stogdill 1990) by which leadership phenomena can be considered.

The degree of each factor's contribution in the moulding of personality has been hotly debated. It is undeniable however that, in our times, the pendulum has swung favourably towards nature, as evidenced by the cross-cultural validity of the Big Five model described above. After all, the human genome has recently been mapped (Bentley *et al.* 2001) and this accomplishment has created an avalanche of discoveries relating to

---

[2]   They discuss these factors as follows: 'Neuroticism represents the tendency to exhibit poor emotional adjustment and experience negative affects, such as anxiety, insecurity, and hostility. Extraversion represents the tendency to be sociable, assertive, active, and to experience positive affects, such as energy and zeal. Openness to Experience is the disposition to be imaginative, nonconforming, unconventional, and autonomous. Agreeableness is the tendency to be trusting, compliant, caring, and gentle. Conscientiousness is comprised of two related facets: achievement and dependability.'

the genetic determinants of many diseases, which were until recently thought of as sporadic and environmentally dependent.[3] Moreover, many other aspects of our behaviour appear to have genetic influences; whether, for example, a person will respond favourably or not to a medicinal drug or who will develop certain unwanted but serious side effects, is partly (if not wholly) genetically determined.[4]

That the environment also plays an important role in shaping behaviour, within the limits set by genes, continues to be considered an axiom. Baby Mozart, for example, was musically endowed by nature. Growing up in a family of musicians and composers probably enhanced his musical career tremendously; if he had been adopted away and raised by farmers, he would still probably have exhibited musical talents and skill. Would he have also grown to become the great composer as know him? Perhaps not. The environment he grew up in helped his genetically inherited talent reach its maximum potential. The nature via nurture proposition of Ridley (2003) becomes relevant here. For example, research on children's desire to take on leadership roles, a biological tendency, has shown that it is contingent upon the ambition levels of parents (Bass 1960, Klonsky 1983). Such findings corroborate the nature–nurture hypothesis.

Moreover, adult adaptability is also contingent on such nature–nurture interplay, because recent advances in the neurosciences have brought about a change in the dogma that the brain is immutable and any damage or neuronal loss is irreplaceable. The current notion is that neuronal plasticity (capacity for reorganization) continues throughout life, so that rehabilitative therapies following a stroke, to use a common example, result in functional if not anatomical improvements. This is the basis of such rehabilitative treatments as physiotherapy, occupational therapy, and speech therapy. This plasticity is much more readily apparent in children whose nervous system is still developing.

Not only does the environment influence and shape behaviour, it must do so at set times during biological growth in order to help the organism reach its predetermined developmental stages. Kittens are born with their eyes shut for the first few days of their life; thereafter the eyes become unsealed and, by the influence of light (the environment), eyesight

---

[3]   Our genome is simply a compilation of all the genes that make up our 23 pairs of chromosomes.

[4]   A whole new discipline called pharmacogenomics has recently sprung out of this observation, which attempts to explain and predict a person's response to drugs in terms of his genetic endowment.

develops. If those eyes remain sealed or are experimentally kept blind-folded past a critical stage for the development of sight, the kittens will remain blind after their eyes open. The sense of vision is programmed genetically. Whether it will develop normally depends on environmental conditions and influences. The same holds true for most of our capabilities and talents such as our intelligence, height, skills, social manners, and ability to lead.

Language dominance (whether it localizes in the left or the right hemisphere), can easily switch sides up until the age of about eight years; in other words, if a child is affected by a process that damages his language centres on one side of the brain, this function can easily go to the opposite hemisphere. Such processes may include trauma, stroke, or epilepsy. That is why surgery to cure intractable seizures is done more easily, and preferably, before the age of eight years, especially if the dominant hemisphere will be affected. Language lateralization is another example of the 'plasticity' of the nervous system that comes about in response to environmental cues.

In the past, left handers were forced to switch to the right hand as their dominant one. From birth to death, genes get environmental cues to activate or deactivate biochemical processes (protein synthesis) and effect changes in behaviour that are better suited for survival and success. This holds true for leaders as well, provided that they are genetically endowed with the capacity to transform into such. Post (2004) reminds us that many revolutionary leaders have experienced social upheavals during their formative adolescent years. Paranoia may thrive during social upheavals precisely because it was nurtured under similar conditions.

Genes determine the limits of our behavioural potential, and the environment our actual achievements. These influences may be positive (think Mozart), or negative (think Hitler). Thus, whether a person acts constructively or destructively will depend, to some extent, on the type of environment in which he finds himself. Paranoid individuals will thrive in an environment of suspicion, of rapid social changes, and political turmoil; under such circumstances they are able to muster the energy and willingness to come forth, declare their (often unfounded) beliefs, and demand that followers submit to them, blindly surrendering their own will and thought processes in servitude to the greater cause, which naturally, is represented by themselves.

The issue of experiential influences on learning and personality development was discussed by Bennis (2003) who includes such factors as broad and continuing education, extensive travel and/or exile, a rich private life, key associations with mentors and groups, and, quite interestingly, idiosyncratic families. I reordered Bennis' sequence of these factors to emphasize *idiosyncratic families*; in other words, families that are outside the typical boundaries of behaviour as would be expected in their particular groups. Oddity was identified previously as a trait common in the paranoid personality disorders and other psychoses. This is behaviour falling outside the range of expected and observable behaviours as we saw in Chapter 7 of this book. It ultimately depends on the activation of the genes that predispose us to such behaviour, but the process depends also on environmental (experiential) cues.

There are times when the paranoid individual's way of thinking is appealing precisely because it reifies the group's collective (and at times unconscious) sensitivities, fears, wishes, and predispositions, and this is partly because, as Hampton and Schroeder Burnham state, 'Paranoia is not just extremism, not just psychosis, not just abnormality' (1990). As we have previously stated, paranoid individuals, having escaped the ravages of full-blown schizophrenia, can actually reach high echelons of their respective professions, owing to their cognitive and communicative abilities, traits that evolved together in archetypal humans. Hampton and Schroeder Burnham also state that 'paranoia is also safety, sanity, and normal when we are in danger. Paranoia galvanizes, stimulates and fuels our competitive natures. Paranoia gives our leaders their motivation and guidance' (ibid.). They go so far as to claim that we all possess a dose of paranoia, some to a greater and some to a lesser degree and those with the least amount are usually naive and are easily taken advantage of by others. In other words, they consider paranoia to be another human trait, just as language is. Post (2004) claims 'in a conspirational milieu, having paranoid traits is not only *not* dysfunctional, it is necessary for survival' in both open as well as closed totalitarian societies, qualifying it with the observation that stress, in combination with the leader's personality, significantly influences the way and the type of decisions made (Porcelli *et al.* 2012). Hitler for example, held even closer to his (paranoid) convictions as the stress of losing the war increased. Whimsical acts such as assuming the command of his army in the field and claiming 'unbounded confidence in myself, so that nothing, whatever it may be, can throw me out of the saddle, so that nothing can shake me' are thus understood as products of a paranoid personality under stress (Bullock 1991). Nixon's paranoia and all-inclusive suspiciousness skyrocketed as the particulars of the Watergate affair were revealed; his 'grandiose fantasies' (Brodie 1981) coupled with his 'poor reality testing' (Loewenberg 1988) induced his eloquent defensive lies just prior to his resignation and political doom.

If we consider the fact that close relatives of schizophrenics have paranoid personalities, but are nevertheless high functioning, then Hampton and Schroeder Burnham's proposition becomes plausible. As they put it:

> Everyone is paranoid, or should be, when it comes to his physical, mental, and emotional well-being. If one has too little paranoia, he or she may be extremely naive, immature and susceptible to control by others. Those who are overly paranoid are generally aggressive, demanding, controlling, and extremely difficult to live with. But they may well be successful in managerial [that is, *leadership*] roles; as corporate executives, or political and religious leaders.

The last sentence quoted above encapsulates the essence of my argument: paranoid individuals, especially those who possess enough energy and intelligence (and are not overtly psychotic), assume the roles of leadership in their societies. Business (economy), politics, the army, and religion are areas in which the paranoid personality thrives. They are also those areas of human activity that define a society and its culture. One may take issue with this position, however, since many of us can lead normal, quiet lives without evidence of paranoid thinking. This may be true, especially in the case of followers or when leaders function under relatively stable circumstances. As we will see later on in this chapter, paranoid leaders tend to deteriorate as their life progresses especially under challenging circumstances. The Sudanese president Jaafar Nimeiri turned to deepening religious beliefs and paranoia as his age advanced and his health deteriorated, to the point of going back on earlier proclamations about respect of heavenly religions; thus, he suppressed ruthlessly his Christian countrymen (Khalid 1985). Former British Prime Minister Tony Blair's turn to religion following his political retirement is also intriguing, if not indicative of worsening guilt regarding his deeds and alliance with George W. Bush while in office.

We should remember, nonetheless, that many students of human behaviour consider normality and abnormality to fall on a continuum and this same point was also made elsewhere in this book. Also, a continuum of degrees of paranoia appears to exist. Hampton and Schroeder Burnham (1990) divide people into three categories depending on their degree of paranoia, stating that those with a high degree tend to dominate the rest and also seem to prosper the most; those with a moderate degree seem to have enough to be able to remain vigilant and protect themselves and their families, as well as lead satisfactory lives; and those with the lowest degree or no paranoia at all (remember the continuum), are situated at the end of the pecking order, are dominated by all the rest, and are frequently taken advantage of. These authors claim that the last category contains very few individuals indeed, and attribute this to evolutionary processes. Whether evolution tends to remove the non-paranoid individuals from our world is debatable. I am of the opinion that non-paranoids have been and always will be with us in order to complete the pecking order. Evolutionary pressures tend to increase or decrease the numbers of certain individuals from a population in a way analogous to the situation we discussed earlier regarding the thalassaemia and sickle-cell anaemia genes in the Mediterranean area and in North Africa.

The leaders we elect personify our deepest collective dreams and wishes. We project onto them our (unconscious?) ideas about whom and what we desire to be and where we are headed. Leadership, then 'is the social counterpart to rationality. People use this process to achieve plans and goals that could not otherwise be achieved' (Price and Hicks 2006). Therefore, if leaders somehow manage to embody and reflect these desires and ideas effectively, they can rise in our social hierarchies by appealing to our innermost ideals and become charismatic. They are capable of communicating through what Denning (2007) calls a hidden pattern of getting people's attention; this they accomplish by stimulating their desire for changing their predicament, and reinforcing that desire with reasons that reflect their listeners' wishes. Elizabeth Faier's view of leadership fits nicely with these notions because she considers it to be 'a process wholly dependent on human action, local problems, social structures, history and systems of social beliefs, values and symbols' (quoted in Wren 2006). All the things, in other words, which make up who the group members are, what they want, and where they are headed. The role of the leader, according to Harvey (2006) is to 'frame stories and events to help the group understand the world, themselves, and other groups, as well as to identify or solve problems'. The story – the narrative in other words – can have energizing effects on a group depending on the way it is told. Thus, the skilful use of language by a leader becomes pivotal in getting his followers' motivation to the level needed to bring about effective action. A person with paranoid tendencies uses language in precisely such a way. Homer's narratives have nourished generations of Greeks throughout history and helped glue together their identity for centuries. St Paul's narratives, on the other hand, galvanized those early Christians into solidifying their beliefs, actions, and faith; they still do so for millions. Paul's letters of interpretation of the story and teachings of Christ effectively spread Christianity beyond anyone's imagination.

Post (2004) in his psychoanalytic approach, asserts that certain 'crucial aspects of the psychology of the leader ... like a key fit and unlock certain aspects of the psychology of their followers', and explains the process by drawing on concepts about narcissism. My views regarding narcissism and paranoia have been expounded earlier. Willner (1984), who does not accept such concepts unconditionally, has distilled the leader–follower relationship in four key observations; the leader is considered akin to being superhuman (think of Turkey's Ataturk); the followers unquestionably believe the leader's statements (think of Khomeini); the followers comply with the leader's directives for action (think of Hitler); and the followers give their leader unqualified emotional support (think of Osama Bin Laden). Leadership, according to Ospina and Sorenson (2006), 'is intrinsically relational and social in nature, is the result of shared meaning-making, and is rooted in context or place. Leadership from this perspective is not only necessary and possible ... but ubiquitous and emergent'. The leader's role is precisely to make, use, or construct explanatory models in this 'meaning-making' process.[5] As Meindl (1990) noted, there is nearly universal consensus that leadership is a function of leaders and followers embedded in a rich web of negotiated meanings and contextual variables. Effective leadership therefore should be considered a phenomenon that, among other functions, achieves a substantial management of meaning (Smircich and Morgan 1982). On the part of followers, Lord and Maher (1991) use the analogous to explanatory models term, schemas, in describing their pre-conceived notions as to what the leader should be like and what he should represent. Such schemas are conveyed and achieve substantial expression through the proper use of language.

Leadership characteristics therefore, along with the core personality profile that determines them, can be studied and assessed through an analysis of verbal behaviour (Landis 2011). This can be accomplished through formal language-analysis tools that nowadays are computerized,[6] or by the observation of casual words that float to the surface without

---

[5] The concept of explanatory models was originally coined by Arthur Kleinman, MD in his book *Patients and Healers in the Context of Culture*, where he uses it to describe congruencies and incongruences between physicians (healers) and patients; congruent explanatory models led to compliance with treatment, in other words with the acceptance of the authority (and leadership) of the healer.

[6] DICTION is a software program explicitly designed to examine the linguistic elements of political leaders. It uses 31 predefined dictionaries, containing over 10,000 search words, to analyse a passage. They are expressly concerned with words 'most frequently encountered in contemporary American public discourse' (Hart 1984). They only contain individual words, which are subjected to statistical procedures and are also corrected for context (Hart 2000). The

conscious effort; these are usually in the form of spontaneous comments or humorous remarks; such utterances are colloquially known as Freudian slips and can give the observer clues about latent traits of a speaker. Such an analysis was performed on President Bush's verbal output before and after the 9/11 crisis (Bligh *et al.* 2004). Six constructs were examined as follows: optimism, collectives, faith, patriotism, aggression, and ambivalence. According to the results of this analysis, 'In the wake of the crisis of 9/11, President Bush's speeches were more likely to reference the American people as a collective, and incorporate more patriotic, faith-based themes. In addition, the President's post-crisis speeches were more aggressive and less ambivalent when compared with those given in the first nine months of his administration.' A significant factor that contributed towards such a change in the president's language must have been an 'awakening' of latent paranoid feelings about the dire situation in which the American nation found itself. In the post-crisis period there was no room for ambivalence or 'softy' outlooks. The enemy was real, identified, and targeted. A job had to be done. The language became crispy clear and to the point. Consider the following excerpt:

> Tonight we are a country awakened to danger and called to defend freedom. Our grief has turned to anger, and anger to resolution. Whether we bring our enemies to justice, or bring justice to our enemies, justice will be done. (Bush 2002b)

Meanings were shared and the American nation approved and followed. We will return to this interplay later on.

At this point, I think it's worth using J. Thomas Wren's (2006) quotations of several of his collaborating authors in describing the process of preparing their book *The Quest for a General Theory of Leadership*, which was a great source for myself in writing this volume. They sum up the points that were expounded above:

> Gill Robinson Hickman ... articulated a model of the leadership process that began with a need for action, followed by a recognition of purpose, communication, concurrence and willingness to participate, and, finally, collective action.

> James MacGregor Burns [contribution was that] 'As a process, leadership begins ... with palpable human wants and needs that can be broadly generalized. Potential leaders ... respond to these wants and legitimize them as needs deserving of recognition and response ... Conflict arises out of the

---

researcher can also create up to 10 customized dictionaries that can be adapted to specific research needs (Bligh *et al.* 2004)

competition of people for economic and psychological satisfactions … the clues to the mystery of leadership lie in a powerful equation: embattled values grounded in real wants, invigorated by conflict, empower leaders and activated followers to fashion deep and comprehensive change in the lives of people.'

Thus, President Bush's attributes of leadership switched overnight from disapproval and indifference to acceptance and applause. Similarly, when the German nation rallied around Hitler's prompts and declarations, it probably saw in him all its ideals reified. He must have awakened in them not only those feelings that were considered sacred, but in addition, all their common fears about their changing world. Hitler was not a normal person; by all measures of normality he was outside its boundaries. Yet he, like scores of other 'abnormal' leaders, managed to persuade his people that he represented their best interests and chances of dominance. This, in turn, symbolized their self-image and future aspirations. He was determined, inflexible, aggressive and paranoid. His paranoia induced his inflexibility, his determination, and what must have sounded as his 'straight talk'; not going around in circles, not beating around the bush. Things were called as they were, and blame was applied where it was (seemingly) due. Shirer (1969) attributes this abhorrent development to the humiliation Germany experienced after World War I. National embarrassment or shame primes people into acting in politically incorrect ways. Following repeated disappointments in its attempt to gain entry into the European Union, Turkey has hardened its stance and aggressive policies in the region of the Eastern Mediterranean, coming into conflict with the EU as a whole but also with individual countries such as Cyprus and Israel.

A psychoanalytic explanation of Hitler's success in rallying the support of German people was the fact that rationalism had induced a repression of their religious feelings (Nolte 1996) which were magnificently expressed by his ritualistic handling of language and his massive populace gatherings, which symbolized, according to Heer (1968), a 'Mass, the celebration of the sacred Great War'. Such claims may hold more truth than one might suspect; Brodie (1960) has shown that religious leaders are frequently delusional, psychotic and megalomaniac just as are political leaders, and have an amazing skill in swaying followers over to their camps. Psychosis and sociopathy can be useful ammunition for rising leaders.

Groups may rally behind leaders, however it is the leaders that lead, make decisions, and bring about change, be it for better or for worse. Post (2006) reminds us of the Cuban missile crisis and the mishandling of intelligence, not only about the actual state of affairs but also, and most importantly, because of 'too much emphasis on rationally analyzing the motives of the Soviets and the Cubans, with insufficient attention paid to the psychology of the two key actors, Khrushchev and Castro'. Added into the equation, we should also place Kennedy's personality and the way he reacted to the crisis. Ghaemi (2011) attributes his early failure (1961–62) and his late success (1962–63) on this affair, on the influence of chronic treatment with steroids and other psychotropic medications; they had resulted in impairment and enhancement of his abilities successively and perhaps induced hypomanic elements during the late phase. Moreover, his Addison's disease may have alternatively caused both depression and psychosis. Such factors most certainly played a role in his style of leadership.

Especially in times of hardship, economic depression, uncertainty about the future, and rapid social turmoil, when values and orthodoxies are questioned, anyone who appears stable, clinging to principles, and willing to fight for his ideas (hence with a propensity to violence, inflexibility, and charisma), will possess those characteristics that will enhance his rise to power. Focusing on a single source of evil, which needs to be cut off in order to cleanse the crowd, will enhance a charismatic leader–follower relationship. Desperation breeds desperate decisions and underscores misjudged choices. Post (2004) predicted that Osama bin Laden was 'on an expansive roll, with messianic grandiosity, ever expanding his vision'. Subsequent events have vindicated Post. Timing as well as context will help shape the nature of a charismatic leader–follower relationship. As Max Weber wrote (1978), there must be a readiness on the part of society to accept and follow a charismatic revolutionary leader.

Charisma is an attribute that is conferred onto a leader by his followers in response to his inspirational conduct. The most conducive means for transmitting inspiration is of course language and the leader's use of it will, to a significant extend, determine the 'amount', so to speak, of charisma that followers will attribute to him. By the term language we mean any form of communication be it verbal, written, electronic, mannerist, or symbolic. Obama, as we will see later on, has capitalized on the wide availability of the Internet and email to get his charismatic/ inspirational points across. In that respect, he actualized the requirements that Conger and Kanungo (1998) considered important in making up the charismatic personality of a leader: the ability to inspire through a compelling vision, the steadfast commitment to that vision, and a demonstration of the attainability of that vision with the support and backing of the group. To that end, the leader must possess extraordinary attributes, or at least be perceived as possessing them by his followers, as initially proposed by Weber (1947).

Language emerges again as an important determinant of the charismatic process since it plays a key role and occupies a central position in its transmission towards, and the perception by, a leader's followers. This has been emphasized by several authors who stressed the gift of using language in an inspirational as well as an emotional manner (Hoyt *et al.* 2006, Riggio 2004). Skilful use of language in persuading and inspiring followers has been used by leaders at all levels, from preachers (Thrall *et al.* 1999) to US presidents (Mio *et al.* 2005). Besides persuading, a charismatic leader should also be effective by raising his followers' sense of worth, self-esteem, and belief in their capability of accomplishment. In that respect, a charismatic leader possesses what MacGregor Burns (1978) calls both transactional as well as transformational leadership styles. The former style refers to elements of social exchange as defined by the leader–follower relationship, while the latter refers to the empowerment that a leader confers onto his subjects in order to raise their level of commitment into a partnership of higher performance and morality (MacGregor Burns 1978). Thus, charisma becomes a means towards the inter-connectedness that characterizes those moments in history when great achievements have occurred. Pericles and the ancient Athenians, as we saw, had reached that point. This process operates at all levels of true and effective leadership enhancing first and foremost, survival.[7]

During times of crisis then, individuals who appear determined to carry on the common cause will prevail. Such people might even (and usually) manage to muster the energy to lead their people to a successful outcome, strengthening in this way the conception of their charismatic personality and visionary leadership. Hollander and Julian state that 'the individual who best fits the followers' shared conceptions will emerge as the group leader' (1969). Reagan carried the 1979 US election with a sweeping victory because he managed to arouse hope, pride, and patriotism in Americans at a time when all these values faired low, as a result of the humiliation that was suffered in Iran. Carter's handling of that crisis, probably as a result of a non-paranoid or low-paranoia personality, appeared to be weak and inadequate; the change that had occurred found him pitifully unprepared to show leadership to a puzzled nation, and this handling cost him the re-election. John Perkins (2004) has characterized Carter as an anomaly compared to his predecessor and

---

[7] Survival here may refer to physical existence or the success of an organization, company or any other social group.

his successor, a 'naively archaic ... throwback to the ideals that molded' the American nation.

Author and filmmaker Michael Moore (2003) explains, in somewhat apologetic tones, why Americans frequently vote in favour of the Republican Party in national elections even though surveys consistently reveal that, in their majority, they espouse liberal ideas: 'Conservatives are real leaders. They have the courage of their convictions. They don't bend, they don't break, and they never give in. They are relentless in pursuit of their ideals ... they actually believe in something.' A. Kubizek (1955), a close associate and biographer of Hitler, recounted that 'the most outstanding trait in my friend's character was ... the unparalleled consistency in everything he said and did. There was in his nature something firm, inflexible, immovable, obstinately rigid, which manifested itself in his profound seriousness and was at the bottom of all his other characteristics.'

In hopeless situations, whoever appears steadfast wins the people's hearts. Language plays a key role here since it is the means by which the dream of new possibilities can be communicated (Bennis 2003). To return to Hitler's personality, it was his insistence for no compromise, his persistence that he be in charge and his self-confidence, all expressed in a captivating language, that kept his political party going in the early 1930s. His unwavering stances finally won him the power he desired and gifted him the directorship of the Nazi Party (Bullock 1991).[8]

A leader should be prepared and able to not only lead his own group, but also lead against other groups as the situation dictates. Reagan appeared ready to do both. A football team leader must solidify cohesiveness within his team, and also come up with strategies to lead against the other team. In turn, followers, or the team, will respond; as the American nation did to the moral, motivational, and emotional uplift by their leader, President Bush (Bass 1998, Burns 1978).

In such a way, a threatening situation, or a changing milieu, will be handled appropriately and effectively. The leader–follower dyad will be effective so long as their relationship rests on common, but also complementary, ground, such that one fulfils the needs and aspirations of the other. The reality of their vicissitudes is thus defined and constructed by 'their social, political, legal and other interactions' (Crotty 1998). To quote from W. Drath, 'leadership happens when a community create a shared understanding of the moral obligations each has with the others to

---

[8] Nationalsozialistische Deutsche Arbeiterpartei was active in Germany from 1920 to 1945.

make sure that these demands are taken care of, so that the common cause is realized' (2001). According to the constructionist view of leadership, the phenomenon revolves around the process of making meaning and is an exchange between a group and an individual (leader), to whom leadership qualities are attributed (Ospina and Sorenson 2006).

A single leader usually emerges, even if the initial action was spontaneously prompted by a multitude. The leader will be necessary to guide and direct further action, as well as manage change, just as recent events in the Arab world have aptly demonstrated. As Bennis (2003) reminds us:

> Learning to lead is, on one level, learning to manage change. As we've seen, a leader imposes (in the most positive sense of the word) his or her philosophy on the organization,[9] creating or re-creating its culture. The organization then acts on that philosophy, carries out the mission, and the culture takes on a life of its own, becoming more cause than effect. But unless the leader continues to evolve, to adapt and adjust to external change, the organization will sooner or later stall.

Jimmy Carter did not fill that role, whereas Reagan did perfectly. Jacob Bronowski (1973) wrote that 'The world can only be grasped by action, not by contemplation.' Americans are now looking upon Obama to fulfil the role in the current global political, economic, and social crisis that exists. Non-interesting (that is, non-paranoid) leaders would not thrive at times of social mobilization. Despite Carter's apparent initial lack of effective handling of the Iranian crisis, and his subsequent replacement by Reagan, he eventually managed to re-emerge as a leader on a larger, worldwide scale through his efforts to advance democracy and human rights around the globe. This development came about as a result of his transformation. To see his world leadership through the eyes of a constructionist, we must consider the process that attributed the role to him: that is the international scene, and the need for respect for democracy and human rights. Thus, Jimmy Carter as a leader and Jimmy Carter's leadership would be distinct and separate entities. His latent leadership in effecting change, to use Hickman and Couto's construct (2006), rested on the world's impulse to create change and was achieved by first imagining that future, which subsequently, created meaning and inspired action.

---

9   The term organization can be applied to any group of people following a leader, from a company to a nation.

The notorious anthropologist Margaret Mead (1955) wrote that 'at times of individual or group crisis, the situation is more favorable for adaptive changes in habitual behaviors, beliefs and attitudes.' And, as Lincoln echoed long ago, 'The dogmas of the quiet past are inadequate to the stormy present ... As our case is new, so we must think anew, and act anew. We must disenthrall ourselves.'[10] Such changes can be funnelled in certain directions by individual leaders who won't 'budge', and as Bennis says, 'chaos is all around us now, but the leader knows that chaos is the beginning, not the end. Chaos is the source of energy and momentum'. Lewin (1951) on the other hand, has proposed, in his field theory, that all interrelated factors, circumstances and players, including leaders, should be accounted for in the equation for social change. In other words, the field of change is far more complicated that the actions of one single leader and the dyadic relationship that forms with followers.

To illustrate this complexity, Robinson Hickman and Couto (2006) describe the case of African Americans' struggle for equality in the early 1950s and how that led to the civil rights movement of Prince Edward County in Virginia. Through a detailed description of events they guide us up to the emergence of Barbara Rose Johns, a local student, whose actions culminated in the organization of a protest that was instrumental in launching the anti-segregation movement for schools, eventually ending public school segregation in the United States. They do this by trying to account for as many other variables as they can that had contributed or played a key role in the succession of events, such as the reaction of parents and teachers, local authorities, the NAACP,[11] and the American nation at large. Their final argument is that Johns emerged as a leader not only as a result of her own individual actions but as a result of multiple interplays at multiple levels. However, and in support of my arguments regarding leaders, it is undeniable that she was instrumental in reordering and reorganizing such variables in a way that facilitated change.

Bass and Stogdill (1990) suggested that transformational leaders can actually halt crises in some situations by disclosing opportunities, arousing courage, and stimulating enthusiasm. There is no doubt that other players showed great leadership in this case, as in other similar ones, but it took the actions of one individual to mould them together into the final result that was achieved. As a person without much authority in herself,

---

[10] Annual message to Congress, Concluding Remarks, Washington DC, 1 December 1862. Delivered prior to Lincoln's great act of leadership, the signing of the Emancipation Proclamation.

[11] National Association for the Advancement of Colored People.

she mediated and directed change by what Ronald Heifetz (1994) calls the 'modulation of distress within a dynamic and shifting environment'. We can speculate about her personality that, being the niece of an outspoken minister, she herself was extraverted and self-confident. After all, she delivered a passionate speech and rallied the support of her fellow students. She was also unyielding in her stance regarding her school and we can therefore infer that she might have also had a paranoid streak in her.

Hampton and Schroeder Burnham (1990), in their study of the paranoid personality in action, described its intransigent nature as follows; 'highly paranoid people are the least comfortable to be with because of their demanding and controlling natures. Yet often others turn to them for advice and support, because of their confident and over-bearing manner.' As the popular cliché goes, you can't live with them, and you can't live without them. One could reasonably conclude that, since this phenomenon occurs time and again, it may be sub-served by genetic programming, having been selected by evolution to maximize our chances of survival. As Cesare Lombroso (1981) noted a 'proud mediocrity' resists the notion that what is common, and thus normal, may not be best. So-called normal people need the guidance and leadership of 'abnormal' individuals in order to attain their goals.

II.

There have been attempts to shy away from the concept of the co-existence of leadership skills and paranoid thinking, especially by authors who claim that leaders can be coached into these roles. They go so far as to suggest that if these individuals are guided to assume certain attributes, then they can perform well in leadership positions. They have developed and proposed assessment tools to be used in would-be leaders in order to assess their style and readiness to assume their roles, and ultimately, to guide trainers to the particular needs of their clients. One such tool is the *Leadership Readiness Index* (Best 2010) which claims to 'provide executive and leadership coaches with a device that can be used to support effective leader development strategies'. Trainees undergoing such tutoring programmes are geared towards industrial and business executive positions. The *Index* takes into account the specific personality characteristics of trainees and attempts to allow trainers to build upon and mould them into effective leadership styles. To achieve this goal it also incorporates known attributes of effective leaders such as Sperry's (2002,

2004) contributions on personality, work style, and leadership potential, as well as effectiveness and readiness (De Vries 2006, Nelson and Hogan 2009).

Of course this positivist thinking may be true, to a certain extent, in view of the evidence for neural plasticity and epigenetics that were discussed earlier. However, this is mostly the case when one deals with business and managerial type positions, which can be coached, taught, and learned up to a point. They can, most likely, be taught to engage in what Lambert *et al.* (1995) call 'leadership acts' but, as Ospina and Sorenson (2006) qualify, 'not roles'. Bolden (2005) expresses the same notions when he writes that 'while the skills associated with effective leadership (for example, communication, interpersonal, strategic thinking) can be cultivated through training, the personality traits that influence leadership style are less amenable to modification'. The issue is not a trivial one because, as the constructionist students of leadership hold, the leader may eventually become irrelevant in the 'reciprocal process that enables participants ... to construct meanings that lead toward a common purpose' (Lambert *et al.* 1995). The basic idea is that any individual in this process may choose to take on leadership acts, so long as they are congruent with the larger group's goals and aspirations. Coaching can help up to a point; followers must be lured over by the (inborn) radiance of the effective leader upon which they bestow the leadership charisma. Pastor (1998) even proposes that the act of leadership itself becomes the property of the group that sustains and nourishes it. In other words, leadership becomes invisible, like blue notes in a jazz composition (Ospina and Sorenson 2006, Sorenson and Hickman 2002), however, blue notes are placed between formal notes by an individual, the composer who's the real leader, while the blue notes may be thought of as representing the leader's style. And that style, contrary to hard constructionist views, is grounded in biology, heredity, and personality styles that colour leadership and promote the leader. Yes, a 'culturally derived and historically situated leadership in context' (Ospina and Sorenson 2006) is important to consider, but not to the exclusion of basic hierarchical phenomena as they are determined by nature, nurturing influences notwithstanding.

There exist a plethora of books, articles, and treatises dealing with the way one may learn leadership skills in order to make it into the business and corporate world. These individuals are not the leaders we are concerned with and in any case, fulfil minor roles in the leadership of their societies. So, for example, Warren Bennis (2003) in the introduction to his book *On Becoming a Leader*, in which he mostly deals with business leaders, claims:

A leader need not possess all the individual skills of the group members. What he or she must have are vision, the ability to rally others, and integrity. Such leaders also need superb curatorial and coaching skills – an eye for talent, the ability to recognize correct choices, contagious optimism, a gift for bringing out the best in others, the ability to facilitate communication and mediate conflict, a sense of fairness, and, always, the kind of authenticity and integrity that creates trust.

This description sounds more like a wish list of the ingredients needed to help leaders ascend their ladder. Kevin Eikenberry (2007) even offers a laundry list of 'what to do things' in order to become a remarkable leader, also holding on to the belief that leaders are made and not born; proper training and self-coaching is all that's needed. However, this cannot always be sufficient, since as we argued before, other attributes, including language, play a paramount role in being a leader. Certainly, some of those characteristics are true and necessary, such as vision, coaching skills, recognizing appropriate choices, and the ability to communicate. Some of the rest of the characteristics, however, remind me of the ubiquitous new age, 'let's be kind to each other' courses that people take to improve themselves and fulfil their potential. But even in these cases the truly successful managers are also paranoid. Their paranoia helps them harness their great need for power so that they put forth their ideas. The energy is there, it just needs to be funnelled in directions that benefit the whole rather than only themselves. McClelland and Burnham (2003) posit the same argument as well and also propose that 'the manager's [leader's] concern for power should be socialized – controlled so that the institution as a whole, benefits'.

I attended one of these workshops as a requirement of my position as Clinic Head and Senior Scientist. What disappointed me during this otherwise worthwhile experience was the interchangeable use of the terms 'leader' and 'manager'. Genuine leadership, however, requires the personality traits that we discussed earlier, in short a degree of paranoia, set in a challenging, changing, environment. As Margaret Hermann (1976) states, a leader distinguishes himself 'in a crisis: this is a pre-eminent occasion for leader personality to come to the fore; how a leader acts in a crisis will often be the measure of his leadership.' This is the time when public sensitivities are heightened; attention is at a maximum and the one who delivers the right messages in a distinctive empathetic manner, will get many followers onto his pecking order.

Greenstein (1987) proposes that the likelihood that a potential leader will have an impact on his system varies according to the degree that the system (a primed environment or social group) is ready for restructuring, the leader's location in the hierarchy, and his personal attributes (that is, characteristics that set him apart as discussed previously). Therefore, 'a profound change in the social climate may permit the paranoid leader who heretofore has been essentially a prophet in the wilderness, operating either alone or with only a small group of loyal followers, to become transformed into a millenarian leader' (Robins and Post 1987). Revolutionary thinking may thus become translated into action as the examples of the toppling of Eastern European dictatorships in the 1990s aptly manifest.

Another way to look at leadership style is what Hook (1943) calls eventful versus event-making leadership. The latter recapitulates the 'Great Man of History' theories that claim history to be driven and shaped by the individual, whereas the former asserts that leadership is reactive to specific times and conditions. Both styles of course can be observed in the same leader.

Nietzsche, who provided the philosophical and social framework for the development of modern-day fascism and racism, held that the individual superhuman (leader) should be allowed to take over and lead all others who should yield to his authority and excellence. In line with Harvey's (2006) third problem of the human condition,[12] Nietzsche was able to dream up his superhuman that, true to his promise, should be given the authority to rule over those lesser humans.

Stephen Denning (2007), despite his targeted insight into the makings of leaders, is also of the opinion that 'once people grasp what is involved in acting and speaking in that way and take the trouble to master it, then they find that *anyone* can drive change, if they want to' (emphasis in original). To want to drive change however is not the wish of the masses but the stuff of leaders who possess the biological determinants, and find themselves in the ripe circumstances, to declare themselves. The wish to effect change is the initial cause and not the result of coaching. I think that this point was espoused adequately in this book so far. In effect, to rise as a leader, there needs to be a group to be led. The dyadic relationship thus formed, defines both the leader and the followers. In other words, the group solidifies an identity by the guidance of the leader; the leader on the other hand, is created, so to speak, by the reaction his followers exhibit to his particular personality style. Even in cases of mass action from discontent, as we recently saw in the Arab world, the multitudes will turn to a leader for practical guidance,

---

[12]   The third problem of the human condition deals with how to wield power. According to Harvey: 'Enabling the conditions for survival, while enlarging the space for freedom and imagination – these are the true and highest ends of leadership, its lasting contribution to the human condition.'

cohesiveness, and group identification of needs. Post (2004) reminds us that 'a leader is not formed until he encounters his followers', and Nancy McWilliams (2010) adds that 'the more chaotic or ambiguous one's situation, the more likely it is to create anxieties about trust and thereby to incite paranoid dynamics'. Regressive responses and paranoia is also predicted by Bion (1967) with regards to unstable and ambiguous environments; it remains to be seen whether the Arab nations will regress into paranoia and seek scapegoats for their tribulations.

Even Bennis later on in his book, and likely unbeknown to him, corroborates this position by identifying four ingredients that leaders should have in order to generate trust in their followers; these include constancy, congruity, reliability, and integrity. The first three are characteristics that help compose the rigid personality of the paranoid individual (or leader); certainly, such persons remain constant in their ideas and 'stay the course' as Bennis says. Paranoid individuals almost never change their minds, even in view of evidence that they are wrong. This is probably a desirable quality that makes them attractive to others, especially when they express ideas tacitly shared by their followers. Their congruity follows, then, from their constancy as explained above. Paranoid individuals act out their thoughts and ideas in a congruent manner. Thus, their actions become self-fulfilling prophesy and this congruency is in itself also attractive to followers. Their reliability comes from their intransigence and their inability to see other points of view.

This is why conservative politicians tend to win elections at times of crisis, the way George W. Bush won a second term in office despite growing discontent with the war in Iraq. The events of 9/11 drastically transformed both the climate of the country and the context surrounding US presidency. Seemingly overnight, the president's approval ratings skyrocketed to a level unparalleled in polling history (Bligh *et al.* 2004). Despite previous disapproval ratings, and the wimp factor epithet of his father that hung over his own reputation, the American public changed its opinion and outlook and demonstrated the willingness to forgo their personal liberties for the greater common good. Shared meanings were expressed by the rediscovered leader who used such themes as 'family, God, and country' with increasing frequency. The terrorist attacks helped solidify the leader–follower relationship and identified the urgency they faced. As we saw previously, in the aftermath of the 9/11 attacks, President Bush's addresses to the American nation became more connected to people as a collective and incorporated more patriotic, faith-based themes (Bligh *et al.* 2004). It was also more specific and goal-directed. Consider the following excerpt:

> Civilized people around the world denounce the evildoers who devised and
> executed these terrible attacks. Justice demands that those who helped or
> harbored the terrorists be punished – and punished severely. The enormity of
> their evil demands it. (Bush 2002a)

The delivery of a message is enhanced by the way a leader uses
language, and this is significantly determined by his biological endowment. In other words, if a leader is born, not made, then his use of
language, a distinctive characteristic of the stuff he's made of, would also
carry its own connotations and nuances, thus giving its possessor unique
qualities. Such uniqueness would be the use of narratives to tell a story
and pass a message across. A message that, according to Couto *et al.*
(2002), 'seeks either to affirm or contest an existing meaning, expresses
the nature and origins of a particular set of social relations that can have
economic, political and/or cultural dimensions'. In other words, the
message has the power to recapitulate a group of followers' goals,
desires, and need for action and change. An example of how powerful a
message can be is the avalanche of Arab mobilization and discontent, in
one country after the other, in response to such basic slogans as freedom,
democracy, God, and justice. The language, in the context of which such
messages are presented, can have a galvanizing effect with consequences
well beyond even the leaders' expectations. To quote from Couto *et al.*
(2002) again, 'narratives [and their messages] fulfill various purposes;
they motivate, define group identity, make limits, provide the building
blocks for imagination and creativity, teach lessons'. The ability to use
stories in order to construct meanings and send messages is a distinct
human characteristic, a by-product of our ability to use language in a
sophisticated manner. Descartes (1967 [1637]) captured this fact quite
eloquently:

> It is a very remarkable fact that there are none so depraved and stupid,
> without even excepting idiots, that they cannot arrange different words
> together, forming of them a statement by which they make known their
> thoughts; while, on the other hand, there is no other animal, however perfect
> and fortunately circumstanced it may be, which can do the same.

Along with storytelling, a distinctive voice is another attribute of all
authentic leaders according to Bennis (2003), which he qualifies further
as a cluster of things including, among others, a sense of purpose and
confidence, characteristics that certainly make up the paranoid individual's language style. In addition, as the same author states, '[leaders]
are able to engage others by creating shared meaning'. This is their
ability to tap into their followers' sensitivities and fears, which at times of

crisis enhance their longing for a charismatic leader. These are times ripe for the rise of messianic movements and fanatical followers. Groups are thus created in solidarity of thought and action. Ospina and Sorenson (2006) hold that 'emerging from collective processes that support it, visible leadership can manifest in strong charismatic individuals'. Lech Wałęsa's Solidarity movement, which ended up, under his leadership and along with other key players such as the Catholic Church, gaining the liberation of Poland comes to mind as an example. Leading strikes under a communist regime, martial law, and rejecting the regimes attempts to co-opt him (*The Economist* 2008) certainly favoured his leadership ascent.

According to Post (2004), 'even the most basic of human needs – the drive for self-preservation – can be suspended in the service of the group, as was horrifyingly evidenced by the phenomenon of Jonestown'. The Reverend Jim Jones tapped into the inequalities that existed between blacks and whites, as well as among poor and rich Americans of both races, and created what appeared at first to be the ideal Christian community. He created a shared meaning for the lives of his people and gave them a sense of purpose and accomplishment in a faraway community that defied such evil doers as the Ku Klux Klan, racism, and the oppressive big government! He was, as Warren Bennis would say, extremely attuned to his followers' feelings and pains, their wants and their needs. His psychopathology of course eventually got in the way and he suspected everyone, to the point of using humiliating means to control his followers and maintain power. Eventually, they ended up in a disastrous conclusion of mass suicide. Why did people follow him to such extremes of behaviour? Moreover, why did they succumb to his wish of mass suicide? Many treatises have attempted to explain this and other similar phenomena. The final answer to these troubling questions was given in Chapter 2 where we exposed and discussed the biological need to form and maintain hierarchies in order to survive and reproduce. In the final analysis, their death by suicide was perceived by them as the means to their ultimate salvation (survival in the nether world) and eternal life. Gaining eternal life by one's death is a central theme of the Abrahamic religions. Trampling down death by death is the main message Christians get in their churches on Easter Sunday. Sadly, the recent events of global terrorist resurgence can be explained, at least in part, on world events that enhanced the rise of paranoid leaders with exquisite abilities to magnetize and control their operatives in their destructive frenzy.

Using the language of vision, shared meaning, and a purpose, while promising future heavenly benefits, they activate the very biological desires of survival (heavenly in this case), where reproduction is no longer useful. Messianic leaders liberate but they also enslave. Jones' paranoia was instrumental in formulating his followers' manifesto and group cohesiveness, but it was also the means for their ultimate demise. After all, 'when the individual identity is subsumed in the ranks or the cult or the blind patriotism ... there inevitably results loss, not gain; harm, not blessing' (Ray 2011). Whether our New Common Era, with its global interdependence and interconnections, will succumb to fanatical leaders or manages to subdue them, remains to be seen.

Along with a distinctive voice, we should re-emphasize the qualification of a distinctive language; these two characteristic are closely associated with one another and help produce effective rhetoric.

Bennis (2003) also identifies four basic characteristics that all leaders should have. Again, even though he uses examples of national politics and political leaders, his main focus is on the development of business leaders, a process that he claims holds also true for great national and messianic leaders. It is important to distinguish the two kinds of leaders, however, in order to avoid concluding (wrongly) that great men of history just happened to be coached into their roles and that with a bit of luck and favourable circumstances, they excelled. The first two, engaging others and a distinctive voice, I agree with, and they have been discussed already. Whether business or national leaders are concerned, these attributes must be in place. His other two characteristics, however, we need to take issue with: integrity is certainly not a trait that all leaders have, either in business or otherwise. Global financial scandals attest to this fact. Integrity is not a characteristic of most aggressive paranoid leaders, and certainly they do not encourage dissent as the same author claims elsewhere. For the paranoid leader you are either with him, or against him. Merkel, the German chancellor, can be ruthless to the point of destroying her opponents (Elliot 2009) in order to get her way. Recently she began to apply her tactics to Southern European nations that are financially strained. If integrity is present it will help the leader accomplish great feats as it did for King; if it is lacking from a person, he still can gain many followers, just as Jones did. Both men had a degree of paranoia: King's, along with his integrity, enabled him to rally African Americans out of discrimination and into mainstream American society; Jones' paranoia, without integrity or adaptive capacity, which constitutes Bennis' fourth leadership attribute, was disastrous as we saw. A benevolent leader might possess adaptive capacity and quickly shift his paradigm to fit a changing world.

A paranoid leader will attempt to change the world (be it a social group or a nation), to fit his paradigm in a give and take, dyadic relationship in which he has the initiative and others follow. Jones and Hitler changed their worlds' attitudes to fit their own pre-conceived notions, just as Pericles swayed his fellow Athenians in ancient Greece. The latter of course had magnificence for Athens in mind whereas the former had self-interests at heart. Volkan (1980) distinguishes between two types of charismatic leaderships: the so-called *reparative* charismatic leadership, which induces beneficial societal transformation, and mentions King as an example; and the so-called *destructive* charismatic leadership like that of Hitler. Perhaps the presence or absence of Bennis' *integrity* is the determining quality that drives these two types of leadership.

Parsons *et al.* (1953) also identifies four strategies an effective leader must employ in order to rally the support of his followers and exhibit leadership: (1) setting direction, that is, pointing the way which the group must follow; (2) actualizing the goals of the enterprise, that is, defining the end point that needs to be reached; (3) sustaining the commitment of the group, that is, obtaining approval and support; and (4) creating adaptive mechanisms, that is, devising and sustaining the process by which the goals will be attained. As Ospina and Sorenson (2006) remind us, 'the potential for leadership exists when there is a collective need to accomplish something'. If the group at large does not recognize this need, the potential leader will not emerge.

Certainly, and the point was made in the introduction of this book, a leader must be seen in the context of his history and culture. But the true leader will shape his culture as well as be shaped by it. This is relevant to field theory discussed earlier in this chapter with regards to how it applied to the desegregation movement of US public schools. Wheatley (1992) emphasizes the reactivity of the receiving follower in shaping the field, in response to the leader's actions, which is then played out in order to effect change. Hickman and Couto (2006) state that 'in leadership terms the efficacy of leaders comes from shaping a field in which others, by their own actions, may participate in energy and forms of the field'. Jerrold M. Post (2004) in his much acclaimed book *Leaders and their Followers in a Dangerous World*, summarizes the swing of the pendulum concerning the role of leaders in a nice way, as follows:

> Early historians tended to depict history as an unfolding of events, with the King, Prime Minister, or President as steward of their nation. When political events occurred, it was a consequence of historical forces. If the role of a leader was described, he tended to be portrayed as being present during these events ... the French sociologist Emile Durkheim emphasized the role of what he termed 'social facts', by which he meant factors external to the individual

leader. Similarly Max Weber ... emphasized the importance of conformity to an organized and uniform system. Such personality factors as motivations and emotions, in contrast to impersonal rationality, were considered hindrances to smooth bureaucratic functioning that needed to be eliminated ... Gordon DiRenzo notes ... 'little concern is shown for the social agents as status role occupants operating within the social systems'.

Later, a shift from this impersonal view of historical systems occurred, to focus on the role of the leader as a *causative agent* in changing history, the so-called Great Man theory of history. And, later on, he adds:

The pendulum that overswung from the view of history as a consequence of power, ignoring the role of leadership, to the 'great man' of history, which emphasized the centrality of leadership, has come to rest with current working model, the leader in context.

Hickman and Couto (2006) add that 'leadership is infinitely more complex than the efforts of any one individual; rather, it is the impact of efforts to influence the actions of leaders and followers opposed to and supportive of the same or related changes'. Clearly, then, Bennis' claim that 'leaders are made, not born, and made more by themselves than by any external means', is at odds with all three concepts of leadership as they were expounded by Post. True leadership is founded by biological determinants that evolved millennia ago in order to consolidate the group hierarchies and enhance survival. Bands of early humans who did not possess the hierarchy-forming gene (that is, the tendency to follow leaders with desirable characteristics) probably left few or no descendants.

III.

Yielding to authority, whether actual or perceived, is a biological phenomenon that has been observed and was confirmed time and again by sociologists and psychologists. Consider the notorious example of the Stanley Milgram experiments (1975); run-of-the-mill, honest and law-abiding citizens were induced to deliver what they thought were electric shocks to subjects as part of what they had thought was a learning via punishment experiment; just because a sturdy, white-jacketed (authoritarian) scientist instructed them to do so they obeyed willingly despite their subjects' cries of pain. What this experiment accomplished, besides ruining Milgram's career at Yale as well as Harvard, was that we have the tendency to follow those we perceive as leaders, in charge, or authoritarian. This fact raises difficult to answer questions regarding the responsibility of followers in a hierarchy of whatever nature; in other words, one begins to wonder whether the German soldiers who followed their officers' orders and carried out scores of atrocities were actually responsible for their acts or could be somehow excused due to our genetic endowment. The same can be asked of their SS officers as well.

To bring the argument to more familiar examples, how much can we blame those terrorists who, having fallen under the spell of a charismatic (but certainly paranoid) leader, engage in despicable acts of violence against innocent people? The Nuremburg trials have posited that the responsibility lies with the one carrying out the act. In other words, a clearly inhuman order should alert whosoever is to carry it out that it is insane and immoral, and therefore not to be followed. Of course, if we are biologically programmed to follow our paranoid leaders to extremes, how can we avoid misbehaving, on their orders, on a grand scale? After all, we have argued that by doing so we probably increase our chances of survival. Well, the issue has become rather complicated if not philosophical. By recognizing the absurdity of a command as well as the paranoid disposition of the leader issuing it, we can practically determine the extent to which reason can take over. It is not easy; millennia of evolution have introduced paranoia into our genetically determined behaviour. Moreover, we have been programmed to follow the more paranoid individuals among us, so that they may see us through our troubles and tribulations. It is, after all, a double-edged sword (Hampton and Schroeder Burnham 1990). Without paranoia, we don't survive; with it we may become extremists. At times of physical danger, this could be an advantage; at times of peace, it could prove destructive.

The biological basis of this phenomenon serves to enhance survival and has thus 'guided' evolutionary pressures to aid the emergence of people who follow authority figures, whereas, at the same time, it has bestowed higher levels of aloofness in those members at the top of social hierarchies. Recent scientific advances in neuroimaging techniques (Beasley *et al.* 2012) have allowed the biological study of social ranking, and an individual's social place in a hierarchy as either dominant or subordinate, in relation to brain structure and function. They consider the mind of leaders–followers in a social rank theory from an evolutionary perspective, possessing a modular structure from which various psychological traits and processes have evolved in order to promote the success of the individual, his group, and the species. Gilbert (2000) proposes social rank theory in explaining responses reflecting a system that appears to have functional underpinnings linking limbic, prefrontal, and striatal structures brain areas (see also Levitan *et al.* 2000), which also sub-serve personality, language, and memory.[13] This evolution-derived system appears to be responding to status information during social exchanges and serves to facilitate cohesion and ranking in social encounters; namely, competition, cooperation or both for access to resources (Gilbert 2000, Levitan *et al.* 2000) and survival enhancement. However, other brain structures may also be implicated, including the visual associative processing areas of the brain (Chiao *et al.* 2009);[14] it therefore becomes clear that a rather complex biopsychosocial process underlies the relationship between the leader and the crowd, with further influences from the particular cultural milieu, historical predicaments, and geopolitical determinants.

Hoyt *et al.* (2006) remind us that the closer the relationship, and the longer its duration, the more power wielded by a legitimate leader over followers. The decades old conflict between the Greeks and Turks of Cyprus had been sustained in part due to the unyielding, paranoid, and intransigent stances of their respective powerful leaders, Archbishop Makarios and Rauf Denktash. That legacy continues on in their political descendants. Part of their amazing popularity was their ability to give out an air of authority, coupled with effective storytelling (that is, language skills) and legitimate goal setting.

I return here to Denning's ideas about telling an effective story. All the ingredients of a convincing and successful leader are to be found in the following quotation:

> The newly emerging narrative is constructed both from the ongoing stories of the people and their organization, and from the new story put forward by the leader. It is born in the listener's minds as a more compelling version of their ongoing life stories. The listeners themselves create the story, they tend to embrace it. What the leader says is mere scaffolding, a catalyst to a creative process going on inside the listeners.

Whereas Denning feels that coaching can cultivate the ability to deliver powerful narratives, my position is that leaders possess innate (genetic) traits, which as argued before, enable them to master language and create the captivating stories by which they win their followers. The quotation above is right on the mark so long as we accept that it is biology and not

---

[13] Limbic and striatal structures are subcortical areas of grey matter that sub-serve emotional responses and behaviour, motor acts, and memory. Prefrontal areas participate in the formation of personality.

[14] That is, the intraparietal sulci of the brain where sensory information from the eyes is integrated with other types of information.

coaching that creates it. It could then apply to a business, a club, or a nation. Nor is it true, as he claims, that charisma is not a necessary ingredient for leadership. I accept that charismatic persons such as Gandhi and King lacked an imposing physical presence. What they had in excess though was a paranoid predisposition that, put to good use, enabled them to lead their people to greener pastures. And in that respect, like any true leader, they helped their people visualize possibilities that had so far been thought of as impossible. Their charisma was not that of a physical presence but of a predisposition that combined personality traits, language skills, and a context, that enabled them to rise and lead. Christ sent a message in such a language, which even though historically he may appear to have failed, galvanized most of the known world of antiquity. To be a leader you must possess the right stuff. Bennis quotes Richard Ferry in having said:

> You can't really create leaders. How do you teach people to make decisions, for example? All you can do is develop the talents people have. I am a great believer in trial by fire, on-the-job-experience. Put them out there in the plants, put them in the markets, send them to Japan and Europe. Train them on the job.

Again, this is an argument, albeit indirect, that leaders are born and not made; to lead they need all the qualities we have mentioned. What Ferry is reiterating here is that leaders are born, not made, they just need to find themselves in the right context in order to develop, mature, and act. If they so happen to combine charisma with the skill of language they can take on the world. Obama tapped into an excellent resource, the Internet and social media, in order to appear that he personally reaches out to individuals in order to affect change. What follows is an excerpt from an electronic message that I received on his behalf as he was gearing up to fight for his health reform proposals. Note the language of mobilization and the hints of an upcoming crisis should his efforts fail.

> Special interests and opponents of health care reform in Washington have made their priority clear: attack President Obama at any cost.
>
> On Friday, GOP Senator Jim DeMint told a special-interest attack group that if they're 'able to stop Obama on this, it will be his Waterloo. It will break him.' And just this morning, Republican Chairman Michael Steele backed up DeMint's statement 100%. At the same time, the Republican National Committee is running deceptive ads to scare Americans away from the reform we need.
>
> Their plan is simple: oppose health care reform as a political ploy to weaken the President and defeat his entire agenda of change. But if we follow the

Republican 'Party of No' and do nothing, we'll not only ensure more of the same, but saddle our children and grandchildren with a growing burden of exploding costs and declining care that they may never overcome.

We can't let this kind of slash and burn politics succeed. We can fight back by collecting as many signatures as possible backing the President's principles for health care reform. A huge response will show Washington and the media that when Republicans try to 'break' the President, Americans are ready to stand up for what's right.

The President has consistently argued that health care reform must: reduce costs, guarantee choice – including the choice of a strong public insurance option – and ensure all Americans have quality, affordable health care. These principles are the key to keeping our country healthy – and protecting our families, businesses, and economy from costs that are spiralling out of control. It's the change the American people voted for and so desperately needed.

But special interests and Republican leaders are so concerned with scoring points that they seem to think health care reform is a political game. They are literally playing politics with our lives and livelihood, and it has to stop.

We know that they will not 'break' President Obama or the movement that supports him. And if we work together, they will not stop us from enacting the real health care reform that Americans need and demand.

Stand with President Obama on health care

http://www.democrats.org/declare

Please declare your support today.

Governor Tim Kaine

Chairman

P.S. – Just this afternoon, President Obama, speaking at a children's hospital, responded to Senator DeMint's comment. Here are his inspiring words:

'Think about that. This isn't about me. This isn't about politics. This is about a health care system that is breaking America's families, breaking America's businesses and breaking America's economy. And we can't afford the politics of delay and defeat when it comes to health care. Not this time, not now. There are too many lives and livelihoods at stake.'

Obama and his inner circle are exhibiting just enough healthy paranoia in their attempt to neutralize their opponents. His message, delivered by proxy (Tim Kaine) is worded in such a way, so as to rouse an emotional reaction in people, but also to get them involved in the struggle. They are asked to write to congressmen, contribute money and effort and consider his potential victory theirs. The issue is hot – health care. The enemy is visible – the GOP. The goal is clear – offer everyone equal access to the goods. The language is captivating, and the stand is unyielding. The time is also ripe; a nation recovering from a financial crisis, in the midst of two major wars abroad, and an uncertain future, make people want to cling to a leader who offers them security and hope. With this strategy, Obama is acting more as a transformational rather that a transactional leader because he attempts to engage his followers in a significant, mutually respective, motivational process, transforming them up to the level of leaders just as MacGregor Burns describes (1978). Leadership by followers may be more symbolic than actual, but this is an effective approach that characterized great leadership for millennia. A degree of paranoia equips such leaders with the galvanizing language that gets attention.

Even though he did not quite put is in such words, Huntington (2002) clearly warns that different world cultures are on an inevitable collision course, precisely because of their differences and the suspicions one has about the others. Suspicion is paranoia. If we are to ever achieve peace, a feat rather impossible in my view, we need to begin to formulate ways and ideas that are tolerant and understanding towards others. Unfortunately, we no longer have the luxury of evolutionary timeframes; it simply takes far too long. We may not survive to see it happen. What, then, can we do to avert our self-destruction? Choosing our leaders wisely would be a start. But how can this be accomplished if we are biologically programmed to pick the crazy ones to lead? Herodotus (1998) prompted us to choose our enemies well, since we end up becoming just like them. Hofstadter (1964) echoed as much centuries later, in describing paranoid strategies of American fringe groups:

> The Ku Klux Klan imitated Catholicism to the point of donning priestly vestments, developing an elaborate ritual and an equally elaborate hierarchy. The John Birch Society[15] emulates Communist cells and quasi-secret operation through 'front' groups, and preaches a ruthless prosecution of the ideological war along lines very similar to those it finds in the Communist enemy.

The same usually holds true about the leaders we choose since they reify our deepest needs, and subsequently, define what we should behave like in order to attain them. Castro's egocentrism (OK, narcissism), has led to

---

[15] A radical right-wing political advocacy society, which has strong anti-communism and anti-governmental sentiments, and supports a constitutional republic (Webb 2010).

such statements as 'It is not my fault that I haven't died yet. My vocation is the revolution. I am a revolutionary, and revolutionaries do not retire' (Bardach 1994), implying that he will remain in power for the rest of his life. Ailing health has finally removed him from office. His paranoia induced his thinking that everyone was out to get him, long after the West had given up trying, and this conviction had spilled over to his followers.

Our discussion should include a reference to Greenleaf's ideas about servant leadership (1977), which suggests that the leader be placed at the bottom of the social hierarchy, as a result of his desire to serve, as opposed to leading in order to promote one's interests. This is how he phrased his conceptualization of servant leadership:

> The servant-leader is a servant first … [and] begins with the natural feeling that one wants to serve, to serve first. Then conscious choice brings one to aspire to lead. That person is sharply different from the one who is a leader first, perhaps because of the need to assuage an unusual power drive or to acquire material possessions.

Perhaps a good example of servant leadership would come from the Christian church and its emphasis on servitude of its functionaries towards their flock. Certainly, even here this is an idealized goal, not always attained; however there are many examples of self-denial and humility on the part of religious leaders. Monks and priests have been known to go to extremes of sacrifice, including their lives, in order to save their followers. The ancient Greek story of King Kodros of Attica, who sacrificed himself for the sake of his country's victory against the Dorians, echoes a similar principle. European languages imply that much for their leaders: in modern Greek the word used for governmental ministers is *upourgos* which roughly translates to 'under-worker' meaning servant, proclaiming perhaps an idealized goal rather than an actual state of affairs. The word 'minister' itself has a similar meaning. Greenleaf goes far enough to deny would-be servant leaders the right to gain excessive property and privileges, just like Plato proposed in his *Republic*. Such extreme situations are usually not attained in most states, a main reason being the fact that such self-denial would be incompatible with the effectiveness seen in paranoid personalities and leaders. As stated above, perhaps the best examples of servant leadership are to be found among religious functionaries such as those seen in Christianity. Even in such circumstances however, the effective servant leader would possess some paranoid qualities. St Paul, to use a familiar example, had certainly paranoid features in his personality, yet he exhibited self-sacrificial leadership. Whatever the style of leadership that emerges in a given group, it requires some paranoia in order to solidify itself.

Another way would be to restructure our educational systems and institutions in order to guide children, who are the future followers and potential leaders, to accept diversity, not only on philosophical premises, but also as a necessary means for biological survival. Ignorance breeds mistrust, mistrust breeds conflict. The programmes of student exchanges between countries can be considered as a step in that direction, helping those who are unable to travel extensively to get to know different cultures, to begin to understand the relativism of their own social systems. The European Union, by accepting different languages and cultures as official and legitimate, strives to form a truly multifaceted society characterized by tolerance and mutual respect.[16] Contrast this effort to the 'melting pot' idea of the US that suppresses national identity, language, and culture by the second generation of immigrants. American society is, on the whole, less tolerant, more bigoted and less patient with foreign cultures despite the fact that it is made up from the most diverse backgrounds. It has also been less tolerant with its own minorities; Hofstadter (1964) discusses this paranoid style in American politics and recounts the suppression and persecution of groups like the Masons, Catholics, international bankers and munitions makers. However, US paranoia may offer a better protection of its national interests, and a more successful 'union' of states, that the European amalgam and wimpy ineffectiveness when it comes to decisive actions (Dickerson and McAllister 2002). The US has a better chance to survive as a nation than the EU and this is beginning to manifest in the way the latter handles its financial troubles and economic policies.

Mark Walker (2006) has studied six schools of thought regarding leadership and tabularized them for easy reference. In order of appearance he includes: the Great Men theory, which is based on traits exhibited by leaders; behavioural leadership with the style of leadership being the determinant of its effectiveness; contingency leadership, which focuses on specific situations and the style they require in order to be effective; cognitive theory leadership in which behaviour is perceived as the result of internal factors of individual leaders; moral leadership with morality being the most desirable purpose of the leader; and finally,

---

[16] The EU experiment is still largely unproven if one judges it from the latest economic policies that the financially healthier North has imposed on the weaker South. Failure in economic solidarity may begin to bring about the first signs of the partnership's eventual breakup.

strategic/transactional leadership where individual decision making leads to goal fulfilment. The last two shift from being leader-centred, to an emphasis on the leader–follower relationship. Obviously individual leaders can employ different styles under different situations, or even combine styles during the same situation depending on the needs of the moment. Moreover, even though there's a hint of sociological evolution in the order presented, some styles may be most appropriate given specific circumstances. Therefore, the leader-centred theories may be more effective when mobilization is necessary during times of crisis. For these styles, a paranoid trait is a basic biological determinant. The various styles have been discussed under various headings in this book.

IV.

Paranoia is present in one form and degree or another, in all of us. It helps us protect our interests, our lives, and our families. On a larger scene, it enhances the formation, solidification, and sustenance of our societies. It is part and parcel of our biology, and as such has directed our physical as well as our cultural evolution through the millennia. It is the 'stuff' that makes our leaders and transforms them into such, as we saw in the many examples mentioned in this book. It is perhaps the *original sin* in our genetic makeup (de Duve 2010) passed down from the 'first man' to posterity. As such, it forms part of our identity. It is also the stuff we need to take heed of, accept it, control it and funnel in directions that will service our humanity. Failure to check it can lead to disastrous consequences as history has repeatedly demonstrated.

Science fiction writers often portray a futuristic existence in which the whole world has come under one global government that is either benevolent and peaceful, or malignant and oppressive. Usually the benevolent version is fighting outsiders who are attempting to usurp our planet. Malignant ones are fighting the people in order to maintain power and dominance. We may or may not achieve a Future Common Era. Whether we do, and which kind it will turn out to be, will depend on our leaders and the licence we grant them in order to bring about our future. Lincoln said that 'the best way to predict your future is to create it'. Science, education, and epigenetics are beginning to show us the way.

Postscript: a personal note

One may wonder what prompted me to write this book. After all, the subject is not something I deal with in my professional or personal life, nor do I consider myself an expert in political psychology. Although I have had formal training in psychiatry, my current field of practice is neurology and within that my expertise is in epilepsy, dementia, and clinical neurophysiology. The subject, however, is not completely un-related to my profession; before I went to medical school I obtained degrees in biology and medical anthropology. The tripartite approach to the book's thesis, which considers genetic, socio-cultural, and psycho-logical inputs, stems from my educational background and biases.

Events in a person's life will influence his attitudes about the world, and at times, induce him to act in certain ways. One such way for some is to write a book and expose facts and feelings. For me too, this was a reaction to a personal event that has affected me deeply; it was a way to undergo a catharsis and healing.

Paranoid people are found in all societies for the reasons exposed in the book. Some rise to be leaders. Others lead their lives and are possibly deemed 'strange' or 'odd' by those around them since, as a result of their psychopathology, they might appear peculiar, intransigent, combative, difficult, different, or plain bad. These are the people who cannot form lasting partnerships at work or in their social circles, and who constantly scan their environment for signs of malice and betrayal. In doing so they are unfailingly bound to clash with colleagues, associates, or former confidants. Once trusted friends may become hated enemies, and once respected partners could end up being despised renegades.

My story begins shortly following my appointment at the post of Consultant Neurologist and Director of the Department of Clinical Neurophysiology at a tertiary care medical centre. Shortly thereafter, a younger doctor was hired as an assistant. A likeable guy, even though a bit odd, he impressed us with his knowledge and skill. At times though, he stubbornly held on to his own opinion, even with evidence to the contrary; his religious beliefs and practices were somewhat extreme, but then that was his own prerogative; he constantly, however, rambled on about corruption everywhere, inadequate behaviours of others, and unethical schemes. He frequently misunderstood our intentions towards him. He always worried that he was cheated out of his fair share; he never quite trusted anyone. And, one day, he suddenly quit his position at the medical centre and went into his own private practice. Distance breeds mistrust among paranoid people. Constructive criticism is regarded as either rejection or open hostility. Honest disagreement with them is perceived as a personal attack, and a second opinion elsewhere (when the paranoid person is a doctor), is a sure sign of betrayal. I inadvertently committed all of the above errors.

At times, while he was still with us, I offered him friendly advice on conduct and professional matters; he was, after all, given a position in my department and I was ultimately responsible for his behaviour. Once I requested that he returned books he had 'permanently' borrowed from the library. I was labelled hostile.

After he quit his job, I was asked to consult on a prominent public figure who had dementia and who, unbeknown to me, had also been seen by my former colleague. He subsequently refused to see that patient again.

I saw another patient he had previously seen, and my diagnosis, rightly or wrongly, differed from his. He flew off the handle accusing me of systematically trying to tarnish his reputation.

I probably also 'offended' him, along with a score of other physicians, in ways I will never surmise. A person with paranoid personality tends to seek and find hidden meanings, agendas, and schemes in the most neutral of behaviours. Such an attitude colours his thinking, conduct, and relationships with others. One day I was informed that he had written a letter accusing me of unprofessional and unethical behaviour. He proceeded to send it to the president of the medical association, the president of the neurological society, the head of a physicians' union and several others. I was eventually exonerated, however the process of investigation, questioning, and suspicions raised about me lasted a few trying years.

During this trying process, I began writing this book and researching the topic of paranoia in everyday life. I inadvertently stumbled upon leadership and paranoia, and subsequently made the connection between paranoia and language endowment. It took me several years to finish writing this book due to my gradual shift in focus as well as my job and family-related responsibilities. Meanwhile, the focus of my writing and its relationship to my paranoid colleague, shifted towards a more scientific exploration of the working of such personalities, and in doing so, I borrowed from my background in the social and the biomedical sciences. I have thus attempted to bring about a synthesis of notions stemming from areas of knowledge that traditionally are kept apart and do not benefit from each other. In the process of doing so I have discovered, and I am proposing, what I believe are the defining elements of the phenomenon of leadership and followership; an evolutionary adaptation which has developed to enhance survival and group cohesion by allowing each party of this dyad to assume its appropriate role; to be effective, leaders must possess certain traits that have been linked through evolution and are found in all societies, past and present; namely, a paranoid predisposition, a mastery of language, and an extroverted personality that induces the leader-to-be to come forth and claim his rightful place in his group's hierarchy. An almost exclusively human illness, schizophrenia plays an instrumental role in supplying such individuals, relatives of schizophrenics, to the general population.

The reader will detect an evolution of ideas and their exposition as he goes through these pages; however, I tried to keep a common underlying theme throughout the book, which was the paranoid personality's bio-psychological makeup, language endowment, and behaviour. Whether I succeeded or not, is for the reader to decide.

References

Ahrweiler, H. (2012). *Why Byzantium*. Athens: Metaixmio Publications.

Alexander, L. G. (1986). 'The impact of crisis-induced stress on decision making', in Soloman, F. (ed.), *The Medical Implications of Nuclear War*. Washington, DC: National Academy Press.

Alexander, R. (1987). *The Biology of Moral Systems*. London: Aldine.

Alexander, R. S. (2001). *Napoleon*. London: Aldine.

Allen, C. (1975). 'The schizophrenia of Joan of Arc', *Hist Med* **6**(3–4), 4–9.

American Psychiatric Association (1994). *Diagnostic and Statistical Manual of Mental Disorders IV-TR*. Arlington, VA: American Psychiatric Press.

Annett, M. (1985). *Left, Right, Hand and Brain: The Right Shift Theory*. London: Lawrence Erlbaum.

Ansari, M. A. and A. Kapoor (1987). 'Organizational context and upward influence tactics', *Organizational Behavior and Human Decision Processes* **40**(1), 39–49.

Ardey, R. (1971). *The Social Contract*. New York: Delta.

Aristotle (2001). 'Aristotle's *Politics*', in Morgan, M. L. (ed.), *Classics of Moral and Political Theory*. Indianapolis, IN: Hackett.

Armstrong, D., W. Stokoe and S. E. Wilcox (1995). *Gesture and the Nature of Language*. Cambridge: Cambridge University Press.

Arsu, S. (2011). 'Drilling off Cyprus will proceed despite warning from Turkey', *The New York Times*, 19 September.

Ashri, E. (1997). 'Noa (Netanyahu) bat 17' ['Noa is 17 years old'], *Ha'aretz 1*, 2 May.

Austen, J. (2005). *Persuasion*. New York: Barnes & Noble Classics.

Ayman, R. and M. M. Chemers (1983). 'The relationship of leader behavior to managerial effectiveness and satisfaction in Iran', *Journal of Applied Psychology* **68**(2), 4.

Badian, E. (1958). *Alexander the Great and the Unity of Mankind*. Indianapolis, IN: Bobbs-Merrill.

Bailey, A., A. Le Couteur, I. Gottesman, P. Bolton, E. Simonoff, E. Yuzda and M. Rutter (1995). 'Autism as a strongly genetic disorder: evidence from a British twin study', *Psychol Med* **25**, 63–77.

Baird, M. (2003). 'North Korea's leaders and strategic decision making', in Schneider, B. and Post, J. (eds), *Know Thy Enemy*. Montgomery, AL: US Air Force Counterproliferation Center, Air War College.

Bales, R. F. and P. E. Slater (1945). 'Role differentiation in small decision making groups', in Parsons, T. and Bales, T. P. (eds), *Family, Localization and Interaction Processes,* New York: Free Press.

Bardach, A. L. (1994). 'Conversations with Castro', *Vanity Fair* **57**(3), March.

Bargh, J. A., P. M. Gollwitzer, A. Lee-Chai, K. Barndollar and R. Trotschel (2001). 'The automated will: nonconscious activation and pursuit of behavioral goals', *J Pers Soc Psychol* **81**(6), 1014–27.

Barnes, B. (2008). 'Jessie Helms: 1921–2008: "Senator No" served 5 times, hailed as saint of new right', *Washington Post,* 5 July.

Barnes, J. (1982). *The Presocratic Philosophers*. London: Routledge Taylor & Francis.

Barrett, W. P. (1932). *The Trial of Jeanne d'Arc: Translated into English from the Original Latin and French Documents*. New York: Gotham House Inc.

Bass, B. M. (1954). 'The leaderless group discussion', *Psychol Bull* **51**, 465–92.

Bass, B. M. (1960). *Leadership, Psychology and Organizational Behaviour*. New York: Harper.

Bass, B. M. (1998). *Transformational Leadership: Industrial, Military and Educational Impact*. Mahwah, NJ: Lawrence Erlbaum Associates.

Bass, B. M. and R. Stogdill (1990). *Handbook of Leadership: Theory, Research, and Managerial Applications*. New York: Free Press.

Beasley, M., D. Sabatinelli and E. Obasi (2012). 'Neuroimaging evidence for social rank theory', *Front Hum Neurosci* **6**, 123.

Beaver, K. M., M. DeLisi, M. G. Vaughn and J. C. Barnes (2010). 'Monoamine oxidase A genotype is associated with gang membership and weapon use', *Compr Psychiatry* **51**(2), 130–4.

Bennis, W. G. (2003). *On Becoming a Leader*. Cambridge, MA: Perseus.

Bentley, D. R., P. Deloukas, A. Dunham, L. French, *et al.* (2001). 'The physical maps for sequencing human chromosomes 1, 6, 9, 10, 13, 20 and X', *Nature* **409**, 942–3.

Benziman, U. (1993). 'Haolam al pi bibi' ['The world according to Bibi'], *Ha'aretz 4*, 30 June.

Best, K. C. (2010). 'Assessing leadership readiness using developmental personality style: a tool for leadership coaching', *International Journal of Evidence Based Coaching and Mentoring* **8**(1), 22–33.

Betros, G. (2012). 'Napoleon the man', *History Review*, August.

Betzig, L. L. (1986). *Despotism and Differential Reproduction: A Darwinian View of History*. New York: Aldine Transaction.

Bion, W. R. (1961). *Experiences in Groups: And Other Papers*. London: Tavistock Publications.

Bion, W. R. (1967). *Experiences in Groups*. New York: Basic Books.

Bird, A. (2007). 'Perceptions of epigenetics', *Nature* **447**, 396–8.

Blaxill, M. F. (2004). 'What's going on? The question of time trends in autism', *Public Health Rep* **119**, 536–51.

Bligh, M. C., J. C. Kohles and J. R. Meindl (2004). 'Charting the language of leadership: a methodological investigation of President Bush and the crisis of 9/11', *J Appl Psychol* **89**, 562–74.

Bloom, H. (1986). *James Boswell's Life of Samuel Johnson*. London: Penguin Classics.

Boas, F. (1912). 'Changes in the bodily dorm of descendants of immigrants', *American Anthropologist* **14**, 530–3.

Boehm, C. (1999). *Hierarchy in the Forest: The Evolution of Egalitarian Behavior*. London: Harvard University Press.

Boinski, S. (1993). 'Vocal coordination of troop movement among white-faced capuchin monkeys, Cebus capucinus', *American Journal of Primatology* **30**(2), 85–100.

Bolden, R. (2005). *What is Leadership Development: Purpose and Practice*, Exeter: University of Exeter Leadership South West.

Bon, G. L. (1969). *The Crowd (1895)*. New York: Ballantine.

Boroditsky, L. (2001). 'Does language shape thought? Mandarin and English speakers' conceptions of time', *Cogn Psychol* **43**, 1–22.

Bouchard, T. J., Jr., D. T. Lykken, M. McGue, N. L. Segal and A. Tellegen (1990). 'Sources of human psychological differences: the Minnesota Study of Twins Reared Apart', *Science* **250**(4978), 223–8.

Breasted, J. H. (1916). *Ancient Times, a History of the Early World: An Introduction to the Study of Ancient History and the Career of Early Man*, Outlines of European History 1. Boston, Ginn and Company.

Breasted, J. H. (1939). *The Dawn of Conscience*. New York: Scripner's.

Brodie, F. M. (1981). *Richard Nixon: The Shaping of His Character*. New York: Norton & Co.

Brodie, F. M. K. (1960). *No Man Knows My History: The Life of Joseph Smith, the Mormon Prophet*. New York: A.A. Knopf.

Bronowski, J. (1973). *Ascent of Man*. London: Little, Brown and Co.

Brown, S., M. J. Martinez and L. M. Parsons (2006). 'Music and language side by side in the brain: a PET study of the generation of melodies and sentences', *Eur J Neurosci* **23**, 2791–803.

Brunell, A. B., W. A. Gentry, W. K. Campbell, B. J. Hoffman, K. W. Kuhnert and K. G. Demurred (2008). 'Leader emergence: the case of the narcissistic leader', *Pers Soc Psychol Bull* **34**(12), 1663–76.

Bullock, A. (1991). *Hitler, A Study In Tyranny*. New York: Harper & Row.

Burns, J. M. G. (1978). *Leadership*. New York: Harper & Row.

Bush, G. W. (2002a). Address to a joint session of Congress and the American people. Available at: http://www.whitehouse.gov/news/releases/2001/09

Bush, G. W. (2002b). National day of prayer and remembrance for the victims of the terrorist attack on September 11, 2001. Available at: http://www.whitehouse.gov/news/releases/2001/09

Butler, C. (2007). *The Flow of History*. Available at: http://www.flowof history.com/

Cann, R. L., M. Stoneking and A. C. Wilson (1987). 'Mitochondrial DNA and human evolution', *Nature* **325**, 31–6.

Carlson, N. (2001). *Physiology of Behavior*. Boston: Allyn and Bacon.

Carlyle, T. (1840). 'On heroes, hero-worship and the heroic in history', in Stern, F. (ed.), *The Varieties of History*, 2nd edn (1972), New York: Vintage books.

Cartledge, P. (2002). *Sparta and Laconia: A Regional History, 1300–362 BC*. New York: Routledge.

Cartwright, S. (1851). 'Report on the diseases and physical peculiarities of the negro race', *The New Orleans Medical and Surgical Journal*, 691–715.

Cavalli-Sforza, L. L. (2001). *Genes, Peoples, and Languages*. Berkeley, CA: University of California Press.

Centers for Disease Control and Prevention (2007). Morbidity and Mortality Weekly Report. Surveillance Summaries. Coordinating Center for Health Information and Service, (CDC), US Department of Health and Human Services. **56**.

Chagnon, N. (1997). *The Yanomamo*. London: Wadsworth.

Chiao, J. Y., T. Harada, E. R. Oby, Z. Li, T. Parrish and D. J. Bridge (2009). 'Neural representations of social status hierarchy in human inferior parietal cortex', *Neuropsychologia* **47**, 354–63.

Chiari, J. (1975). *Twentieth-Century French Thought: From Bergson to Lévi-Strauss*. London: Elek.

Chomsky, N. (1965). *Aspects of the Theory of Syntax*. Hong Kong: MIT Press.

Chomsky, N. (1979). *Language and Responsibility*, New York: Harvester.

Chomsky, N. (1986). *Knowledge of Language: Its Nature, Origin, and Use*. New York: Praeger Special Studies.

Chrysostom, St John (1886). 'On the priesthood; ascetic treatises; select homilies and letters; homilies of the statutes', in Schaff, P. (ed.), *A Select Library of the Nicene and Post-Nicene Fathers of the Christian Church,* Grand Rapids, MI: WM. B. Eedermans Publishing Co.

Ciobanu, C. (2004). 'Mikhail Gorbachev: the decay of socialism and the renaissance of Eastern Europe (from the perspective of an insider)', *East European Politics and Societies* **18**(1), 45–69.

Ciulla, J. B. (2004). *Ethics, the Heart of Leadership*. Westport, CT: Praeger.

Clancy, T. (1991). *The Sum of All Fears*. London: HarperCollins.

Clayton, P. A. (2006). *Chronicle of the Pharaohs: The Reign-by-Reign Record of the Rulers and Dynasties of Ancient Egypt*. London: Thames & Hudson.

Cleitarchus (2004). *History of Alexander: 310–301 BC*, in Heckel, W. and Yardley, J. C. (eds), *Historical Sources in Translation, Alexander the Great*. Malden, MA: Blackwell Publishing.

Conger, J. (1991). 'Inspiring others: the language of leadership', *Academy of Management Executive* **5**, 31–45.

Conger, J. A. and R. N. Kanungo (1998). *Charismatic Leadership in Organizations*. Thousand Oaks, CA: Sage Publications.

Conquest, R. (1973). *The Great Terror: Stalin's Purge of the Thirties*. New York: Macmillan Books.

Copeland, E. S. (2009). 'A bipolar world: from the inside looking out', *Rochester Medicine* Spring/Summer, 36–7.

Costa, P. T., Jr. and R. R. McCrae (1988). 'Personality in adulthood: a six-year longitudinal study of self-reports and spouse ratings on the NEO Personality Inventory', *J Pers Soc Psychol* **54**(5), 853–63.

Couto, R. A. (1992). *Public Leadership Education: The Role of the Citizen Leader*. Dayton, OH: The Kettering Foundation.

Couto, R. A., E. A. Faier, D. A. Hicks and G. R. Hickman (2002). 'The integrating leadership project: gold team report', cited in Hickman and Couto (2006) as unpublished paper.

Craig, W. J. (1914). *The Complete Works of William Shakespeare*. London: Oxford University Press.

Crotty, M. (1998). *The Foundations of Social Research: Meaning and Perspective in the Research Process*. Thousand Oaks, CA: Sage Publications.

Crow, T. J. (1997a). 'Is schizophrenia the price that Homo sapiens pays for language?', *Schizophr Res* **28**(2-3), 127–41.

Crow, T. J. (1997b). 'Schizophrenia as failure of hemispheric dominance for language', *Trends Neurosci* **20**(8), 339–43.

Crow, T. J., L. R. Crow, D. J. Done and S. J. Leask (1996). 'The perils of hemispheric indecision', unpublished paper.

Custers, R. and H. Aarts (2010). 'The unconscious will: how the pursuit of goals operates outside of conscious awareness', *Science* **329**, 47–50.

Dalrymple, T. (2007). *In Praise of Prejudice: The Necessity of Preconceived Ideas*. New York: Encounter Books.

Damásio, A. R. (1994). *Descartes' Error: Emotion, Reason, and the Human Brain*. New York: Quill.

Darwin, C. (1846). *Journal of Researches Into the Natural History and Geology of the Countries Visited During the Voyage of H.M.S. Beagle Round the World: Under the Command of Capt. Fitz Roy, R.N*. New York: Harper & Brothers.

Darwin, C. (1859). *On the Origin of Species*. London: John Murray.

Dawkins, R. (1976). *The Selfish Gene*. Oxford: Oxford University Press.

Dawkins, R. (2006). *The God Delusion*. London: Bantam Press.

de Charmettes, P. A. L. B. (1817). 'Histoire de Jeanne d'Arc, surnommée la Pucelle d'Orléans', in Bertrand, A. (ed.), *The Story of Joan of Arc, Known as the Maid of Orleans, Based on Her Own Statements, 144 Depositions from Eye-witnesses, and Manuscripts in the Royal Library in the Tower of London*. Bertrand.

De Cremer, D. and M. Van Vugt (2002). 'Intra and intergroup dynamics of leadership in social dilemmas: a relational model of cooperation', *Journal of Experimental Social Psychology* **38**, 126–36.

de Duve, C. (2010). *Genetics of Original Sin*. New Haven, CT: Yale University Press.

de Launay, J. (1968). *De Gaulle and His France: A Psychopolitical and Historical Portrait*. New York: Julian Press.

De Neve, J. E., S. Mikhaylov, C. T. Dawes, N. A. Christakis and J. H. Fowler (2013). 'Born to lead? A twin design and genetic association study of leadership role occupancy', *Leadersh Q* **24**(1), 45–60.

De Vries, M. K. (2006). 'Lured to the dark side', *Director* **60**(3), 44–8.

de Waal, F. B. M. (1996). *Good Natured: The Origins of Right and Wrong in Humans and Other Animals*. Cambridge, MA: Harvard University Press.

Denning, S. (2007). *The Secret Language of Leadership: How Leaders Inspire Action Through Narrative*. San Francisco, CA: Jossey-Bass.

Descartes, R. (1637). 'Discourse on method (Pt. V)', in Ross, E. H. a. G. (ed.), *The Philosophical Works of Descartes,* Vol. 1. Cambridge: Cambridge University Press.

DeVries, K. (1999). *Joan of Arc: A Military Leader*. Stroud: Sutton Publishing.

Diamond, J. (1998). *Guns, Germs and Steel*. London: Vintage.

Dickerson, F. and J. F. O. McAllister (2002). 'Bush Blair and the Eurowimps', *Time*, 1 April.

Digman, J. M. (1989). 'Five robust trait dimensions: development, stability, and utility', *J Pers* **57**(2), 195–214.

Dirks, K. T. and D. L. Ferrin (2002). 'Trust in leadership: meta-analytic findings and implications for research and practice', *J Appl Psychol* **87**(4), 611–28.

Dobzhansky, T. G. (1937). *Genetics and the Origin of Species*. New York, Columbia University Press.

d'Orsi, G. and P. Tinuper (2006). "'I heard voices ...": from semiology, a historical review, and a new hypothesis on the presumed epilepsy of Joan of Arc', *Epilepsy Behav* **9**(1), 152–7.

Drath, W. (2001). *The Deep Blue Sea: Rethinking the Source of Leadership*. San Francisco, CA: Jossey-Bass.

Dunbar, R. I. M. (1993). 'Coevolution of neocortical size, group size and language in humans', *Behavioral and Brain Sciences* **16**(04), 681–94.

Dunbar, R. M. (2004). *Gossip, Grooming, and the Evolution of Language*. London: Faber & Faber.

Eagly, A. H. and S. J. Karau (2002). 'Role congruity theory of prejudice toward female leaders', *Psychol Rev* **109**, 573–98.

Eikenberry, K. (2007). *Remarkable Leadership: Unleashing Your Leadership Potential One Skill at a Time*. San Francisco, CA: Jossey-Bass.

Elliot, M. (2009). 'Who needs charisma?', *Time* **174**(2), 28–30.

Enard, W., M. Przeworski, S. E. Fisher, C. S. L. Lai, V. Wiebe, T. Kitano, A. P. Monaco and S. Paabo (2002). 'Molecular evolution of FOXP2, a gene involved in speech and language', *Nature* **418**, 869–72.

Enard, W., S. Gehre, K. Hammerschmidt, S. M. Holter, T. Blass, *et al.* (2009). 'A humanized version of Foxp2 affects cortico-basal ganglia circuits in mice', *Cell* **137**, 961–71.

Engels F. (1978 [1894]). 'Letter to H. Starkenburg', in Tucker, R. C. (ed.), *The Marx-Engels Reader*, 2nd edn. New York: Norton.

English, R. (2011). 'Hammurabi: First King Of Beer', *Drink Me Magazine* **16**, 18–20. Available at: http://drinkmemag.com/category/magazine-articles/issue-16/

Falk, E. B., M. B. O'Donnell and M. D. Lieberman (2012). 'Getting the word out: neural correlates of enthusiastic message propagation', *Front Hum Neurosci* **6**, 313.

Faulks, S. (2005). *Human Traces*. London: Hutchinson.

Fiedler, F. E. (1972). 'The effects of leadership training and experience: a contingency model interpretation', *Administrative Science Quarterly* **17**(4), 453–70.

Follett, M. P. (1951). *Creative Experience*. New York: Peter Smith.

Foner, E. (1990). *A Short History of Reconstruction*. New York, Harper Perennial.

Forrest, W. G. G. (1968). *A History of Sparta 950–192 B.C.* New York: W.W. Norton & Co.

Foucault, M. (1978). *The History of Sexuality: An Introduction*, translated Robert Hurley. New York: Pantheon Books.

Foundas, A. L., C. M. Leonard and K. M. Heilman (1995). 'Morphologic cerebral asymmetries and handedness. The pars triangularis and planum temporale', *Arch Neurol* **52**(5), 501–8.

Freeman, D., K. Pugh, A. Antley, M. Slater, P. Bebbington, *et al.* (2008). 'Virtual reality study of paranoid thinking in the general population', *Br J Psychiatry* **192**(4), 258–63.

French, J. R. P. and B. Raven (1959). 'The bases of social power', in Cartwright, D. (ed.), *Studies in Social Power.* Ann Arbor, MI: Institute of Social Research.

Freud, S. (1921). 'Group psychology and the analysis of the ego', in Strachey, J. (ed.), *The Standard Edition of the Complete Works of Sigmund Freud, Beyond the Pleasure Principle, Group Psychology and other Works.* London: Hogarth Press.

Freud, S. (1964). 'Moses and monotheism', in Strachey, J. (ed.), *The Standard Edition of the Complete Works of Sigmund Freud, Beyond the Pleasure Principle, Group Psychology and other Works.* London: Hogarth Press.

Fukuyama, F. (1998). 'Women and the evolution of world politics', *Foreign Affairs*, **77**(5), 25–40.

Galanter, M. (1980). 'Psychological induction into the large-group: findings from a modern religious sect', *Am J Psychiatry* **137**(12), 1574–9.

Galanter, M., R. Rabkin, J. Rabkin and A. Deutsch (1979). 'The "Moonies": a psychological study of conversion and membership in a contemporary religious sect', *Am J Psychiatry* **136**, 165–70.

Galili, L. (1995). 'Haish shemazkir lay or lama hu roze et hashilton' ['The man who reminds the chairman why he wants power'], *Ha'aretz*, 2, 16 March.

Galton, F. (1869). *Hereditary Genius: An Inquiry Into Its Laws and Consequences.* London: Macmillan & Co.

Gardner, H. (1995). *Leading Minds: An Anatomy of Leadership.* New York: Basic Books.

Gay, P. (1988). 'Psychoanalysis in history', in Runyan, W. M. K. (ed.), *Psychology and Historical Interpretation.* New York: Oxford University Press.

Gazzaniga, M. S. (2008). *Human: The Science Behind What Makes Us Unique.* New York: HarperCollins.

Gentilucci, M., P. Bernardis, G. Crisi and R. Dalla Volta (2006). 'Repetitive transcranial magnetic stimulation of Broca's area affects verbal responses to gesture observation', *J Cogn Neurosci* **18**(7), 1059–74.

George, A. L. and J. George (1956). *Woodrow Wilson and Colonel House: A Personality Study.* New York: John Day Publications.

Geschwind, D. H. (2008). 'Autism: many genes, common pathways?', *Cell* **135**, 391–5.

Ghaemi, S. N. (2011). *A First-Rate Madness: Uncovering the Links Between Leadership and Mental Illness*, New York: Penguin Group.

Giddens, A. (1976). *New Rules of Sociological Method: A Positive Critique of Interpretative Sociologies*. New York: Basic Books.

Gifford, J. (2010). *History Lessons: What Business and Management Can Learn from the Great Leaders of History*. London: Marshall Cavendish International.

Gilbert, P. (2000). 'Varieties of submissive behavior as forms of social defense: their evolution and role in depression', in Sloman, P. and Gilbert, P. (eds), *Subordination and Defeat: An Evolutionary Approach to Mood Disorders and their Therapy*. Mahwah, NJ: Lawrence Erlbaum Associates.

Goldberg, L. R. (1990). 'An alternative "description of personality": the big-five factor structure', *J Pers Soc Psychol* **59**(6), 1216–29.

Gough, H. G. (1988). *Manual for the California Psychological Inventory*. Palo Alto, CA: Consulting Psychologists Press.

Granovetter, M. (1978). 'Threshold models of collective behavior', *The American Journal of Sociology* **83**(6), 1420-1443.

Green, Z. G. (2006). 'Preliminary ideas about a General Theory of Leadership', unpublished manuscript (2002), quoted in Goethals, G. R. and G. J. Sorenson (eds), *The Quest for a General Theory of Leadership*, Northampton, MA, USA and Cheltenham, UK: Edward Elgar.

Greenleaf, R. K. (1977). *Servant Leadership: A Journey Into the Nature of Legitimate Power and Greatness*. New York: Paulist Press.

Greenstein F. (1987). *Personality and Politics: Problems of Violence, Influence and Conceptualization*. Princeton, NJ: Princeton University Press.

Hachinski, V. (1999). 'Stalin's last years: delusions or dementia?', *Eur J Neurol* **6**(2), 129–32.

Hall, R. H. (2012). *The Ancient History of the Near East* Lecturable, ebook.

Halpern, B. L. and K. Lubar (2003). *Leadership Presence: Dramatic Techniques to Reach Out, Motivate, and Inspire*. New York: Gotham Books.

Hampsey, J. C. (1954). *Paranoia and Contentment: A Personal Essay on Western Thought*. Charlottesville, VA: University of Virginia Press.

Hampton, W. H. and V. Schroeder Burnham (1990). *The Two-Edged Sword: A Study of the Paranoid Personality in Action*. Santa Fe, NM: Sunstone Press.

Harkins, P. (1999). *Powerful Conversations: How High Impact Leaders Communicate*. New York: McGraw-Hill Education.

Hart, R. P. (1984). *Verbal Style and the Presidency: A Computer-Based Analysis*. Orlando, FL: Academic Press.

Hart, R. P. (2000). *DICTION 5.0: The Text-Analysis Program*. Thousand Oaks, CA: Sage.

Hartmann, H. (1958). *Ego Psychology and the Problem of Adaptation*. New York: International Universities Press.

Harvey, M. (2006). 'Leadership and the human condition', in Goethals, G. R. and Sorenson, G. J. (eds), *The Quest for a General Theory of Leadership,* Northampton, MA, USA and Cheltenham, UK: Edward Elgar.

Hauser, M. D., N. Chomsky and W. T. Fitch (2002). 'The faculty of language: what is it, who has it, and how did it evolve?', *Science* **298**, 1569–79.

Hawking, S. W. (1988). *A Brief History of Time: From the Big Bang to Black Holes*. London: Bantam Books.

Hayman, S. E. and G. E. Tesar (1993). *Manual of Psychiatric Energencies*. Philadelphia, PA: Lippincott Williams and Wilkins.

Heer, F. (1968). *Glaube des Adolf Hitler: Anatomie einer Politischen Reliogiositat*. Munich, Germany: Esslingen.

Heifetz, R. A. (1994). *Leadership Without Easy Answers*. Cambridge, MA: Harvard University Press.

Heilman, M. E. (2001). 'Description and prescription: how gender stereotypes prevent women's ascent up the organizational ladder', *Journal of Social Issues* **57**(4), 657–74.

Henker, F. O. (1984). 'Joan of Arc and DSM III', *South Med J* **77**(12), 1488–90.

Hermann, M. (1976). 'When leader personality will affect foreign policy', in Rosenau, J. N. (ed.), *In Search of Global Patterns*. New York: Free Press.

Herodotus (1998). *The Histories*, R. Waterfield (ed.). Oxford: Oxford Paperbacks Press.

Heston, L. L. (1970). 'The genetics of schizophrenic and schizoid disease', *Science* **167**, 249–56.

Hickman, G. R. and R. A. Couto (2006). 'Causality, change and leadership', in Sorenson, G. and Goethals, G. (eds), *The Quest for a General Theory of Leadership*. Northampton, MA, USA and Cheltenham, UK: Edward Elgar.

Hillman, J. (1995). *Kinds of Power: A Guide to its Intelligent Uses*. New York: Currency Doubleday.

Hobbes, T. (1651). *Leviathan*, Richard Tuck (ed.). Cambridge: Cambridge University Press.

Hofstadter, R. (1964). 'The paranoid style in American politics', *Harper's Magazine*, November, 77–86.

Hogan, R., G. J. Curphy and J. Hogan (1994). 'What we know about leadership: effectiveness and personality', *Am Psychol* **49**, 493–504.

Hogg, M. A. (2001). 'A social identity theory of leadership', *Pers Soc Psychol Rev* **5**(3), 184–200.

Holladay, S. J. and W. T. Coombs (1993). 'Communicating visions: an exploration of the role of delivery in the creation of leader charisma', *Management Communication Quarterly* **6**, 405–27.

Holladay, S. J. and W. T. Coombs (1994). 'Speaking of visions and visions being spoken: an exploration of the effects of content and delivery on perceptions of leader charisma', *Management Communication Quarterly* **8**, 165–89.

Hollander, E. P. (1985). 'Leadership and power', in Lindzey, G. and E. Aronson (eds), *Handbook of Social Psychology*. New York: Random House.

Hollander, E. P. (1993). 'Legitimacy, power and influence. A perspective on relational features of leadership', in Chemers, M. M. and R. Ayman (eds), *Leadership Theory and Research: Perspectives and Directions*. San Diego, CA: Academic Press.

Hollander, E. P. and J. W. Julian (1969). 'Contemporary trends in the analysis of leadership processes', *Psychol Bull* **71**, 387–97.

Hollister, C. W. and A. C. Frost (2003). *Henry I*. New Haven, CT: Yale University Press.

Holmes, S. (2008). 'Jessy Helms dies at 86: conservative force in the Senate', *The New York Times*, 5 July.

Hook, S. (1943). *The Hero in History: A Study in Limitation and Possibility*. New York: John Day.

Horrobin, D. F. (1998). 'Schizophrenia: the illness that made us human', *Med Hypotheses* **50**(4), 269–88.

Horrobin, D. F. (2001). *The Madness of Adam and Eve: How Schizophrenia Shaped Humanity*. New York: Bantam.

House, R. J. and R. N. Aditya (1997). 'The social scientific study of leadership: quo vadis?', *Journal of Management* **23**(3), 409–73.

Hoyt, C. L., G. R. Goethals and R. Riggio (2006). 'Leader-follower relations: group dynamics and the role of leadership', in Goethals, G. R. and Sorenson, G. J. (eds), *The Quest for a General Theory of Leadership*. Northampton, MA, USA and Cheltenham, UK: Edward Elgar.

Huntington, S. P. (2002). *The Clash of Civilizations and the Remaking of World Order*. London: Free Press.

Hyde, H. N. J. (1990). 'Embassy Moscow: paying the bill', *Congressional Record*, E3555.

Iacoboni, M., L. M. Koski, M. Brass, H. Bekkering, R. P. Woods, *et al.* (2001). 'Reafferent copies of imitated actions in the right superior temporal cortex', *Proc Natl Acad Sci USA* **98**(24), 13995–9.

Iacoboni, M., R. P. Woods, M. Brass, H. Bekkering, J. C. Mazziotta and G. Rizzolatti (1999). 'Cortical mechanisms of human imitation', *Science* **286**, 2526–8.

Ilies, R., M. Gerhardt and H. Le (2004). 'Individual differences in leadership emergence: integrating meta-analytic findings and behavioral genetics estimates', *International Journal of Selection and Assessment* **12**(3), 207–19.

Insch, G. S., J. E. Moore and L. D. Murphy (1997). 'Content analysis in leadership research: examples, procedures, and suggestions for future use', *The Leadership Quarterly* **8**(1), 1–25.

Isaacson, W. (2007). *Einstein: His Life and Universe*. London: Simon & Schuster.

Jackson, R. H. (2003). *That Man: An Insider's Portrait of Franklin D. Roosevelt*. New York: Oxford University Press.

Jaynes, J. (1990). *The Origin of Consciousness in the Breakdown of the Bicameral Mind*. Boston, MA: Houghton Mifflin.

Jones, J. S. and S. Rouhani (1986), 'Human evolution. How small was the bottleneck?', *Nature* **319**, 449–50.

Judge, T. A. and J. E. Bono (2000). 'Five-factor model of personality and transformational leadership', *J Appl Psychol* **85**, 751–65.

Judge, T. A., J. E. Bono, R. Ilies and M. W. Gerhardt (2002). 'Personality and leadership: a qualitative and quantitative review', *J Appl Psychol* **87**(4), 765–80.

Kafka, F. (2011). *The Trial*. New York: Tribeca Books.

Kagan, D. (1998). *Pericles of Athens And The Birth Of Democracy*. New York, Free Press.

Kandel, E., J. Schwartz and T. Jessell (2000). *Principles of Neural Science*. New York: McGraw-Hill.

Kanner, L. (1943). 'Autistic disturbances of affective contact', *Nervous Child* **2**, 217–50.

Kanner, L. (1949). 'Problems of nosology and psychodynamics of early infantile autism', *Am J Orthopsychiatry* **19**, 416–26.

Karlsson, J. L. (1966). *The Biologic Basis of Schizophrenia*. Springfield, IL: Thomas.

Karlsson, J. L. (1974). 'Inheritance of schizophrenia', *Acta Psychiatr Scand Suppl* **247**, 1–116.

Karlsson, J. L. (2001). 'Mental abilities of male relatives of psychotic patients', *Acta Psychiatr Scand* **104**(6), 466–8.

Kelloway, E. K. and J. Barling (2000). 'What we have learned about developing transformational leaders', *Leadership & Organization Development Journal* **21**, 355–62.

Kelman, H. C. (1958). 'Compliance, identification, and internalization: three processes of attitude change', *Journal of Conflict Resolution* **2**(1), 51–60.

Kernberg, O. F. (1975). *Borderline Conditions and Pathological Narcissism*. New York: J. Aronson.

Kety, S. S., P. H. Wender, B. Jacobsen, L. J. Ingraham, L. Jansson, *et al.* (1994). 'Mental illness in the biological and adoptive relatives of schizophrenic adoptees. Replication of the Copenhagen Study in the rest of Denmark', *Arch Gen Psychiatry* **51**, 442–55.

Khalid, M. (1985). *Nimeiri and the Revolution of Dis-May*. London: KPI.

Kimhi, S. (2002). 'Benjamin Netanyahu: a psychological profile using behavior analysis', in Valenty, L. and Feldman, O. (eds), *Political Leadership for the New Century*. Westport, CT: Greenwood.

King, A. J., D. D. Johnson and M. Van Vugt (2009). 'The origins and evolution of leadership', *Cell Biology* **19**(19), 911–16.

Kipnis, D., S. M. Schmidt and I. Wilkinson (1980). 'Intraorganizational influence tactics: explorations in getting one's way', *Journal of Applied Psychology* **65**(4), 440–52.

Kirk, U., J. Downar and P. R. Montague (2007). 'Interoception drives increased rational decision-making in meditators playing the Ultimatum Game', *Frontiers in Neuroscience* **10**, 779–86.

Kirkpatrick, S. A. and E. A. Locke (1991). 'Leadership: do traits matter?', *Academy of Management Executive*, **5**, 48–60.

Kleinman, A. (1981). *Patients and Healers in the Context of Culture: An Exploration of the Borderland Between Anthropology, Medicine, and Psychiatry*. Berkeley, CA: University of California Press.

Klonsky, B. G. (1983). 'The socialization and development of leadership ability', *Genetic Psychology Monographs*, **108**.

Kluckhohn, C. and H. A. Murray (1953). 'Personality formation: the determinants', in Kluckhohn, C., Murray, H. and Schneider, D. (eds), *Personality in Nature, Society and Culture*. New York: Knopf.

Knapp, M. (2007). *Mental Health Policy and Practice Across Europe: The Future Direction of Mental Health Care*. New York: McGraw-Hill International.

Kohler, E., C. Keysers, M. A. Umiltà, L. Fogassi, V. Gallese and G. Rizzolatti (2002). 'Hearing sounds, understanding actions: action representation in mirror neurons', *Science* **297**, 846–8.

Kohut, H. (1971). *The Analysis of the Self: A Systematic Approach to the Psychoanalytic Treatment of Narcissistic Personality Disorders*. New York: International Universities Press.

Kohut, H. (1984). *How Does Analysis Cure?* Chicago, IL: University of Chicago Press.

Konovsky, M. A. and S. D. Pugh (1994). 'Citizenship behavior and social exchange', *Acad Manage J* **37**, 656–69.

Korman, A. K. (1968). 'The prediction of managerial performance: a review', *Personnel Psychology* **21**(3), 295–322.

Kraepelin, E. (1920). 'Die Erscheinungsformen des Irreseins', translated by H. Marshall as 'Patterns of mental disorder', in Hirsch, S. R. and Shepherd M. (eds), *Themes and Variations in European Psychiatry.* Bristol: Wright.

Kraybill, D. B., K. M. Johnson-Weiner and S. M. Nolt (2013). *The Amish.* Baltimore, MD: Johns Hopkins University Press.

Kubizek, A. (1955). *The Young Hitler I Knew.* Boston, MA: Houghton Mifflin.

Lambert, L., D. P. Zimmerman and J. E. Cooper (1995). *The Constructivist Leader.* New York: Teachers College Press.

Lammers, J., D. A. Stapel and A. D. Galinsky (2010). 'Power increases hypocrisy: moralizing in reasoning, immorality in behavior', *Psychol Sci* **21**(5), 737–44.

Landis, J. (2009, 2010, 2011). 'The verbal behavior and personality assessment of the Syrian President Bashar al-Assad', comments on blogsite www.styriacomment.com, beginning 21 March 2009. Accessed 22 September 2012.

Langer, E. J. and J. Roth (1975). 'Heads I win, tails it's chance: the illusion of control as a function of the sequence of outcomes in a purely chance task', *Journal of Personality and Social Psychology* **3**(6), 951–5.

Lasswell, H. D. (1930). *Psychopathology and Politics.* Chicago, IL: University of Chicago Press.

Launay J. (1968). *De Gaulle and his France: A Psychological and Historical Portrait*, translated Dorothy Albertyn. New York: Julian Press.

Le Bon, G. (1969 [1895]). *The Crowd.* New York: Ballantine.

Le Couteur, A., A. Bailey, S. Goode, A. Pickles, S. Robertson, *et al.* (1996). 'A broader phenotype of autism: the clinical spectrum in twins', *J Child Psychol Psychiatry* **37**(7), 785–801.

Leakey, R. E. and R. Lewin (1993). *Origins Reconsidered.* New York: Anchor Books.

Lee, D. and H. Seo (2007). 'Mechanisms of reinforcement learning and decision making in the primate dorsolateral prefrontal cortex', *Ann N Y Acad Sci* **1104**, 108–22.

Levine, J. M. and R. L. Moreland (1998). 'Small groups', in Gilbert, D., Fiske, S. and Lindzey, G. (eds), *The Handbook of Social Psychology,* 4th edn, vol. 2. Boston, MA: McGraw-Hill.

Levitan, R. D., G. Hasey and L. Sloman (2000). *Major Depression and the Involuntary Defeat Strategy: Biological Correlates.* Mahwah, NJ: Lawrence Erlbaum Associates.

Lewin, K. (1951). *Field Theory in Social Science: Selected Theoretical Papers.* New York: Harper.

Lewis, H. S. (1974). *Leaders and Followers: Some Anthropological Perspectives.* Reading, MA: Addison-Wesley.

Lewis, T. (1984). *Late Night Thoughts on Listening to Mahler's Ninth Symphony.* New York: Bantam Doubleday Dell.

Lieb, J. (2008). 'Two manic-depressives, two tyrants, two world wars', *Med Hypotheses* **70**(4), 888–92.

Lindholm, C. (1990). *Charisma.* London: Basil Blackwell.

Linebaugh, P. (2008). *The Magna Carta Manifesto: Liberties and Commons for All.* Berkeley, CA: University of California Press.

Locke, J. (1988). *Two Treatises of Government*, Peter Laslett (ed.). Cambridge: Cambridge University Press.

Loewenberg, P. (1988). 'Psychoanalytic models of history: Freud and after', in Runyan, W. M. K. (ed.), *Psychology and Historical Interpretation.* New York: Oxford University Press.

Lombroso C. (1981). *The Man of Genius.* New York: Scribner's Sons.

Lord, R. G. and K. J. Maher (1991). *Leadership and Information Processing: Linking Perceptions and Performance.* Boston, MA: Unwin Hyman.

Lord, R. G., R. J. Foti and C. L. De Vader (1984). 'A test of leadership categorization theory: internal structure, information processing, and leadership perceptions', *Organizational Behavior and Human Performance* **3**, 343–78.

Lord, R. G., C. L. de Vader and G. M. Alliger (1986). 'A meta-analysis of the relation between personality traits and leadership perceptions: an application of validity generalization procedures', *Journal of Applied Psychology* **71**(3), 402–10.

Machiavelli, N. (2001a [1531]). 'Discourses on the first ten books of Titus Livius', excerpts reprinted in Morgan, M. L. (ed.), *Classics of Moral and Political Theory*, 3rd edn. Indianapolis, IN: Hackett.

Machiavelli, N. (2001b [1532]). *The Prince*, in Morgan, M. L. (ed.), *Classics of Moral and Political Theory*, 3rd edn. Indianapolis, IN: Hackett.

MacIntyre, A. (1994). *Is Patriotism a Virtue?* Belmont, CA: Wadsworth.

Mackowiak, P. (2007). *Post Mortem: Solving History's Great Medical Mysteries.* Washington, DC: ACP Press.

Maddi, S. R. (1986). *Personality Theories: A Comparative Analysis.* Chicago, IL: Dorsey Press.

Magiorkinis, E., K. Sidiropoulou and A. Diamantis (2010). 'Hallmarks in the history of epilepsy: epilepsy in antiquity', *Epilepsy Behav* **17**(1), 103–8.

Makiya, K. (1998). *Republic of Fear: The Politics of Modern Iraq.* Berkeley, CA: University of California Press.

Malinowski, B. (1961). *Argonauts of the Western Pacific.* New York: E. P. Dutton & Co.

Markus, Y. (1992). 'Gonev laem at hamiflaga' ['Stealing the party from them'], *Ha'aretz 1*, 14 August.

Markus, Y. (1996). 'Shuvo shel Netanyahy' ['The return of Netanyahu'], *Ha'aretz 1*, 1 March.

Markus, Y. (1997). 'Iekahim mimashber ahad' ['Four lessons from one crisis'], *Ha'aretz 1*, 30 November.

Martin, R. E. and J. Q. Wickham (1996). 'Membrane docosahexaenoic acid content influences A-type phospholipase activity in PC12 cell nerve growth cones', *Society for Neuroscience* **22**(37).

Martin, T. R. (1996). *Ancient Greece: From Prehistoric to Hellenistic Times.* New Haven, Yale University Press.

Marx, K. (1978 [1845]). *Theses on Feuerbach*, in Tucker, R. C. (ed.), *The Marx-Engel Reader*, 2nd edn. New York: Norton.

Marx, K. (1978 [1857–8]). *The Grundrisse*, in Tucker, R. C. (ed.), *The Marx-Engel Reader*, 2nd edn. New York: Norton.

Marx, K. (1937 [1869]). *The Eighteenth Brumaire of Louis Bonaparte*, translated by Padover, S. Moscow: Progress Publishers.

Mayer, R. C., J. H. Davis and F. D. Schoorman (1995). 'An integrative model of organizational trust', *Academy of Management Review* **20**, 709–34.

McAllister, D. J. (1995). 'Affect- and cognition-based trust as foundations for interpersonal cooperation in organizations', *Academy of Management Journal* **38**, 24–59.

McCarthy, A. C. (2010). 'War-power paranoia', *National Review*, 15 November.

McClary, A. (1975). *Biology and Sociology.* New York: Macmillan.

McClelland, D. C. and D. H. Burnham (2003). 'Power is the great motivator', *Harv Bus Rev* **81**, 117–26.

McCrae, R. R. and P. T. Costa (1997). 'Personality trait structure as a human universal', *Am Psychol* **52**(9145021), 509–16.

McNeill, W. H. (1995). *Keeping Together in Time: Dance and Drill in Human History.* Cambridge, MA: Harvard University Press.

McWilliams, N. (2010). 'Paranoia and political leadership', *Psychoanalytic Review* **97**(2), 239–61.

Mead, M. (1955). *Cultural Patterns and Technical Change.* New York: Mentor Books.

Meindl, J. R. (1990). 'On leadership: an alternative to the conventional wisdom', in Cummings, B. and Staw, L. (eds), *Research in Organizational Behavior.* Greenwich, CT: JAI Press.

Milgram, S. (1975). *Obedience to Authority: An Experimental View.* New York: Harper Colophon.

Mineka, S., M. Davidson, M. Cook and R. Keir (1984). 'Observational conditioning of snake fear in rhesus monkeys', *J Abnorm Psychol* **93**, 355–72.

Mio, J. S., R. E. Riggio, S. Levin and R. Reese (2005). 'Presidential leadership and charisma: the effects of metaphor', *Leadership Quarterly* **16**(2), 287–94.

Mitani, J. C., D. P. Watts and S. J. Amsler (2010). 'Lethal intergroup aggression leads to territorial expansion in wild chimpanzees', *Curr Biol* **20**, 507–8.

Montagu, A. (1968). 'The new litany of innate depravity or original sin revisited', in Montagu, A. (ed.), *Man and Aggression.* New York: Oxford University Press.

Moore, M. (2003). *Dude, Where's My Country?* New York: Warner Books Publications.

Morgan, E. (1997). *The Aquatic Ape Hypothesis.* London: Souvenir Press.

Morris, D. (1969). *The Human Zoo.* New York: McGraw-Hill.

Mowry, B. J., D. P. Lennon and C. N. De Felice (1994). 'Diagnosis of schizophrenia in a matched sample of Australian aborigines', *Acta Psychiatr Scand* **90**(5), 337–41.

Mulder, M., J. R. Ritsema van Eck and R. D. de Jong (1970). 'An organization in crisis and non-crisis conditions', *Human Relations* **16**, 317–34.

Murakami, H. (2013). *1Q84.* New York: Vintage International.

Myers, D. G. and G. D. Bishop (1971). 'Enhancement of dominant attitudes in group discussion', *J Pers Soc Psychol* **20**(3), 386–91.

Myers, D. and Kaplan, M. (1976). 'Group induced polarization in simulated juries', *Personality and Social Psychology Bulletin* **2** (1), 63–6.

Nasar, S. (1998). *A Beautiful Mind: The Life of Mathematical Genius and Nobel Laureate John Nash.* London: Simon & Schuster.

Nasrallah, H. A. (1985). 'The unintegrated right cerebral hemispheric consciousness as alien intruder: a possible mechanism for Schneiderian delusions in schizophrenia', *Compr Psychiatry* **26**(3), 273–82.

Natarajan, D. and D. Caramaschi (2010). 'Animal violence demystified', *Front Behav Neurosci* **4**, 9.

Nelson, E. and R. Hogan (2009). 'Coaching on the dark side', *International Coaching Psychology Review* **4**, 9–21.

Nesse, R. (2004). 'Cliff-edged fitness functions and the persistence of schizophrenia', *Behavioral and Brain Sciences* **27**(6), 862–3.

Nicholson, N. (2000). *Managing the Human Animal*. London: Thomson.

Niebuhr, G. A. (1994). 'To churches dismay, priest talks of "justifiable homicide" of abortion doctors', *New York Times* A12, 24 August.

Nisbett, A. (1976). *Konrad Lorenz*. London: Dent.

Nolte, E. (1996). *Three Faces of Fascism: Action Francaise, Italian Fascism, National Socialism*. New York: Henry Holt & Co.

Norman, W. T. (1963). 'Toward an adequate taxonomy of personality attributes: replicated factors structure in peer nomination personality ratings', *J Abnorm Soc Psychol* **66**, 574–83.

Nye, J. S. (2004). *Soft Power: The Means to Success in World Politics*. New York: Public Affairs.

Oh, K. D. and R. C. Hassig (2000). *North Korea through the Looking Glass*. Washington, DC: Brookings Institution Press.

Oloyede, O. B., A. T. Folayan and A. A. Odutuga (1992). 'Effects of low-iron status and deficiency of essential fatty acids on some biochemical constituents of rat brain', *Biochem Int* **27**(5), 913–22.

Oppenheimer, S. (2004). *The Real Eve: Modern Man's Journey Out of Africa*. New York: Carroll & Graf.

Osman, A. (2002). *Moses and Akhenaten: The Secret History of Egypt at the Time of the Exodus*. Rochester, VT: Bear & Co.

Ospina, M. B., J. Krebs Seida, B. Clark, M. Karkhaneh, L. Hartling, *et al.* (2008). 'Behavioural and developmental interventions for autism spectrum disorder: a clinical systematic review', *PLoS One* **3**.

Ospina, S. and G. L. J. Sorenson (2006). 'A constructionist lens on leadership: charting new territory', in Goethals, G. R. and G. J. Sorenson (eds), *The Quest for a General Theory of Leadership*. Northampton, MA, USA and Cheltenham, UK: Edward Elgar.

Parsons, T., R. F. Bales and E. A. Shils (1953). *Working Papers in the Theory of Action*. Glencoe, IL: Free Press.

Pastor, J. C. (1998). *The Social Construction of Leadership: A Semantic and Social Network Analysis of Social Representations of Leadership*. Ann Arbor, MI: University of Michigan Dissertation Services.

Payne, E. A. (1992). *The Pharaohs of Ancient Agypt*. New York: Random House.

Perkins, J. (2004). *Confessions of an Economic Hit Man*. San Francisco, CA: Berrett-Koehler.

Pinker, S. (2002). *The Blank Slate: Denying Human Nature in Modern Life*. New York: Penguin.

Pinker, S. (2011). *The Better Angels of Our Nature: Why Violence Has Declined*. New York: Penguin.

Plato (2001). *Republic*, in Morgan, M. L. (ed.), *Classics of Moral and Political Theory*. Indianapolis, IN: Hackett.

Plomin, R. and E. Colledge (2001). 'Genetics and psychology: beyond heritability', *European Psychologist* **6**, 229–40.

Porcelli, A. J., A. H. Lewis and M. R. Delgado (2012). 'Acute stress influences neural circuits of reward processing', *Front Neurosci* **6**, 157.

Post, J. M. (1973). 'On aging leaders: possible effects of the aging process on the conduct of leadership', *J Geriatr Psychiatry* **7**(1), 109–16.

Post, J. M. (1980). 'The seasons of a leader's life: influences of the life cycle on political behavior', *Political Psychology 2* **2**(3Q), 35–49.

Post, J. M. (2004). *Leaders and Their Followers in a Dangerous World: The Psychology of Political Behavior*. New York: Cornell University Press.

Post, J. M. and R. S. Robins (1995). *When Illness Strikes the Leader: The Dilemma of the Captive King*. New Haven, CT: Yale University Press.

Postmes, T. and R. Spears (1998). 'Deindividuation and anti-normative behavior: a meta analysis', *Psychological Bulletin* **123**(3), 238–59.

Powell B. (2012). 'Meet Kim Jong Un', *Time Magazine*, 179(**8**), 16–23.

Premack, D. and G. Woodruff (1978). 'Does the chimpanzee have a theory of mind?', *Behavioral and Brain Sciences* **1**(4), 515–26.

Price, T. L. (2006). *Understanding Ethical Failures in Leadership*. New York: Cambridge University Press.

Price, T. L. and D. A. Hicks (2006). 'A framework for a general theory of leadership ethics', in Goethals, G. R. and Sorenson, G. J. (eds), *The Quest for a General Theory of Leadership*. Northampton, MA, USA and Cheltenham, UK: Edward Elgar.

Pyysiainen, I. and M. Hauser (2010). 'The origins of religion: evolved adaptation or by-product?', *Trends Cogn Sci* **14**, 104–9.

Raaflaub, K. A. (2007). 'The breakthrough of demokratia in mid-fifth century Athens', in Raaflaub, K. A., Ober, L., Wallace, R., Cartledge, P. and Farrar, C. (eds), *Origins of Democracy in Ancient Greece*. Berkeley, CA: University of California Press.

Raven, B. (1965). 'Social influence and power', in Steiner, I. D. and Fishbein, M. (eds), *Current Studies in Social Psychology*. New York: Society for the Psychological Study of Social Issues, Holt, Rinehart and Winston.

Rawls, J. (1971). *A Theory of Justice*. Cambridge, MA: Harvard University Press.

Rawls, J. (1999). *The Law of Peoples: with 'The Idea of Public Reason Revisited'*. Cambridge, MA: Harvard University Press.

Ray, D. (2011). *The Reassuring Universe*. Ebook, Quantum Embrace Books.

Reader, J. (1988). *Man on Earth*. London: William Collins.

Redford, D. B. (1987). 'The monotheism of the heretic pharaoh: precursor of Mosiac monotheism or Egyptian anomaly?', *Biblical Archaeo Review* **13**(3), May–June.

Richey, S. W. (2003). *Joan of Arc: The Warrior Saint*. Westport, CT: Praeger.

Ridley, M. (2003). *Nature Via Nurture: Genes, Experience, and What Makes Us Human*. New York: HarperCollins.

Ridolfi, R. (1968). *The life of Francesco Guicciardini*. New York: Alfred A Knopf.

Riggio, R. E. (2004). 'Charisma', in Goethals, G. R., Sorenson, G. J. and Burns, J. M. G. (eds), *Encyclopedia of Leadership*. Thousand Oaks, CA: Sage.

Rimland, B. (1964). *Infantile Autism: The Syndrome and Its Implications for a Neural Theory of Behavior*. New York: Appleton Century Crofts.

Ringo, J. L., R. W. Doty, S. Demeter and P. Y. Simard (1994). 'Time is of the essence: a conjecture that hemispheric specialization arises from interhemispheric conduction delay', *Cereb Cortex* **4**(4), 331–43.

Rizzolatti, G. and M. A. Arbib (1998). 'Language within our grasp', *Trends Neurosci* **21**(5), 188–94.

Robins, R. (1984). 'Paranoia and charisma', paper presented to the Annual Meeting of the International Society of Political Psychology, Toronto, Canada.

Robins, R. S. and J. M. Post (1987). 'The paranoid political actor', *Biography* **10**(1), 1–19.

Rohde, D. L. T., S. Olson and J. T. Chang (2004). 'Modelling the recent common ancestry of all living humans', *Nature* **431**, 562–6.

Ronson, J. (2011). *The Psychopath Test*. Oxford: Pan Macmillan.

Ropper, A. H. and R. J. Brown (2005). *Adams and Victor's Principles of Neurology*. New York: McGraw-Hill Education.

Rosenblum, K. E. and T. M. C. Travis (2008). *The Meaning of Difference: American Constructions of Race, Sex and Gender, Social Class, Sexual Orientation, and Disability*. New York, McGraw-Hill Higher Education.

Roth, M. T. (2000). *Law Collections from Mesopotamia and Asia Minor*. Atlanta, GA: Scholars Press.

Rousseau, D. M., S. B. Sitkin, R. S. Burt and C. Camerer (1998). 'Not so different after all: a cross-discipline view of trust', *Academy of Management Review* **23**, 393–404.

Rousseau, J. J. (2001 [1755]). 'Discourse on the origin and foundations of inequality among men', in Morgan, M. L. (ed.), *Classics of Moral And Political Theory,* 3rd edn. Indianapolis, IN: Hackett.

Rousseau, J. J. (2001 [1762]). 'On the social contract, or principles of political right', in Morgan, M. L. (ed.), *Classics of Moral And Political Theory,* 3rd edn. Indianapolis, IN: Hackett.

Roy, J. J. E. (2010). *Histoire de Jeanne D'Arc (1840).* Kessinger Publishing.

Runyan, R. McKinley (1988a). 'A historical and conceptual background to psychohistory', in Runyan, R. McKinley (ed.), *Psychology and Historical Interpretation.* New York: Oxford University Press.

Runyan, R. McKinley (1988b). 'Reconceptualizing the relationships between history and psychology', in Runyan, R. McKinley (ed.), *Psychology and Historical Interpretation.* New York: Oxford University Press.

Rushton, J. P., D. W. Fulker, M. C. Neale, D. K. Nias and H. J. Eysenck (1986). 'Altruism and aggression: the heritability of individual differences', *J Pers Soc Psychol* **50**(6), 1192–8.

Rutter, M., J. Kreppner, C. Croft, M. Murin, E. Colvert, *et al.* (2007). 'Early adolescent outcomes of institutionally deprived and non-deprived adoptees. III. Quasi-autism', *J Child Psychol Psychiatry* **48**(12), 1200–7.

Sagan, C. (1977). *Dragons of Eden: Speculations of the Evolution of Human Intelligence.* New York: Ballantine Books.

Samuelson, C. D., D. M. Messick, C. Rutte and H. Wilke (1984). 'Individual and structural solutions to resource dilemmas in two cultures', *J Pers Soc Psychol* **47**(1), 94–104.

Schmitt, D. P. and J. J. Pilcher (2004). 'Evaluating evidence of psychological adaptation: how do we know one when we see one?', *Psychol Sci* **15**, 643–9.

Schrödinger, E. (1944). *What is Life?: Mind and Matter?* Dublin: Trinity College.

Shavit, H. (1996). 'Mizrah Tihon hadash? Eize raayon meshashea' ['New Middle East? What a ridiculous idea'], *Ha'aretz* 18, 22 November.

Sherif, M. and G. Murphy (1936). *The Psychology of Social Norms.* New York: Harper.

Sherman, W. T. (1889). *Memoirs of General William Sherman,* 2nd edn. New York: D. Appleton & Co.

Shirer, W. L. (1969). *The Collapse of the Third Republic: An Inquiry into the Fall of France.* New York: Simon & Schuster.

Simon, H. A. and H. Guetzkow (1955). 'A model of short- and long-run mechanisms involved in pressures toward uniformity in groups', *Psychol Rev* **62**, 56–68.

Singer, P. (1972). 'Famine, affluence and morality', *Philosophy and Public Affairs* **1**(1), 229–43.

Smircich, L. and G. Morgan (1982). 'Leadership: the management of meaning', *J Appl Behav Sci* **18**, 257–73.

Smith, A. (1776). *The Wealth of Nations*. London: Strahan and T. Cadell.

Snow, C. P. (2001 [1959]). *The Two Cultures*. London: Cambridge University Press.

Sober, E. and D. S. Wilson (1998). *Unto Others: The Evolution and Psychology of Unselfish Behavior*. Cambridge, MA: Harvard University Press.

Sorenson, G. H. and G. R. Hickman (2002). 'Invisible leadership: action on behalf of a common purpose', proceedings of the International Leadership Association, James MacGregor Burns Academy of Leadership.

Spalding, D. A. (1873). 'Instinct: with original observations on young animals', *Macmillan's Magazine* **27**, 282–93.

Spector, T. (2012). *Identically Different: Why You Can Change Your Genes*. London: Weidenfeld & Nicolson.

Sperry, L. (2002). 'From psychopathology to transformation: retrieving the developmental focus in psychotherapy', *The Journal of Individual Psychology* **58**(5), 398–421.

Sperry, L. (2004). *Executive Coaching: The Essential Guide for Mental Health Professionals*. New York: Brunner-Routledge.

Stoddard, T., T. Kliengklom and T. Ben-Zeev (2003). 'Stereotype threat, assimilation, and contrast effects and subtlety of priming', paper presented at the Annual Society for Personality and Social Psychology Conference, Los Angeles.

Stogdill, R. M. (1950). 'Leadership, membership and organization', *Psychological Bulletin* **47**, 1–14.

Stogdill, R. M. (1957). *Leader Behavior: Its Description and Measurement*. Columbus, OH: Ohio State University College of Administrative Science.

Stoneking, M., S. T. Sherry, A. J. Redd and L. Vigilant (1992). 'New approaches to dating suggest a recent age for the human mtDNA ancestor', *Philos Trans R Soc Lond B Biol Sci* **337**, 167–75.

Strathearn, L. (2009). 'The elusive etiology of autism: nature or nurture?', *Frontiers in Behavioral Neuroscience* **3**, doi: 10.3389/neuro.08.011.2009

Takahashi, A., I. M. Quadros, R. M. de Almeida and K. A. Miczek (2012). 'Behavioral and pharmacogenetics of aggressive behavior', *Curr Top Behav Neurosci* **2**, 73–138.

Team, R. D. C. (2009). *A Language and Environment for Statistical Computing*. Vienna: R Foundation for Statistical Computing.

Terman, L. M. (1904). 'A preliminary study in the psychology and pedagogy of leadership', *Journal of Genetic Psychology* **11**, 413–51.

The Economist (1990). 'Lech Wałęsa', 22 September.

The Economist (2008). 'Lech Wałęsa: History's tentacles', 26 June.

Thrall, B., B. McNicol and K. McElrath (1999). *The Ascent of a Leader*. San Francisco, CAP: Jossey-Bass.

Thucydides (1974). *History of the Peloponnesian War*. London: Penguin.

Tiger, L. and R. Fox (1971). *The Imperial Animal*. New Brunswick, NJ: Transaction Publishers.

Tomasello, M. (1999). *The Cultural Origins Of Human Cognition*. Boston, MA: Harvard University Press.

Trigger, B. G., B. G. Kemp, D. O'Conner and A. B. Lloyd (2001). *Ancient Egypt, a Social History*. Cambridge: Cambridge University Press.

Trivers, R. (2000). 'The elements of a scientific theory of self-deception', *Ann N Y Acad Sci* **907**, 114–31.

Trommershauser, J. (2011). 'Frontiers research topic on the neurobiology of choice', *Front Neurosci* **5**, 119.

Tucker, R. C. (1965). 'The dictator and totalitarianism', *World Politics* **17**, 555–83.

Tucker, R. C. (1973). *Stalin as Revolutionary, 1879–1929: A Study in History and Personality*. New York: Norton.

Tucker, R. C. (1981). *Politics as Leadership*. Columbia, MO: University of Missouri Press.

Tullberg, M., E. Fletcher, C. DeCarli, D. Mungas, B. R. Reed, *et al.* (2004). 'White matter lesions impair frontal lobe function regardless of their location', *Neurology* **63**, 246–53.

Tupes, E. C. and R. E. Christal (1961). *Recurrent Personality Factors Based on Trait Ratings. (Technical Report ASD-TR-61-97)*. Lackland Air Force Base, TX: US Air Force.

Turnbull, C. (1972). *The Mountain People*. New York: Simon & Schuster.

Tylor, E. B. (1889). *Primitive Culture: Researches Into the Development of Mythology, Philosophy, Religion, Language, Art and Custom, by Edward B. Tylor*. London: John Murray.

Van de Meiroop, Marc (2005). *King Hammurabi of Babylon: A Biography*. Malden, MA: Blackwell.

Van Vugt, M. (2006). 'Evolutionary origins of leadership and followership', *Pers Soc Psychol Rev* **10**(4), 354–71.

Van Vugt, M. and D. De Cremer (1999). 'Leadership in social dilemmas: the effects of group identification on collective actions to provide public goods', *Journal of Personality and Social Psychology* **76**(4), 587–99.

Van Vugt, M., R. Hogan and R. B. Kaiser (2008). 'Leadership, follower-ship, and evolution: some lessons from the past', *Am Psychol* **63**(3), 182–96.

Ventura-Junca, R. and L. M. Herrera (2012). 'Epigenetic alterations related to early-life stressful events', *Acta Neuropsychiatrica* **24**(5), 255–65.

Verter, Y. (1996). 'Netanyahu yeshalem beyoker al haitalelot bezarbaat habekhirim', omrim balikud' ['Likud sources: Natanyahu will pay high price for maltreatment of the four senior members'], *Ha'aretz 3*, 17 June.

Verter, Y. (1997). 'Netanahu: Novil et israel leshnat alpaim ume'ever la' ['Netanyahu: we will lead Israel to the year 2000 and beyond'], *Ha'aretz 3*, **3**, 18 April.

Vicario, C. M. (2013). 'FOXP2 gene and language development: the molecular substrate of the gestural-origin theory of speech?', *Front Behav Neurosci* **7**, 99.

Volkan, V. M. (1980). 'Narcissistic personality organization and "repara-tive" leadership', *Int J Group Psychother* **30**(2), 131–52.

Volkan, V. M. and N. Itzkowitz (1984). *The Immortal Ataturk: A Psychobiography*. Chicago, IL: University of Chicago Press.

Volkan, V. M. (1982). 'Remarks at symposium on Ataturk and narcissis-tic leaders', Annual Meeting of the International Society of Political Psychology, Washington, DC.

Volman, I., M. L. Noordzij and I. Toni (2012). 'Sources of variability in human communicative skills', *Front Hum Neurosci* **6**, 310.

Vygotsky, L. S. (1986). *Thought and Language*. Cambridge, MA: MIT Press.

Wagenknecht, D. (1995). 'Recasting Moses: narrative and drama in the dumbshow of Freud's "The Moses of Michelangelo"', *American Imago* **52**(4), 439–61.

Wainscoat, J. S., A. V. Hill, A. L. Boyce, J. Flint, M. Hernandez, *et al.* (1986). 'Evolutionary relationships of human populations from an analysis of nuclear DNA polymorphisms', *Nature* **319**(3003580), 491–3.

Walker, M. C. (2006). 'The theory and metatheory of leadership: the important but contested nature of theory', in Goethals, G. R. and Sorenson, G. J. (eds), *The Quest for a General Theory of Leadership*. Northampton, MA, USA and Cheltenham, UK: Edward Elgar.

Warner, R. (1972). *History of the Peloponnesian War*. London: Penguin Books.

Watson, D. and L. A. Clark (1997). 'Extravension and its positive emotional core', in Hogan, R., Johnson, J. A. and Briggs, S. R. (eds), *Handbook of Personality Psychology*. San Diego, CA: Academic Press.

Webb, C. (2010). *Rabble Rousers: The American Far Right in the Civil Rights Era*. Athens, GA: University of Georgia Press.

Weber, M. (1947). *The Theory of Social And Economic Organization*. New York: Free Press.

Weber, M. (1963). *The Sociology of Religion*. Boston, MA: Beacon Press.

Weber, M. (1978). *Economy and Society*. Berkeley, CA: University of California Press.

Weber, M., H. H. Gerth and C. W. Mills (1946). *From Max Weber: Essays in Sociology*. New York: Oxford University Press.

West-Eberhard, M. J. (2003). *Developmental Plasticity and Evolution*. Oxford: Oxford University Press.

Wheatley, M. J. (1992). *Leadership and the New Science: Learning about Organization from an Orderly Universe*. San Francisco, CA: Oxford University Press.

Whitehead, A. N. (1979). *Process and Reality*. Detroit, MI: Free Press.

Whitener, E., S. Brodt, M. A. Korsgaard and J. Werner (1988). 'Managers as initiators of trust: an exchange relationship for understanding managerial trustworthy behavior', *Academy of Management Journal* **23**, 513–30.

Whorf, B. L. and J. B. Carroll (1956). *Language, Thought, and Reality: Selected Writings of Benjamin Lee Whorf*. Cambridge, MA: Technology Press of Massachusetts Institute of Technology.

Wigan, A. L. (1844). *A New View of Insanity: The Duality of the Mind*. London: Longman, Brown, Green and Longmans.

Williams, J. M., E. V. Lonsdorf, M. L. Wilson, J. Schumacher-Stankey, J. Goodall and A. E. Pusey (2008). 'Causes of death in the Kasekela chimpanzees of Gombe National Park, Tanzania', *Am J Primatol* **70**(8), 766–77.

Willner, A. R. (1984). *The Spellbinders: Charismatic Political Leadership*, New Haven, CT: Yale University Press.

Wilson, E. O. (1975). *Sociobiology: The New Synthesis*. Boston, MA: Harvard University Press.

Witelson, S. F. and D. L. Kigar (1988). 'Asymmetry of brain function follows asymmetry in anatomical form: gross, microscopic, postmortem and imaging studies', in Boller, F. and Grafman, J. (eds), *Handbook of Neuropsychology*. London: Elsevier.

Wolfe, B. D. (1948). *Three Who Made a Revolution*. Boston, MA: Beacon Press.

Wood, M. (1997). *In the Footsteps of Alexander the Great: A Journey from Greece to Asia*. Berkeley, CA: University of California Press.

Wrangham, R. W. and D. Peterson (1996). *Demonic Males: Apes and the Origins of Human Violence*. Boston, MA: Houghton Mifflin.

Wren, J. T. (2006). 'A quest for a grand theory of leadership', in Goethals, G. R. and Sorenson, G. J. (eds), *The Quest for a General Theory of Leadership*. Northampton, MA, USA and Cheltenham, UK: Edward Elgar.

Yao, J. K., D. P. van Kammen and J. A. Gurklis (1996). 'Abnormal incorporation of arachidonic acid into platelets of drug-free patients with schizophrenia', *Psychiatry Res* **60**(1), 11–21.

Yarmolinski, A. (2007). 'The challenge of change in leadership', in Couto, R. A. (ed.), *Reflections on Leadership*. Lanham, MD: University Press of America.

Yedioth Ahronoth (1996). 'Netanyahu sipur haim, ['Netanyahu life story'], 21 June.

Yukl, G. A. (2002). *Leadership in Organizations*. Upper Saddle River, NJ: Prentice Hall.

Yukl, G. A. and C. M. Falbe (1990). 'Influence tactics and objectives in upward, downward, and lateral influence attempts', *Journal of Applied Psychology* **75**(2), 132–40.

Zeisberg, M., M. Khurana, V. H. Rao, D. Cosgrove, J. P. Rougier, *et al.* (2006). 'Stage-specific action of matrix metalloproteinases influences progressive hereditary kidney disease', *PLoS Med* **3**(4), e100.

Zieger, K. (2008). 'High throughput molecular diagnostics in bladder cancer – on the brink of clinical utility', *Mol Oncol* **1**, 384–94.

Zuman, P. and G. Somer (2000). 'Polarographic and voltammetric behavior of selenious acid and its use in analysis', *Talanta* **51**, 645–65.

Index